THE PHILOSOPHY OF SYMBOLIC FORMS

Volume 4

By the same author

AN ESSAY ON MAN

THE MYTH OF THE STATE

THE PROBLEM OF KNOWLEDGE

THE PHILOSOPHY OF SYMBOLIC FORMS

  VOLUME 1: LANGUAGE

  VOLUME 2: MYTHICAL THOUGHT

  VOLUME 3: THE PHENOMENOLOGY OF KNOWLEDGE

KANT'S LIFE AND THOUGHT

SYMBOL, MYTH, AND CULTURE

THE PHILOSOPHY OF SYMBOLIC FORMS

VOLUME FOUR: THE METAPHYSICS OF SYMBOLIC FORMS

Including the text of Cassirer's manuscript on Basis Phenomena

BY ERNST CASSIRER

Edited by
John Michael Krois and Donald Phillip Verene

Translated by John Michael Krois

NEW HAVEN AND LONDON : YALE UNIVERSITY PRESS

Published with assistance from the Ernst Cassirer Publications Fund.

Copyright © 1996 by Yale University.
All rights reserved.
This book may not be reproduced, in whole or in part, including illustrations, in any form (beyond that copying permitted by Sections 107 and 108 of the U.S. Copyright Law and except by reviewers for the public press), without written permission from the publishers.

Set in Granjon Roman type by Keystone Typesetting, Inc., Orwigsburg, Pennsylvania.
Printed in the United States of America

Library of Congress catalog card number: 52-13969
ISBN 0-300-06278-8 (cloth)
       0-300-07433-6 (pbk.)

A catalogue record for this book is available from the British Library.

The paper in this book meets the guidelines for permanence and durability of the Committee on Production Guidelines for Book Longevity of the Council on Library Resources.

10 9 8 7 6 5 4 3

Contents

Acknowledgments	vii
Introduction by John Michael Krois and Donald Phillip Verene	ix

PART I. On the Metaphysics of Symbolic Forms (1928)

Chapter 1: "Geist" and "Life"	3
Chapter 2: The Problem of the Symbol as the Fundamental Problem of Philosophical Anthropology	34
1. The Problem of Philosophical Anthropology	34
2. Life and Symbolic Form	56

PART II. On Basis Phenomena (c. 1940)

Chapter 1: Presentation of the Problem	115
1. The Objective Character of Perception	115
2. The Objective Character of the Expressive Function	122
Chapter 2: Basis Phenomena	127
1. Basis Phenomena (Primary Phenomenon)	127
2. Overview of Basis Phenomena	136
3. Relation of Basis Phenomena to Psychology	143
4. Relation of Basis Phenomena to Metaphysics	153
5. Significance of Basis Phenomena for Theory of Knowledge	166

PART III. Symbolic Forms: For Volume Four (c. 1928)

Section 1. For the Introduction	193
1. The Concept of the Whole	193
2. The Problem of Knowledge as the Problem of Form	194
Section 2. "Geist" and "Life"	200
1. "Geist" and "Life": Heidegger	200
2. Heidegger and the Problem of Death	205

| 3. Time in Bergson and Heidegger | 209 |
| Section 3. For the Concluding Chapter | 211 |

| Appendix: The Concept of the Symbol: Metaphysics of the Symbolic (c. 1921–1927) | 223 |
| Index of Personal Names | 235 |

Acknowledgments

THIS edition and translation is the beneficiary of the work of the many persons who aided in the preparation of the manuscript and production of the German edition (Felix Meiner, 1995; see the "Vorwort des Herausgebers"). We are grateful for this, as it has made our task much easier than we anticipated when we originally proposed this volume to Yale University Press in 1986. In relation to the American edition, we wish to thank specifically Randall E. Auxier for his assistance in locating the English editions and quotations that correspond to those used by Cassirer. We thank Hannelore Krois and Molly Black Verene for their technical assistance in checking various parts of the manuscripts and the translation. We are most grateful for the sympathetic understanding and support of the Cassirer Committee of Yale University, Yale University Press, and Judith Calvert, under whose editorial supervision this volume was brought to press. We wish to thank the daughter of Ernst Cassirer, Anne Appelbaum, for her interest and helpfulness to us, for more than a decade, in the matter of her father's papers. We also thank Peter Cassirer of the University of Göteborg.

Introduction

John Michael Krois and Donald Phillip Verene

WHEN Ernst Cassirer died in 1945, he left a quantity of unpublished papers that derive from various periods in his career. Some of those from the last decade of his life were published in 1979 in *Symbol, Myth, and Culture*.[1] The texts that appear here, edited and translated into English for the first time, relate to Cassirer's plan to bring out a fourth volume of *The Philosophy of Symbolic Forms*.[2] This English edition is connected to the recently published German edition of that fourth volume, *Zur Metaphysik der symbolischen Formen*, which appeared as volume 1 of Cassirer's *Nachgelassene Manuskripte und Texte*.[3]

In the remarks that follow, we have made no attempt to introduce Cassirer's philosophy generally. A picture of the development of Cassirer's philosophy and its basic ideas can be found in Charles W. Hendel's introduction in volume 1 of *The Philosophy of Symbolic Forms* and in Cassirer's own "Introduction and Presentation of the Problem," which follows in that

1. *Symbol, Myth, and Culture: Essays and Lectures of Ernst Cassirer, 1935–1945*, ed. Donald Phillip Verene (New Haven: Yale Univ. Press, 1979; paperback 1981). Italian trans., *Simbolo, mito e cultura* (Rome and Bari: Laterza, 1981); Japanese trans. (Kyoto: Minerva, 1985). Hereinafter cited as *SMC*.

2. *Philosophie der symbolischen Formen*, 3 vols. (Berlin: Bruno Cassirer, 1923–1929). Vol. 1, *Die Sprache* (1923); vol. 2, *Das mythische Denken* (1925); vol. 3, *Phänomenologie der Erkenntnis* (1929). Reprinted: 3 vols. (Darmstadt: Wissenschaftliche Buchgesellschaft, 1964). English trans.: *The Philosophy of Symbolic Forms*, 3 vols., trans. Ralph Manheim (New Haven: Yale Univ. Press, 1953–1957). Vol. 1, *Language* (1953); vol. 2, *Mythical Thought* (1955); vol. 3, *The Phenomenology of Knowledge* (1957). Hereinafter cited as *PSF*, accompanied by the volume number and page numbers of the English edition.

3. *Zur Metaphysik der symbolischen Formen*, ed. John Michael Krois, Vol. 1 of Ernst Cassirer, *Nachgelassene Manuskripte und Texte*, ed. John Michael Krois and Oswald Schwemmer (Hamburg: Felix Meiner, 1995).

volume.[4] Our aim is to offer the reader an understanding of the origin and some editorial details of the materials presented here and how they fit with Cassirer's conception of his major work. Readers familiar with the first three volumes of this work or with *An Essay on Man*,[5] or both, will quickly recognize many of the themes that Cassirer develops here, especially in Part I. They will also find that Cassirer's discussion of the "basis phenomena" in Part II contains some of the most original material in the volume, and perhaps in his thought as a whole.

Cassirer's Unpublished Conclusion to The Philosophy of Symbolic Forms

At the end of his preface to the third volume of *The Philosophy of Symbolic Forms*, Cassirer wrote that he hoped to bring out "a special future publication" under the title *"Life" and "Geist"*[6]—*Toward a Critique of Contemporary Philosophy* ("Leben" und "Geist"—zur Kritik der Philosophie der Gegenwart). This publication would take the place of a "concluding section" (*Schlussabschnitt*)[7] that Cassirer had planned for volume 3 but decided not to include. That section would be a critical discussion "defining and justifying the basic attitude of the Philosophy of Symbolic Forms toward present-day philosophy as a whole."[8] Volume 3 appeared in 1929 without the concluding section. It was written, however, and is Part I of this volume.

Cassirer gives two reasons for changing his mind about including this section. The first was length: "to avoid making the present volume even longer than it is." Volume 1 of *Philosophie der symbolischen Formen* was 305 pages, volume 2 was 336 pages, and volume 3 was 571 pages—without it. The manuscript of the "concluding section" contains 284 pages; adding it

4. *PSF*, 1: 1–114.

5. *An Essay on Man: An Introduction to a Philosophy of Human Culture* (New Haven: Yale Univ. Press, 1944).

6. The difficulties of rendering *Geist* into English are well known to readers of German philosophy. *Geist* may be understood as "mind" and as "spirit." Its meaning for Cassirer involves various senses of both words and sometimes is best indicated by "culture." In this volume "geist" often occurs as an English word, in the same way that other terms of German philosophy are now in use in English, such as "dasein." In some instances, *Geist* is "intelligence" where that seems specific to the context. See *The Oxford English Dictionary*, 2d ed., s.v. "Geist."

7. Manheim translates Cassirer's term *Schlussabschnitt* as "final chapter," but an *Abschnitt* can include more than one chapter. See *PSF*, 3: xvi.

8. *PSF*, 3: xvi.

would have created much too long a book. The second reason was content: "to avoid weighing it [volume 3] down with discussions which, in the last analysis, lie outside the territory prescribed by its specific problem."[9] The topics he wrote about were hardly touched upon in the three volumes of *The Philosophy of Symbolic Forms*: philosophical anthropology and the question of the "metaphysics of symbolic forms." These do not have directly to do with his analyses of either specific cultural symbolic forms (such as language or myth) or with the "phenomenology of knowledge." That Cassirer would discuss "life" in a text about metaphysics follows from his conception of the history of metaphysics. Even in the general introduction to volume 1, Cassirer said that the "Philosophy of Life" is the contemporary form of metaphysics.[10] By *Lebensphilosophie* he meant not just what historians of philosophy usually mean by that term, that is, Bergson, Dilthey, Simmel; Cassirer further associates this term with post-idealistic philosophy generally, from Schopenhauer, Kierkegaard, and Nietzsche to Heidegger. The "concluding section" was supposed to show how Cassirer's philosophy relates to this "Philosophy of Life" as the newest form of metaphysics. Hence its topics indeed went beyond that of volume 3: the "phenomenology of knowledge."

Prior to the discovery of the manuscript of this fourth volume, Cassirer's one work on geist and life was thought to be a lecture he delivered in 1929. In the spring of that year, Cassirer and Martin Heidegger met for their famous encounter at the *Hochschulkurse* in Davos, Switzerland.[11] Cassirer and Heidegger were the most famous of the professors from various European countries who presented lectures as part of a series of short courses in this Swiss resort. In addition to a special seminar in which Cassirer and Heidegger exchanged views, each offered his own course of lectures, which were summarized in a little newspaper, the *Davoser Revue*. The *Revue* reports that Cassirer also delivered a special lecture on geist and life in Max Scheler's philosophy.[12] A version of this was subsequently published in *Die neue Rundschau* (1930)[13] and was translated into English and printed in

9. Ibid.

10. *PSF*, 1: 111–114.

11. The meetings, held at the Grand Hotel and Belvedere, Davos-Platz, lasted from Sunday, March 17, to Saturday, April 6, 1929.

12. Cassirer's lecture was titled "Geist und Leben in der Philosophie Schelers," according to the report published in the *Davoser Revue* 4: 7 (April 15, 1929): 198.

13. See *Die neue Rundschau* 1 (1930): 244–264.

place of "The Philosopher's Reply" in the Library of Living Philosophers volume on Cassirer[14] begun in the early 1940s and published in 1949, three years after his death. Until the emergence of his papers, this lecture and its subsequent publication were apparently the only fulfillment of Cassirer's announcement[15] of a study of geist and life in contemporary philosophy. This brief work, however, is about Scheler's anthropology; it can no longer be considered the text of what Cassirer announced as a critical discussion of "present-day philosophy as a whole."

As mentioned above, Cassirer left a large quantity of papers and manuscripts from his entire career. Some are notes and drafts for works Cassirer had published; some are notes and fully written-out lectures for courses he had taught; others are manuscripts, in varying stages of completion, of unpublished texts. Among them was a package of manuscripts marked "Symbolic Forms, Volume IV," which contained the "concluding section" to Volume 3, drafts labeled "symbolische Formen. Zu Band IV," and a manuscript entitled "Basis Phenomena" (*Basisphänomene*), plus notes. The two larger manuscripts as well as parts of the drafts marked "Symbolic Forms. For Volume IV" are published here in English translation.

Cassirer's preface to volume 3 of *The Philosophy of Symbolic Forms*, dated July 1929, states that "the manuscript of the volume was completed at the end of 1927 and that publication was delayed only because at that time I still planned to include the final, critical section."[16] In a letter to his cousin, Kurt Goldstein, dated February 13, 1928, Cassirer wrote that he hoped to finish volume 3 during the coming semester break (at German universities, usually February to April).[17] He did complete the manuscript, entitled

---

14. See "'Spirit' and 'Life' in Contemporary Philosophy," in *The Philosophy of Ernst Cassirer*, ed. Paul Arthur Schilpp (Evanston, Ill.: Library of Living Philosophers, 1949), pp. 857–880.

15. Charles Hendel added a footnote to Cassirer's preface in the English translation, stating that Cassirer meant his 1930 essay; see *PSF*, 3: xvi n. 3.

16. *PSF*, 3: xvii.

17. Joint letter from Toni and Ernst Cassirer to Kurt Goldstein (no address) [Hamburg], dated February 13, 1928, the last page from Ernst Cassirer, who explains why he had to turn down Goldstein's invitation: "Aber es sprachen doch zu viele Gründe dagegen: vor allem der Wunsch den dritten Band der symbol. F. in diesen Ferien zum Abschluss zu bringen. Ich hatte schon für den Februar auf diesen Abschluss gehofft, der dann aber durch die Semester-Arbeit hinausgeschoben worden ist" (But many things would be against this: most of all the wish to bring the third volume of the symbolic forms to completion during this vacation. I had hoped to finish it already this February, but then the semester's work delayed this). The letter

"Zur Metaphysik der symbolischen Formen" (Part I of this volume), on "16/IV 28" (that is, 16 April 1928). It was to be the "concluding section" for volume 3 mentioned in the preface. The first sentence sounds like the start of a "concluding section": "When we look back at the end of the long path of our investigations...." Also, some footnotes refer to passages in volume 3 as though this text were part of that volume. Yet on page 241 of the manuscript there is a footnote reference to volumes 1 and 3, as though volume 3 were a different work. By this point, Cassirer probably no longer regarded his large manuscript as part of volume 3. Even though the 284-page manuscript was finished on April 16, 1928, Cassirer evidently had no time to work further on the project during the next semester or summer vacation, as he explained in a letter he wrote on December 29, 1928, to Aby Warburg.[18] The German manuscript of volume 3, also in the Beinecke collection,[19] shows that sections were renumbered and considerably reorganized before they attained their final form. The book appeared in 1929 without the "concluding section," for the reasons specified.

Cassirer's Papers

Cassirer had written *The Philosophy of Symbolic Forms* at the University of Hamburg, but with the rise of Nazism he left Germany in spring 1933. He taught for two years at Oxford University, and in 1935 he accepted a position at the University of Göteborg, Sweden, where he remained for six

---

is in the Kurt Goldstein Collection, Box 1, folder Correspondence with Ernst Cassirer, in the Rare Book and Manuscript Library, Columbia University.

18. Cassirer wrote: "Ich hatte mir vorgenommen, den Abschluss des dritten Bandes der 'symbol. Formen' noch in diesem Jahre zu erzwingen. Ganz ist dies nun freilich nicht gelungen—denn bei der Rückkehr zu der Arbeit, die ich viele Monate nicht berührt hatte, zeigte sich doch alsbald, wie vieles zu erweitern, zu berichtigen, schärfer und klarer zu fassen war. Aber nun glaube ich doch, nachdem ich die letzten drei Monate ganz dieser Arbeit gewidmet habe, endlich Land vor mir zu sehen" (I had planned to force completion of the third volume of the "symbolic forms" still during this year. But this has not been fully achieved—for upon returning to my work on it, which I had left untouched for many months, I soon saw how much had to be expanded, altered, more sharply and clearly formulated. But now, after having devoted myself entirely to this work the last three months, I think I finally have land in sight). Cassirer to Warburg, Hamburg, December 29, 1928. The letter is in Zettelkasten 10, "Ikonologie Probleme," in the archives of the Warburg Institute, London. We thank Claudia Naber, Berlin, for bringing this letter to our attention.

19. The manuscript of volume 3 of *Philosophie der symbolischen Formen* is in box 29, folder 551 through box 31, folder 598 in the Beinecke collection.

years before coming to the United States in late spring 1941, at the invitation of the Department of Philosophy at Yale University. He taught for three years at Yale. He died suddenly in spring 1945, when he was on visiting appointment at Columbia University.

He had left the bulk of his writings in Sweden, upon his departure for the United States.[20] His widow, Toni Cassirer, visited Sweden in summer 1946 and returned to New York with her husband's papers.[21] She intended to organize them with the help of other émigré scholars and friends, but this was never done. She copied the titles of the manuscripts onto the covers of the packets into which they were bundled. After Toni Cassirer's death in 1961, Charles W. Hendel, who as chairman of Yale's philosophy department had been instrumental in bringing Cassirer to the United States, obtained the papers from the Cassirer family and took them to Yale. They were kept inaccessible in the basement of Sterling Library. A contract signed on February 20, 1964, by a representative of Cassirer's heirs and Yale University legally transferred to Yale University Press the ownership of the papers and the literary rights. The Press had an inventory of them made in October 1965. The packages were numbered with red ballpoint pen as they were taken from their containers. The numbering was not intended to have any significance regarding either the chronology or the subject matter

---

20. They were left with his son, Georg. The Cassirers left Sweden on May 20, 1941. As late as March 27, 1941, Cassirer was still uncertain about where to deposit his manuscripts. He wrote to the philosopher Åke Petzäll, in Lund: "Die Frage der Bibliothek ist jetzt einigermassen geklärt; die Bücher werden in den Räumen der Högskolas untergebracht werden können. Schwieriger ist es für die fertigen, aber noch ungedruckten Manuskripte eine Vorsorge zu treffen" (The question of the library is now clarified; the books can be stored in rooms at the college. More difficult is the matter of finding a place to store the finished but as yet unpublished manuscripts). Cassirer to Astrid and Åke Petzäll, Göteborg, March 27, 1941. The letter is in the Petzäll's private correspondence at the Lund University Library.

21. See Charles Hendel's preface to Cassirer, *The Problem of Knowledge: Philosophy, Science, and History since Hegel*, trans. W. H. Woglom and C. W. Hendel (New Haven: Yale Univ. Press, 1950). "It was only after his [Cassirer's] death that the copy of the manuscript was obtained by Mrs. Cassirer on a visit to Sweden in 1946" (p. vii). In a letter to Theodor Litt from Göteborg dated July 7, 1946, Toni Cassirer writes that she now had to decide where to live, but that "zuerst gehe ich jedenfalls nach New York zurück, wo ich für meines Mannes Nachlass wichtige Dinge zu ordnen habe und wo meine Tochter und Schwester lebt und viele unserer Freunde, die meinem Manne gerade in letzter Zeit sehr nahe gestanden haben" (no matter what, I am first going to go back to New York, where I have important things to put in order for my husband's papers and where my daughter and sister live and many of our friends, who were close to my husband, especially during the recent past). The letter is in the Theodor Litt Archive of the Heinrich Heine Universität, Düsseldorf.

of the manuscripts in the 219 packages, but it lets us be relatively sure of the state of the papers at Cassirer's death.

Many packets contained several different manuscripts. A few packets consisted of a small number of pages; others contained texts hundreds of pages long. The papers were later transferred to Yale's Beinecke Rare Book and Manuscript Library, where they were kept as a deposit of Yale University Press. The papers remained unexamined by any Cassirer scholar until 1972, when Verene went through all of them. Krois first saw them in 1973. On January 19, 1987, the Cassirer papers became the property of the Beinecke Library. The literary rights remained with Yale University Press. Archiving and cataloging were completed in fall 1991. The old numbering was retained; added to this was a new system for numbering folders. The Cassirer papers were alphabetized by title. Today the papers occupy 1,141 folders in fifty-nine boxes. About two-thirds of this mass of papers consists of manuscripts of Cassirer's published works. The other third is unpublished materials: invited lectures, course lectures, and drafts for larger works, as well as research notes, a small collection of correspondence, and a few personal papers. Most of Cassirer's papers are handwritten, but a few are in typescript: some in English, such as chapters of *An Essay on Man* and *The Myth of the State*, and some in German, such as the perfectly typed texts of the two essays that were translated into English for the volume *Kant, Rousseau, and Goethe* (1945).

Cassirer's Original Title of The Philosophy of Symbolic Forms

Cassirer intended to call the whole of *The Philosophy of Symbolic Forms* by the title he used for the third volume: "Phenomenology of Knowledge" (*Phänomenologie der Erkenntnis*). In a very large package that contains drafts and notes for volume 1 (MS 159) there is a handwritten text of Cassirer's "Foreword" (*Vorwort*) to the first volume. It has a cover page with two lines centered in the middle of the page: Ernst Cassirer / Phaenomenologie der Erkenntnis. In the upper right-hand corner is a stamp of the publishing house, Bruno Cassirer Verlag, showing its Berlin address, and with the date, 3 April 1923, in pencil. There is also a request in pencil for corrections (perhaps referring to proofs returned with the original). Following the text of Cassirer's "Vorwort" is a title page in Cassirer's hand, labeled in the upper right-hand corner: "manuscript of the title page" (*Manuskript zum Titelblatt*). This title page reads: "Phenomenology of Knowledge / Fundamental Features of a Theory of Spiritual Forms of Expression / By / Ernst Cassirer /

Cassirer's April 1923 title page
(Beinecke Rare Book and Manuscript Library, Yale University)

INTRODUCTION

First Part / Linguistic Thought / Berlin 1923 / Bruno Cassirer Publisher" (see fig.).[22]

The first volume of Cassirer's work appeared in 1923 with the title *Philosophie der symbolischen Formen. Erster Teil, Die Sprache*. Cassirer's foreword in the published volume is dated April of that year. The existence of this manuscript title page indicates that at a very late point in the publishing process the general title was changed from "Phenomenology of Knowledge: Fundamental Features of a Theory of Spiritual Forms of Expression" to "Philosophy of Symbolic Forms" (and the title of the first volume was changed from "Das sprachliche Denken" to "Die Sprache").[23]

The manuscript title page suggests that from the start Cassirer saw his philosophy of symbolic forms as a type of phenomenology. In explaining his use of "Phenomenology of Knowledge" as the title of the third volume of *The Philosophy of Symbolic Forms*, Cassirer states in his preface that he means "phenomenology" in the sense that Hegel uses it in *Phenomenology of Spirit* (1807) and not in the "modern" (Husserlian) sense. Cassirer identifies his approach with Hegel's view that phenomenology is the basis of all philosophical knowledge and it must encompass all cultural forms—"the True is the whole."[24] Cassirer also says that he intends his phenomenology, like Hegel's, to provide the individual with a "ladder" that will lead him from the world of "immediate" consciousness to the world of "pure knowledge." Cassirer makes clear that he does not intend a complete identification with Hegel's phenomenology, but he does endorse its fundamentals.

In various places throughout his works Cassirer expresses disagreements with Hegel's system, principally with what he understands to be the power of Hegel's dialectic to compromise the individual forms of consciousness for the sake of a smooth overall progression of forms. Cassirer does not wish to abandon the idea of dialectic and has his own version of dialectic, especially using it as a way to understand the inner life of a symbolic form. In his general introduction to volume 1, Cassirer says that the forms of Hegel's phenomenology culminate in the single form of logic; only logic,

---

22. "Phaenomenologie der Erkenntnis. / Grundzüge einer Theorie der geistigen Ausdrucksformen. / Von / Ernst Cassirer / Erster Teil: / Das sprachliche Denken. / Berlin 1923 / Bruno Cassirer Verlag."

23. This change from (literally translated) "Linguistic Thought" to "Language" expresses a shift in orientation from thinking in a medium to the medium itself.

24. *PSF*, 3: xiv.

the form of the concept, cognitive knowledge, has the right to autonomy.[25] Cassirer aims to preserve the independence of each form.

In the contents of volume 1 of *The Philosophy of Symbolic Forms*, Cassirer keeps the term "phenomenology" in his general heading: "On the Phenomenology of Linguistic Form" (Zur Phänomenologie der sprachlichen Form), and in his foreword he says he wishes to follow the first volume with a sketch of a "phenomenology of mythical and religious thought." The first part of Cassirer's "phenomenology of knowledge" of volume 3 is concerned with the phenomenon of "expression" (*Ausdruck*), which involves the first phase of his theory of language and his conception of mythical consciousness. These lead directly back to Cassirer's use of "forms of expression" (*Ausdrucksformen*) in the above-mentioned manuscript title page. The existence of this manuscript title page helps to make clear how strongly Cassirer understood his conception of knowledge and the symbol to be tied to a phenomenology that could show how they are grounded in and develop from a primitive or "immediate" form of consciousness. Besides his objection that Hegel's phenomenology leads to the dominance of the one form of logic over other forms, Cassirer objects that it does not begin by setting its "ladder" low enough in consciousness.[26] Hegel's phenomenology, he says, begins at the level of the "thing" and its "qualities." Cassirer begins at the more immediate level of mythical consciousness. Mythical thought is formative of the "expressive function" (*Ausdrucksfunktion*) of consciousness, which all other forms of knowing require as their ground.[27]

Cassirer's early title for his major work emphasizes that his aim was to show the relation of knowledge (*Erkenntnis*) to more immediate forms of expression (*Ausdrucksformen*) by means of a phenomenology. But all forms of expression and knowledge lead back to something more fundamental. The expressive function is the most basic manifestation of mind or geist, but geist, Cassirer says, is a transformation of life. What, then, is life? Cassirer's attempt to understand the "expressive function" apparently led him, in Sweden in 1940, to develop his doctrine of *Basisphänomene*, the foremost of which is life. In addition to Cassirer's explicit adaptation, in the text on basis phenomena, of Goethe's notion of the *Urphänomen*—a term that recurs in all three volumes of *The Philosophy of Symbolic Forms*—he

25. *PSF*, 1: 83–84.
26. *PSF*, 2: xvi.
27. *PSF*, 3: 67.

was thinking of Carnap's notion of *Basis* as expressed in *Der logische Aufbau der Welt* (1928), a work that Cassirer had known in manuscript.[28]

The Manuscripts (Envelope 184)

When in 1986 we examined envelope 184 for this edition, it contained three file folders, 184a, 184b, and 184c, that were of American origin and appeared to have been provided by librarians. Part I of the present volume is from MS 184b (today in box 31, folders 606–610). This handwritten manuscript is on folded sheets numbered continuously from 1 to 284. Its title page reads "On the Metaphysics of Symbolic Forms" (Zur Metaphysik der symbolischen Formen). The last page has the date, in Cassirer's hand, of April 16, 1928. Cassirer had two chapters: "Chapter One: 'Geist' and 'Life'" (Erstes Kapitel: "Geist" und "Leben") and "Chapter Two: The Problem of the Symbol as the Fundamental Problem of Philosophical Anthropology" (Zweites Kapitel: Das symbolproblem als Grundproblem der philosophischen Anthropologie).

Preceding the continuous text are pages of rough notes entitled "'Leben' und 'Geist' / I: Historischer Teil." Cassirer's title page of "Zur Metaphysik der symbolischen Formen" has "Teil," without a number, written above the title. This suggests that he conceived the total work as having two main parts, a historical part and a systematic part. The pages of notes marked as the historical part in MS 184b and related pages of notes in MS 184a show that Cassirer intended to trace the question of life and geist from ancient philosophy involving Plato, Aristotle's doctrine of *nous*, Plotinus, and Augustine through the Renaissance to Descartes and modern philosophy to the Romantic concept in Fichte, Schelling, and Hegel, and then to the views of Dilthey.

There is also rough material for the critique of recent philosophy, which would likely belong in the project Cassirer announced in the preface to the third volume of *The Philosophy of Symbolic Forms*. Preparatory work includes critiques of Klages, Kleist, Scheler, and Heidegger. Some of these notes (part of MS 184a) are marked "Material: Scheler Lecture/Vienna 1928!" (Material: Scheler-Vortrag/Wien 1928!). This suggests that a ver-

---

28. This follows from his correspondence with Moritz Schlick. In a letter dated April 4, 1927, Cassirer tells Schlick that he recommended Carnap's book to his cousin and publisher, Bruno Cassirer. The letter is in the "Wiener Kreis Stichtung," Rijksarchief in Noord-Holland, Haarlem. Cassirer discusses Carnap's *Aufbau* several times in his unpublished papers.

sion of the lecture that Cassirer gave in Davos in 1929 and that was published in 1930 was presented as early as 1928 in Vienna.

Part II of this volume is from MS 184c (today in box 31, folders 599, 603–604). This material falls into two parts. The first consists of ninety pages on the problem of basis phenomena. It is the only manuscript in 184c that has a continuous narrative. Then come seventy-four pages of assorted working materials and notes on a variety of topics, written on various kinds of paper and alphabetized by headings at the top of the pages. Cassirer's papers include several such alphabetically ordered batches of notes on different topics.

The most recent literature cited or mentioned in the basis phenomena text is from the mid-1930s, the latest being Folke Leander's study *The Philosophy of John Dewey* (1939). The entire manuscript (184c) has a cover sheet wrapped around it, reading "Problem of Knowledge / Vol. IV" (Erkenntnisproblem / Bd. IV); it also has the abbreviation "Allg.," that is, "Allgemein" (General). These conflicting labels raise the question whether the material of MS 184c was intended as part of a fourth volume of Cassirer's *The Problem of Knowledge* (*Das Erkenntnisproblem*) or of a fourth volume of *The Philosophy of Symbolic Forms*. One thing is clear: the content of MS 184c is systematic and bears no resemblance to the historical studies in *The Problem of Knowledge*.[29] Filed with MS 184c is a large folded piece of green wrapping paper, with the words "Symbolic Forms IV / Preliminary Studies" (Symbolische Formen IV / Vorarbeiten). This wrapper also has "Manuskript an Prof. Cassirer, föreningsgatan 11" (Cassirer's address in Sweden). It originally held the entire contents of MS 184; the folds show that it had been wrapped around such a large package, and "184" is in the same red ballpoint ink used to number all the papers. The a, b, and c folders apparently were introduced later.

Toni Cassirer, in *Mein Leben mit Ernst Cassirer*,[30] writes that in the late spring of 1940, when the possibility of Hitler occupying Sweden had greatly intensified, they left Göteborg a few days after the finish of Cassirer's university lectures, to vacation in the country. She reports that despite the grave political situation Cassirer suddenly commenced work on a new project. While they were on a walk one morning, Cassirer explained that

29. The English translation appeared before the original German: *Das Erkenntnisproblem in der Philosophie und Wissenschaft der neueren Zeit*, vol. 4 (Stuttgart: W. Kohlhammer, 1957).

30. Toni Cassirer, *Mein Leben mit Ernst Cassirer* (Hildesheim: Gerstenberg, 1981). Completed several years after Cassirer's death, this work originally circulated in mimeographed typescripts.

this was actually the fourth volume of the symbolic forms (". . . dass diese neue Arbeit eigentlich den vierten Band der symbolischen Formen bedeutete").[31] This, we think, likely was the text *"Basisphänomene"* in MS 184c. Toni Cassirer also says that when they returned from their six weeks in the country, the manuscript of his new book was finished, *The Logic of the Humanities* (*Zur Logik der Kulturwissenschaften: Fünf Studien*, 1942). At the same time, she reports, the fourth volume of *The Problem of Knowledge* was begun.[32] As Charles Hendel states in his preface to the English translation of the fourth volume of *The Problem of Knowledge*, and as Toni Cassirer confirms, Cassirer wrote it "from 9 July to 26 November 1940," the dates he affixed at the end of the manuscript. Such intense activity was not unusual: it was Cassirer's habit to work on several things at once. This accounts for his enormous corpus of published work, nearly 125 items ranging from short articles to very large books. Cassirer's Swedish years, like his American ones, were an especially creative time. He was rethinking the fundamental ideas of his earlier work, both systematic and historical, and presenting them in new ways to new audiences.

Part III of the present volume is from MS 184a (today in box 31, folders 600–602). In contrast to 184b and 184c, it contains no long, continuous main text. Stylistically, the texts in 184a are unfinished—they are compressed, notelike, and seem to jump from one topic to another. This material was probably written at different times, but none of the literature mentioned is later than 1928.[33] Many of the works are also cited in 184b.[34] Manuscript 184a has a title page in Cassirer's hand: "Symbolische Formen / Zu Band IV."

It contains sets of pages entitled "For the Introduction" (Zur Einleitung) and "For the Concluding Chapter" (Zum Schluss-Kapitel). Their telegraphic sentences seem intended for rewriting and expansion, unlike the

---

31. Ibid., p. 270.

32. Ibid., p. 271.

33. In 184a, Plessner, *Die Stufen des Organischen und der Mensch*, and Uexküll, *Theoretische Biologie*, 2d ed., are both from 1928.

34. Cited in both 184a and 184b are Lévy-Bruhl, *Das Denken der Naturvölker* (1926); Lord Byron, *Manfred* (the same passage is quoted); Nicholas of Cusa, *De ludo globi*; Epicurus's εἴδωλον-theory; Fiedler, *Aphorismen aus dem Nachlass* (1914); Klages, *Vom kosmogonischen Eros* (1922); Litt, *Individuum und Gemeinschaft*, 2d ed. (1924); Lumholtz, *Symbolism of the Huichol Indians* (1900); Plessner, *Die Stufen des Organischen und der Mensch* (1928); Scheler, *Die Sonderstellung des Menschen* (1927); Spengler, *Der Untergang des Abendlandes* (1918); Uexküll, *Theoretische Biologie* (1920), 2d ed. (1928), and his *Umwelt und Innenwelt der Tiere*, 2d ed. (1921); Volkelt, *Über die Vorstellung der Tiere* (1914).

chapters of MS 184b, which have the appearance of being finished. These sets of pages are reprinted here at the end of Part III, but the reader may wish to look at them in connection with the finished text of Part I.

In MS 184a there is also a short but pointed critique of Heidegger, with the heading "'Geist' und 'Leben' (Heidegger)."[35] It relates to Cassirer's criticisms of Heidegger in their seminar at Davos (1929)[36] and in lectures from Cassirer's American years published in *Symbol, Myth, and Culture*.[37] Cassirer's essay on Scheler and this critique of Heidegger are representative of the critical assessment of contemporary philosophy that Cassirer had planned to write.

This volume concludes with an appendix from envelope 107 (now box 29, folders 546–548), labeled in Cassirer's hand: "Vorarbeiten zum / III Band / symb. Formen" (preliminary drafts for the third volume of the Symbolic Forms). We here publish only material from folder 548. Its title and content are closely connected with the texts from MS 184b containing the unpublished concluding section for volume 3 of *The Philosophy of Symbolic Forms*. The rest of the material in envelope 107 appears to be drafts for the published version of that book. The work published here is undated. The latest literature cited is early: Max Frischeisen-Köhler's review in *Kant-Studien* (1921) of Rickert's book *Die Philosophie des Lebens* (1920). These texts are written in three different colors of ink on four kinds of paper; it seems likely that Cassirer produced them between 1921 and 1927.

A Fourth Volume of The Philosophy of Symbolic Forms

Why did Cassirer not complete and publish a fourth volume of *The Philosophy of Symbolic Forms*? In other unpublished papers, Cassirer made cross-references to the texts in envelope 184 by the designation "Phil. d. s. F. IV" (four times in envelope 119, texts written circa 1939),[38] but he never men-

---

35. This text was first published both in German and in English translation by John Michael Krois. "Cassirer's Unpublished Critique of Heidegger," *Philosophy and Rhetoric* 16 (1983): 147–166.

36. See "Davoser disputation zwischen Ernst Cassirer und Martin Heidegger," Heidegger, *Kant und das Problem der Metaphysik, Gesamtausgabe*, vol. 3 (Frankfurt am Main: Klostermann, 1991), pp. 274–296.

37. *SMC*, pp. 229–230; see also *The Myth of the State* (New Haven: Yale Univ. Press, 1946), pp. 368–369.

38. These cross-references are detailed in the manuscript description in the German edi-

tions this project in publications. Toni Cassirer says nothing about it in her biography beyond what is mentioned above. One reason for Cassirer's not writing a fourth volume in 1929–1930 is that he was extremely busy as rector of the University of Hamburg. After that he was on leave to work on *The Philosophy of the Enlightenment* (1932). On January 30, 1933, Hitler became chancellor of Germany. On May 2, 1933, the Cassirers left Hamburg, never to live in Germany again. These were war years, and the explanation for Cassirer's not finishing this project may be the same as the reason he gave later, in the United States, for not producing a work on art—the "malice," or *Ungunst*, of the times.

Among scholars in the United States who knew Cassirer and his work, the impression grew that an unwritten volume was needed to complete *The Philosophy of Symbolic Forms*, and that this was on art. Cassirer continually mentions the triad of art, myth, and religion throughout the three volumes, but there is no separate treatment of art. This impression that there should be a volume on art persisted even after Cassirer's death, especially since the one thinker most immediately to carry on from Cassirer's work was Susanne Langer, who, although she was never his student and met him only after he came to the United States, developed a conception of symbolism formulated in terms of aesthetic theory.

Langer's widely read *Philosophy in a New Key* (1942) and her translation of Cassirer's *Language and Myth* (1946) were a valuable route for many American readers into the philosophy of the symbol prior to the publication of *The Philosophy of Symbolic Forms* in English in the 1950s. Her book on aesthetics, *Feeling and Form*, which is dedicated to Cassirer, appeared in the same year as the first volume of *The Philosophy of Symbolic Forms*, translated in 1953 by Ralph Manheim. In a letter of May 13, 1942, to Paul Schilpp, written during the preparation of the Library of Living Philosophers volume on his work, Cassirer noted that in the first sketch ("*im ersten Entwurf*") of his *Philosophy of Symbolic Forms* he had considered a volume on art, but the "malice" (*Ungunst*) of the times had caused him to put it off again and again. He says that he now intends to present his theory of aesthetics.[39] This apparently became the chapter on art in *An Essay on Man*,

---

tion; see Cassirer, *Zur Metaphysik der symbolischen Formen* (Hamburg: Felix Meiner, 1995), pp. 305–307.

39. Cassirer's letter to Schilpp, New Haven, May 13, 1942, is in the Library of Living Philosophers collection at the University of Southern Illinois Library, Carbondale.

which is connected to three other manuscripts on art published in *Symbol, Myth, and Culture*.[40]

The lack of a separate volume on art is not a fundamental objection in the critical reception of Cassirer's philosophy of symbolic forms. It may be a lack in the system, perhaps partially remedied by his chapter in *An Essay on Man*, but it is not an objection to its validity. Perhaps the strongest critical point persistently raised in relation to Cassirer's thought is: How are his symbolic forms, which are forms of culture, metaphysically or ontologically grounded? This is the question with which Heidegger in his own way concludes his 1928 review of the second volume of *The Philosophy of Symbolic Forms*.[41] The ground for Cassirer's conception of symbolic forms is also apparently the question that Cassirer's American students were immediately asking him in his seminar, "Philosophy of Language and the Principles of Symbolism," at Yale in spring 1942, as can be seen from the way he concludes the manuscript from this seminar in *Symbol, Myth, and Culture*.[42] Cassirer himself raises this question as part of the general problem of the position of philosophical idealism in his lecture to the Warburg Institute, "Critical Idealism as a Philosophy of Culture" (1936), which also appears in *Symbol, Myth, and Culture*.[43]

As to the grounds of the various symbolic forms or their total system of internal relations, Cassirer in the first part of *An Essay on Man* defines man as *"animal symbolicum"* and suggests, on the basis of Jakob von Uexküll's biology of the world of the organism, that the human organism has a "symbolic" system, which falls between the "receptor" and "effector" systems that it shares with all other organisms.[44] But this anthropological answer did not dispel the perception that the strongly epistemological orientation of Cassirer's conception of symbolic forms is non- or even antimetaphysical. The unpublished texts of the fourth volume of *The Philosophy of Symbolic Forms* remained Cassirer's fullest answer.

The 1928 text of this fourth volume was clearly intended to be the sequel to the published third volume. But what was Cassirer's intention in writing the basis phenomena manuscript (1940)? Was this to be a new start on the project of the fourth volume, as his above-mentioned comment to Toni Cassirer during their walk in Sweden suggests, and as one aspect of the

40. *SMC*, pp. 145–215.
41. *Deutsche Literaturzeitung*, 21 (1928): 1011–1112.
42. *SMC*, pp. 194–195.
43. Ibid., pp. 64–72.
44. *An Essay on Man*, pp. 23–26.

labeling of the manuscript package tends to support? Even a cursory look into the fourth volume of *The Problem of Knowledge* excludes the "basis phenomena" as a draft for a part of that work, which deals exclusively with historical materials. Could it have been written as a draft of an essay for *The Logic of the Humanities*, intended perhaps to be a sixth added to the "five studies" therein. When compared closely with these essays, the "basis phenomena" seems very different in subject matter and in approach. It seems most to be a text in which Cassirer is reflecting in a new way on issues relevant to his "phenomenology of knowledge" of the third volume of *The Philosophy of Symbolic Forms*. In the end, however we assess Cassirer's intention, the piece exists to be read and considered in itself as a statement of his ideas that are of special importance for the grounding of his philosophical position.

Editorial Principles and the German Edition

The American edition of this volume was conceived and begun several years before the start of the German edition, while the editors were together at Emory University in the 1980s. The existence of texts for a fourth volume of *The Philosophy of Symbolic Forms* was discovered during Verene's work on the papers at the Beinecke Library in the 1970s, which resulted in *Symbol, Myth, and Culture*. None of the material of this fourth volume was published in that collection, but the existence of an envelope containing those papers (MS 184) was noted and described in an appendix. Discovery of the full structure and import of this material goes back to Krois's work in preparing his study of Cassirer.[45] Formal arrangements to publish this fourth volume of Cassirer's major work were made with Yale University Press and the Cassirer Committee at Yale in 1986.

The American edition was from the beginning planned to be different from the publication of the manuscripts in their original language, which would reproduce them in a manner close to their original format. This full critical edition was published in spring 1995, in commemoration of the fiftieth year since Cassirer's death. The Cassirer specialist will find in the German edition all technical material and discussions relevant to the state and editing of the manuscripts. The American edition is aimed at the philosophical reader who wishes to study the major ideas of Cassirer's

---

45. John Michael Krois, *Cassirer: Symbolic Forms and History* (New Haven: Yale Univ. Press, 1987).

philosophy of symbolic forms through all four volumes. The format of this translation has been made insofar as possible to fit with that of the Manheim translation of the first three volumes. All notes are in a single system of enumeration, and those that are substantially Cassirer's own are so identified. The editorial footnotes reproduce many from the German edition and add others. The texts of Parts I and II and the Appendix correspond in full to the German edition. The materials in Part III are moderately abridged for two reasons. They are so schematic and fragmented that a translation would not be useful, and Cassirer discusses the same points fully in the main texts. Section 1 is complete. Section 2 does not include some material on Klages and Simmel, discussed more fully in Part I, but does include all of Cassirer's remarks on Heidegger. Section 3 does not include some sketches of matters systematically treated in Part I.

Our procedure for bringing this volume into English has been to follow what the Cassirer Committee at Yale originally advised when the papers for *Symbol, Myth, and Culture* were in preparation—to make as readable a text as possible given the state of the manuscripts and to remain true to Cassirer's thought. This is an ideal that cannot be perfectly attained, but it has been the central principle that has guided the preparation of this volume.

PART I

On the Metaphysics of Symbolic Forms
1928

Chapter One

"Geist" and "Life"

WHEN we look back at the end of the long path of our investigations[1] in order to compare and unify the many aspects of all we have seen at different stages, even the attempt at such a unification meets with a difficulty resulting from the problem and method of our investigation itself. For in the course of our investigation we saw with increasing intensity how that particular sphere of meaning which we are accustomed to calling the theoretical "world" contains far greater tensions and divisions than we usually admit. It in no way possesses the simple character and well-unified intellectual organization that we usually attribute to it. Of course, if we compare this theoretical sphere as a complete world to the world of morality or the world of art, it appears to be a self-contained and completely closed form, an entity with an unmistakable and unique character. Here the firm borderlines emerge as Kant had drawn them with critical and analytic mastery. The realm of "being" is sharply and clearly differentiated from that of the "ought"; the world of "nature" stands opposed to the world of "freedom." Between them both, related to each of them and yet separate, is the realm of the "beautiful" with its specific nature.

The cosmos of "reason," its divisions and specificity, its universal character and systematic structure, is revealed to us in this trinity of theoretical, practical, and aesthetic meaning. Measured against this fundamental order, the differences in structure found within specific main areas may now appear to be of relatively little moment. As important as these differences are from the standpoint of content, a philosophical investigation, which is

1. Part I was originally written to provide a conclusion for vol. 3 of *The Philosophy of Symbolic Forms*, hence the reference here to the "end" of Cassirer's investigations. In subsequent references to that three-volume work (originally published in German, 1923–1929), abbreviated *PSF*, the volume and page number will be cited from the translation by Ralph Manheim (New Haven: Yale Univ. Press, 1953–1957).—Eds.

3

not concerned so much with the content of the world as with its pure form, must look beyond them. The pure form of the theoretical, ethical, and aesthetic cannot itself be divided. It is essentially a unity, consisting in nothing other than the rule of a universal and strictly homogeneous regularity, in an a priori principle of strict necessity and generality. Critical analysis formulates this principle, not by following the boundless variety of the various twisting paths taken in the development of thought, but by simply looking at the fruits of this development, its highest and most mature result. Only by reference to this is it possible to make visible the determining basis of each form-world, to determine the categories upon which it "rests," as the conditions of its possibility. The course of the analysis of theoretical knowledge in the *Critique of Pure Reason* begins with "experience." At the outset this is taken to be something immediately "given," yet this analysis is never directed toward this given as such; rather, it is directed to the pure concept of experience as it is presented to us in rigorous natural science, in mathematical knowledge of nature. In this the general "form" of knowledge is discovered, which then, in retrospect, illuminates the stages of "perception" and "intuition." This goal is what makes them significant and gives them a theoretical content. The essence of theoretical thought does not emerge in its preparatory and transitional stages but only in its goal, in its completion and the perfection of its achievements. This end gives theoretical thinking its state of completion and makes it possible for us to know it. In it, its form becomes an *actus purus*; it attains its proper and true "reality."

As needed and fruitful as this perspective—this clear and conscious concentration on the pure "telos" of theoretical knowledge—proves to be, the "philosophy of symbolic forms" cannot stop here. Its concern is not merely to take stock of forms, to assess them, so to speak, for what they are as static magnitudes. It is concerned, rather, with the dynamics of the giving of meaning, in and through which the growth and delimitation of specific spheres of being and meaning occur in the first place. It seeks to understand and illuminate the riddle of the becoming of form as such—not so much as a finished determination but rather with determination as a process. This process does not follow a single, predefined course leading from a specific beginning to an equally fixed end, which has been determined in advance. Thought does not flow here in a finished riverbed which has been made for it; rather, it must find its own way—it must first dig its own bed for itself. This movement of thought searching for itself is not limited at the outset to a single, particular direction. Instead, distinctly different approaches emerge in it, different centers of power and different tendencies. Such tendencies, such basic types, not so much of the "world," as of theoretical attitudes toward the world, were what we sought to show in language, in myth, and finally in scientific knowledge, and which we sought to differentiate sharply from one another. Each of these attitudes had to be interpreted according to its own original principle, the "categories" unique to it had to be sought out. But now, after these particular directions have been sorted out, after phenomenological analysis has sought to bring out the basic forms of linguistic, mythic, and scientific thought, the need for synthesis seems to exert its demand on us all the more urgently and insistently.

The analysis had to be directed primarily and narrowly to knowledge of differences—but should not these differences at the same time refer us to an overarching whole which embraces them all, as aspects, and connects them together? Certainly this connection may not be conceived as a mere alignment in which the characteristic principles of form as found in the structure of myth, language, and theoretical knowledge are again mixed together and leveled off. The different "niveau levels" as such must be upheld unconditionally and without limitations, but here we face the question whether these are to be accepted simply as a fact or whether they can be made understandable, if their significance and intellectual necessity can be conceptually grasped. It seems as if this question has been answered as soon as it has been sharply and clearly formulated. For we do not need to search for long—so it seems—to find the comprehensive species, the *genus proximum*, that embraces all those specific differences we have uncovered and defines them all. We are in possession of that genus, to be sure, by recourse to that level of experience that remains relatively free from the abstract distinctions of reflection as required by and brought about through the progressive differentiation of the different areas of culture. In opposition to them it remains an undifferentiated unity, the unity of the "natural world-picture." If we investigate this natural world-picture, we find it abounding again in all those features that we saw at work in the formative activity of language, myth, and knowledge—but here this abundance is not yet dissected and divided. It presents itself to us, so to speak, as a uniform and simple beam of light, which has not yet been refracted and dispersed by different mediums of meaning. In the previous investigations[2] we sepa-

2. Cassirer is referring here to *PSF*, vol. 3, *The Phenomenology of Knowledge*, which is organized under three major headings, "expression," "representation," and "signification." He discusses these three terms and his use of them, in "The Problem of the Symbol and its

rated the dimension of "expression" from that of "representation" and of "signification," and we have used this tripartite division as a kind of ideal system of relations. By reference to it we were able to establish and, so to speak, read off the unique character of the form of myth, the form of language, and the form of pure knowledge. The "natural" world-picture extends into all these dimensions and lives and moves in all of them without, however, consciously distinguishing between them or "having" them *as* different. It is implemented by and permeated with the symbolic function of expression as well as by representation and signification.

But this organization and division, the "One, Two, Three"[3] that the philosopher brings to the contents of these functions, to the living web of thought, is something quite foreign to it. Taken in itself it is a whole and closed, and it is a living whole by virtue of the fact that here a single step stirs a thousand threads[4] and that all these threads flow unseen. Instead of the *discretio* of forms, which thought subsequently differentiates, we have here a continuous crossing over and crossover, a constant unbroken movement from one extreme to the other. Anaxagoras said of natural objects that each of them is a *panspermia*,[5] that is, they are not composed of individual discrete elements; rather, every physical whole contains the germs and seeds of all elements. This claim about the organization of nature, the structure of *physis*, applies in a more radical and deeper sense to products of culture. We may not conceive of their separations and their inner differences in such a way that the individual instances seem, to use Anaxagoras's

---

Place in the System of Philosophy," trans. John Michael Krois, *Man and World* 11 (1978): 411–428.—Eds.

3. See Goethe, *Faust, Goethe's Collected Works*, vol. 2, ed. and trans. Stuart Atkins (Boston: Suhrkamp/Insel, 1984), p. 49, lines 1918–1922, 1928–1933: "Days on end will be used to teach you / that what you once did as a single act, / as easily as you eat or drink, / must really be done as one-two-three / . . . nonetheless the philosopher comes / and proves to you it had to be thus: / the first was so, the second so, / and hence the third and fourth are so; / but if there were no first and second / the third and fourth could never exist." All citations from Goethe's *Faust* given in English are in this edition. The line numbers in this translation follow those in Johann Wolfgang von Goethe, *Goethes Werke*, hrsg. im Auftrage der Grossherzogin Sophie von Sachsen, 133 vols. in 143, in 4 Abteilungen (Weimar: Hermann Böhlau, 1887–1919); *Faust* appears in Abt. 1, vol. 14, *Faust* II in vol. 15.1. Goethe is hereinafter cited in German from this edition, abbreviated *WA* (*Weimarer Ausgabe*), unless otherwise stated.—Eds.

4. See Goethe, *Faust*, line 1924.—Eds.

5. The word πανσπερμία does not occur in Anaxagoras, but has been attributed to him since Aristotle. See Anaxagoras, in Hermann Diels, *Die Fragmente der Vorsokratiker*, 4th ed. (Berlin: Weidmann, 1922), frag. A 45 (Diels, vol. 1, p. 386) for a reference in Aristotle *Physics* 203a.—Eds.

characteristic and pregnant comparison, "like they were cut off with an axe."[6] The actual "concrete" reality of geist consists rather in the fact that all its different basic aspects mesh with one another and coalesce, that, in the true sense of the word, they are "concrescent." It seems therefore as though we needed only to return to this original basic unity, to this primary, concrete lived experience, for all the "artificial" distinctions of reflection again to be suspended so that we can override these distinctions and have access to an essential unity. When the world of culture differentiates itself—its objective meaning and content—into more and more distinct "levels" and when these levels finally threaten more and more to become alienated from each other, this gulf and alienation have a definite limit set from the beginning by the opposing side of "subjectivity." All these different forms and directions of culture meet and come together again and again in creative subjectivity itself. In the manner in which the objective products of culture unfold from this subjectivity, by which they break away and come to confront it, they then possess an inner commonality which they cannot abandon or disown no matter how greatly their goals may come to diverge. Even the freest, truly autonomous acts of the intellect still possess here, amid the high-handedness that they assert among themselves, a natural bond and ties. No matter how far they appear to be removed from one another when seen from the standpoint of the pure "Idea," the standpoint of objective meaning, such divergences are brought together again if we regard them in perspective, from the viewpoint of subjectivity.

Hence, the worldview of myth seems to be incompatible with that of science—and yet myth and science become entwined in a peculiar way if we conceive them both as efforts of the human mind. They are, even where they appear to be direct opposites, still developments and expressions of that essence of "humanity" that we can only conceive and define as ἓν διαφερόμενον ἑαυτῷ.[7] We seem immediately to regain the unity that the finished products are lacking if instead of looking at these, we look at the way they were produced, the way they came forth. It is this coming forth, this act of breaking away from the simple basis of nature and life that attests to the essence of the human mind and its being, which, amid all its conflicts, remains identical with itself. The divergent rays meet again as

---

6. Anaxagoras frag. B 8 (Diels, vol. 1, p. 403). Kathleen Freeman, *Ancilla to the Pre-Socratic Philosophers: A Complete Translation of the Fragments in Diels* (Cambridge, Mass.: Harvard Univ. Press, 1948), p. 84. In subsequent references to the fragments of the pre-Socratics, the Diels citation will be followed by a page number from Freeman.—Eds.

7. "different from itself."—Eds.

soon as we direct them to this focus, the focal point of subjectivity, and let them assemble in it.

Yet the solution that seems to suggest itself to us here in truth reflects a new expression and a new conception of the problem. For if we conceive the objective conflicts between the "forms" to be resolved in the unity of "life," this does not really eliminate the dialectic; rather, it pushes it back further into the concept of life itself. It is this very dialectic to which metaphysics was led again and again in the nineteenth and early twentieth centuries and with which it has struggled by constantly developing new conceptual instruments. The opposition between "Leben" and "Geist" is the hub of this metaphysics; it proves to be so definitive and decisive that it gradually comes to absorb into itself and eliminate all the other pairs of metaphysical terms that have been coined in the history of metaphysics. The opposites of "Being" and "Becoming," of "One" and "Many," "Matter" and "Form," "Soul" and "Body" all appear now to have been dissolved into this one completely fundamental antithesis. Problems of widely divergent origin and character flow into it from all sides. As if they were led by secret subterranean forces, multifarious and highly divergent intellectual undertakings are directed again and again to this particular metaphysical center. Here, at this point of unification, the philosophy of nature meets the philosophy of history; here ethics and the theory of value interweave with epistemology and the philosophy of science. Thinkers of such divergent intellectual character and different background as Nietzsche and Bergson, as Dilthey and Simmel, have engaged in this movement to transform basic metaphysical oppositions. It is a mistake and a misunderstanding of this movement, to make oneself blind to its origin and its true intellectual significance by thinking that it can be dismissed as a mere intellectual "fad."[8] For no matter how one may judge its final systematic contribution, its motives are unmistakably rooted in a fundamental and basic stratum of our modern sense of life and our specifically modern sense of culture. An inner tension and polar opposition in this sense of life and of culture strive for expression in it. Of all the thinkers who are part of this movement, perhaps no one has so strongly felt its origin and brought it so clearly to consciousness as Simmel has done.

It is typical of Simmel's intellectual character and his aims that he does not rest until he has transformed this felt polarity into a polarity of thought,

---

8. Heinrich Rickert, *Die Philosophie des Lebens. Darstellung und Kritik der philosophischen Modeströmungen unserer Zeit* (Tübingen: [J. C. B. Mohr (Paul Siebeck),] 1920).—Cassirer.

until he has reduced it to its simplest logical formula. Such a formula will not, of course, resolve the basic metaphysical opposition to which it is directed; it can only designate and articulate it from a particular angle. This designation can consist in nothing other than logical paradoxes. As an example of such a paradox, as an intellectual oxymoron, Simmel coined the concept "transcendence of life." Life as such appears to mean nothing other than a pure kind of internal being; in fact its basic character appears to be defined by this very Being-in-itself and Remaining-in-itself. Whatever may proceed from its richness and activity, it remains at the same time closed within this eternally flowing abundance; it possesses its content and its meaning only as part of this process of life itself, not as something opposed to it or in any way approaching it from outside. The concept of Life is distinguished from the concept of Being in the older metaphysics and from its "ontology" by virtue of this one basic feature: it recognizes no substantiality other than that which consists of pure actuality alone. Yet this "immanence" of life is only one of its aspects; another, which is diametrically opposed to it, appears to be insolubly connected to it. As little as life can ever change its character, since this very change itself remains *its* work and its own activity, so it too can never be wholly absorbed in any of its forms, conceived as a closed and complete totality. The notion that it could ever attain its goal, so that it could then be immobile and come to rest, is no less impracticable than the one that its goal, the telos of its movement, lies in principle outside itself. Rather, life's actual movement consists in the oscillation between two extreme phases. It is never at one with itself except by being beyond itself at the same time. The peculiar and unique act of erecting and breaking through its boundaries provides the only absoluteness we can attribute to its character. To the extent that "life" can be defined at all, it always has two complementary definitions. "Life," as Simmel summarizes his basic thesis, "is at once flux without pause and yet something enclosed in bearers and contents, formed about midpoints, individualized, and therefore always a bounded form which continually jumps its bounds. That is its essence."[9] The essence of concrete life as it takes place is (not something that is added onto its being, but that of which its being consists), "that *transcendence is immanent in life.*"[10]

9. Georg Simmel, "The Transcendent Character of Life," in Simmel, *Individuality and Social Forms*, trans. and ed. Donald N. Levine (Chicago: Univ. of Chicago Press, 1971), p. 363.—Eds.

10. [Georg] Simmel, "Die Transzendenz des Lebens," *Lebensanschauung: Vier metaphysische Kapitel*, Munich[: Duncker & Humblot,] 1918, pp. 1ff.—Cassirer. "The Transcendent

In this inner and necessary duality life seems to be not only the original source of geist but also its archetype and prototype. For the same duality is present in a newly heightened form in the being of geist. The heightening and magnification consist in geist not merely having this duality as part of itself, but in the fact that geist is also aware of this duality. "That we are cognizant of our knowing and our not knowing ... and so forth into the potentially endless—this is the real infinity of vital movement on the level of intellect. Every limit is herewith transcended but of course only as a result of the fact that it is fixed, that is, that there exists something to transcend. It is only with this self-transcending movement that geist shows itself to be something absolutely vital."[11] We will not here follow the general metaphysical views that Simmel attaches to this definition of the concept of geist; rather, we will regard it only in terms of our own basic problem, that of the "philosophy of symbolic forms." Simmel himself points in this direction by further giving the original antithesis of "life" and "geist" another expression, by transforming it into the antithesis of "life" and "idea" or of "life" and "form." Again life appears here as that which, in one and the same indivisible act, brings about and eliminates form, which it both furthers and negates, which it both creates and destroys. When they are taken as principles in the shaping of the world, there is a deep contradiction between the processes of life and form, taken in themselves. Form is limitation, hence separation and differentiation, the assertion of an independent content of its own as enduring in being, so that it is set off from the continual process of becoming. But on the other hand, if we take becoming itself in its entirety and in its unbroken unity, not even the concept of such separation, in any strict sense, seems to be conceivable.

We cannot even speak here of an unceasing destruction of forms because something that could be destroyed could not come about on the basis of the complete dynamics of becoming. In this way individuality, which is a necessary condition of every fixed form, must escape the continuity of the stream of life, which does not permit any closed forms. Between life and form, between continuity and individuality there is irreconcilable opposition. That reality appears to overcome this opposition at every moment,

---

Character of Life," p. 363. The passage in its entirety reads "It [the category of 'the reaching out of life over itself'] has been described here only in a schematic and abstract way. I have presented only the bare pattern of the concretely filled life, insofar as its essence (not that something might be added to its being, but rather directly constitutive of its being) may be expressed by the formula that *transcendence is immanent in life.*"—Eds.

11. Simmel, "The Transcendent Character of Life," p. 358.—Eds.

that in it the indiscernible becomes fact,[12] does not offer a true resolution of this conceptual antinomy. Rather, it is only an expression of the undeniable demand for such a solution, which our means of thought can never adequately fulfill. The life of geist cannot represent itself except in forms of some kind, yet it can never put its totality into form and confine this totality to its limits. "As life it needs form; as life, it needs more than form. Life is thus caught up in a contradiction, that it can only be accommodated in forms, and yet it cannot be accommodated in form. . . . The fact that our ideas and cognitions, our values and judgments stand completely apart from the creative life in their meaning, their objective intelligibility and historical effectiveness—exactly this is what is the characteristic of human life. Just as transcending its current, limited form within the plane of life itself is more-life, which is nevertheless the immediate, inescapable essence of life itself, so does transcendence into the level of objective content . . . constitute the more-than-life, inseparable from life, and the very essence of mental life."[13]

If we take these observations as our starting point, which expresses one of the central problems of modern "philosophy of life," in fact with exemplary precision and clarity, we are then surprised to realize that this modern metaphysics diverges from the older one in its goal, but not in the way it pursues it; it differs in the content of its presuppositions but not in its method. For it too proceeds by first observing and firmly fixing certain opposites that are found in the world of experience, in the world of the "given," in order then to free these opposites from the relativization and limits to which they are subjected in the sphere of finite existence, and it then projects them into the infinite. By the power of this method of projection, the infinite becomes the point in which all divergencies, all opposites and contradictions, as they are found in the realm of the finite, are supposed to be dissolved while they at the same time all become concentrated to the highest degree. The last, unconditioned Being that thought can attain does not exclude these contradictions, but takes them up and contains them within itself—whereby, of course, it acquires a completely "irrational" character that can no longer be logically determined.

The modern concept of "life" must be forced by the course of metaphysical thinking to follow the same path taken by the concept of God in the

12. Goethe, *Faust* II, lines 12104–12109: "All that is transitory / is only a symbol; / what seems unachievable / here is seen done; / what's indiscernible; / here becomes fact."—Eds.

13. Simmel, pp. 22ff.—Cassirer. Simmel, "The Transcendent Character of Life," pp. 370–371.—Eds.

older metaphysics. In the concept of God, the notion of the *coincidentia oppositorum*[14] develops with systematic necessity and consistency out of that of absolute totality. God is that subject which should unite all reality and hence everything that can be expressed in a specific predicate, but this subject then also becomes the center and pivot of all those predicates which exclude each other in the empirical sphere and also do so in accordance with the laws of logical reflection. All names apply to it because and insofar as none apply to it; in it the absolute position and the absolute negation coincide.[15]

Simmel attains the basic concept of his metaphysics, the concept of the absoluteness of life, by means of a completely analogous double step in thought. The logical difficulty posed by the principle of identity, namely that life is at once itself and not itself because it is supposed to be more than it is itself, is, as he emphasizes, only a matter of expression. In truth, this contradiction does not apply to Being, nor to the reality of life itself, but only to our thought about this reality, which must necessarily make distinctions and separations, whereas in reality all is contained with complete, seamless indifference. "It is . . . an ex post facto reconstruction of immediately lived life to characterize it as a unity of boundary-setting and boundary-transcending, of individual centeredness and reaching out beyond its own periphery, for the very act of designating this point of unity necessarily breaks it up. According to abstract formulation, the constitution of life in its quantity and quality and the transcendence of this quality and quantity can only touch each other at this point, whereas the life which goes on there includes within itself both sides, constitution and transcendence, as a real unity."[16] Between "immediately lived life" and its interpretation and verbal expression we have thus the same contradiction that exists in "rational theology" between God's Being, which is supposed to be a pure "beyond"—a fundamental transcendence opposed to everything cognizable—and the thought of God.

---

14. The medieval concept of God as the unity of opposites has its source in 1 Cor. 15:28, where God is described as ἐν πᾶσι πᾶτα ("everything to everyone").—Eds.

15. A reference to the logic of the coincidence of opposites as developed by Pseudo-Dionysius Areopagita, in *De Divinis Nominibus* 872 A 4–9. The concept of the *coincidentia oppositorum* is central in the philosophy of Nicholas of Cusa, but he does not use it in a way representative of such medieval modes of thought. See Cassirer, *The Individual and the Cosmos in Renaissance Philosophy*, trans. Mario Domandi (New York: Harper Torchbooks, 1964), pp. 8–10.—Eds.

16. Simmel, "The Transcendent Character of Life," p. 370.—Eds.

Here as there, pure, absolute Being cannot do without the organ of its visibility, the medium by means of which it not only exists but also grasps itself in itself. No matter how one tries to distinguish this visibility itself from that which becomes visible in it, this distinction remains itself as a kind of vision, a specific kind of "view." Just as all "negative theology" in its dispensing with the *logos* is itself an act, a deed of *logos*, so too is the return to the pure immediacy of life only possible by a particular act of "seeing," of the "intuition" of life. And this intuition can never go behind the world of forms per se because it is itself nothing other than a way of giving form. Simmel's metaphysics differs from many of the modern kinds of "irrationalism" in that it clearly sees through this basic situation. As much as he repeatedly insists on this turn toward life, it is also just as clear to him that this is inseparably bound to what he terms the "turn to the idea." This consists for him in the fact that what appeared at first to be a pure creation of life, to be integrated into and at the service of its continuing course, is not bound exclusively to this state of affairs, but rather proves to have its own significance and autonomous meaning. The realm of the "idea" is made accessible to us and arises for us by the forms and functions that life has brought about for its own sake, out of its own dynamics to become independent and definite, so that life serves them, and submits itself to their order; this is what gives them their final value and significance. Only after this change has taken place do the great intellectual categories, which previously seemed passive in contrast to life, become productive in the true sense; their own objective forms are now the dominants which take over the matter of life, which now must follow them.[17]

We now stand at the point where this modern metaphysics of life bears directly on our own basic systematic problem. For what is here described as "rotation of the axis of life,"[18] is nothing other than the particular turn-

17. Simmel, "Die Wendung zur Idee," in *Lebensanschauung: Vier metaphysische Kapitel* (Munich and Leipzig: [Duncker & Humblot,] 1918), see esp. pp. 38f.—Cassirer.

18. Simmel, "Die Wendung zur Idee," p. 38: "And now the great turnabout occurs by which the realm of ideas arises: the forms or functions, which life brought forward on its own and for its own sake, now become so independent and definitive, that life now turns about and serves them, subordinates its goals under them so that the success of this subordination becomes just as important as a final source of value and meaning as the realm of ideas previously did fitting these forms into the economy of life. The great intellectual categories are based of course on life, even when they are still caught up in it, and remain on its plateau. As long as they do, they remain passive toward it, submissive, and subservient to it, because they fit themselves into its demands and must modify themselves according to how they serve it. Only with that great rotation of the axis of life do they actually become truly productive."—Eds.

about, the intellectual peripeteia, that it experiences as soon as it catches sight of itself in the medium of a "symbolic form." The "turn to the idea" requires in every case this turn to "symbolic form" as its precondition and necessary access. But if we pose the question once at *this* level, then we do not merely contrast the "immediacy" of life to the "mediacy" of thought and intellectual consciousness in general as rigid opposite poles; rather, we regard only the process of their mediation as it takes place in language, myth, and knowledge. In this way the problem assumes another form and character. Not some absolute beyond all mediation, but only such mediation can lead us out of the theoretical antinomies. The more that Simmel enters into the abstraction of "form," the more this abstraction, this region of the self-significant and the absolute, the high-handed idea, appears to him as the opposite of the concrete life process with its individual richness and individual turbulence.

When life reaches out to the generality of the "idea," it seems thereby to move beyond its own reality, it seems to have to dare, in a way, to jump over its own shadow. But it is characteristic of this limitation that even this so broadly conceived observation is unable to overcome the fact that again and again *spatial* analogies are mixed unnoticed into this description of "transcendence." It is as though what is "this side" and what is "beyond," what "remains-in-itself" and what "goes-beyond-itself," the "inner" aspect of life and its "externalization," despite all reassurances to the contrary, are repeatedly understood in their most literal senses. The region of life and of form seem to be like two domains of reality which are at odds with each other over the entire space of Being and both of which on the other hand are supposed completely to fill this entire space without any gaps. Simmel attributes the conflict that arises from this way of looking at things to the "impotence of the concept," which is incapable of grasping the unbroken unity of the absolute, which contains no oppositions. But is this really a limitation of thought in general or perhaps only a limitation imposed by a particular type of thought? Does the contradiction apply to logical categories as such, or is it something that applies only to a particular type of spatial, spatializing thinking?

Simmel has never concealed the purely symbolic character that all his descriptions and comparisons carry, but beyond this his portrayal is always subject to the danger that its content and form, and what he intends as a symbol, unnoticeably becomes a metaphor and serves as a metaphor. The gulf which opens up here is not that between the realm of the metaphysical or the real and the realm of "meaning"; rather, it is that between meaning in its ideal purity and meaning as image and imagistic expression. The actual source of the aporias and antinomies which Simmel uncovers is not so much the conversion of a basic and original metaphysical relationship into conceptual symbols as it is their translation into spatial schemata. If we begin with the "opposition" of the unlimited and the limit, of idea and life, then it is no longer possible to make understandable how these two necessarily determine each other, how they are to become correlative to each other. Yet it is this very correlation that is the primarily certain and the primarily given while their separation is something later, a mere construction of thought. The question of how life "achieves" form, how form comes to life, is therefore, of course, unsolvable. This is not because there is an unbridgeable gulf between them, but because the hypothesis of "pure" form (as well as the hypothesis of "pure" life) already contains a contradiction within itself. No matter how deeply we enter into the realm of organic processes or how high we go into the sphere of intellectual creativity, we never find these two subjects, these two substances, so to speak, whose "harmony" and metaphysical relationship are being questioned here. We meet up with completely formless life as seldom as we meet up with a completely lifeless form. The distinction that we draw between them in thought does not refer therefore to two metaphysical potentialities, each of which "is in itself and is conceived through itself";[19] instead, we only meet up with two accents that we fix in the process of becoming. Becoming is in its essence neither mere life nor mere form; rather, it is the becoming of form—γένεσις εἰς οὐσίαν, as Plato said.[20]

If this becomes evident by observing the forces of nature, it becomes clear and unmistakable in all truly intellectual energies. For they all exist only by virtue of being activated and by giving shape to themselves in this activation. Perhaps the clearest example of this situation confronts us in the

19. This is Spinoza's definition of substance. See Spinoza, *Ethica*, pt. I, def. 3, *Opera quotquot reperta sunt*, ed. J. van Vloten and J. P. N. Land, 3d ed., 4 vols. (The Hague: Martinus Nijhoff, 1914), vol. 1, p. 37: "Per substantiam intelligo id, quod in se est, et per se concipitur." *The Ethics*, trans. Samuel Shirley, ed. Seymour Feldman (Indianapolis: Hackett, 1982), p. 31: "By substance I mean that which is in itself and is conceived through itself; that is, that the conception of which does not require the conception of another thing from which it has to be formed."—Eds.

20. "coming-into-being." See Plato *Philebus* 26D8. All subsequent references to Plato follow the *Collected Dialogues of Plato*, ed. Edith Hamilton and Huntington Cairns, Bollingen Series 71 (New York: Pantheon Books, 1961). The Greek text is cited from *Platonis Opera Omnia*, Recensuit et commentariis instruxit Godofredus Stallbaum, 12 vols. (Gotha and Erfurt, 1827–1842).—Eds.

structure of language. Of course here too one normally makes a distinction between the creative process of language as such and the forms that are thereby created, and in this distinction we take note of the form, of how the synthetic structure and grammatical "categories" of language not infrequently stand opposed to the living movement of language so as to restrict and inhibit it. But this external dualism is refuted again and again as soon as we conceive of language in Humboldt's sense, not as an *ergon*, but as an *energeia*,[21] not merely as something that has become what it is, but which is continuously shaping itself. Humboldt emphasized repeatedly that language never really exists except in its immediate performance. Even what we are accustomed to calling its "inner form" has its true actuality only in the variety of the changing and constantly renewing acts in which language is formed. "Language," if it is not to be some mere abstraction, truly consists of these acts, and it is by virtue of them that it always arises anew. The individual speech act does not hereby take place when the speaker merely reaches into a world of completely finished forms from which a selection has to be made but which otherwise must be treated as given, like a minted coin. The speech act is never in this sense an act of mere assimilation; rather, it is, in however small a way, a creative act, an act of shaping and reshaping. It is a completely one-sided and insufficient conception of this act to regard it as though the subject was inhibited and constricted at every turn and with every step by a world of forms as something already present, as though it had to struggle against them to make its way. Here the form does not prove to be such an impediment, but an organ that is always ready, in fact, an organ whose value rests on its being modifiable and mutable in the highest measure. In no way are we governed here by that antithesis, that unbridgeable gulf between what "life" demands and what "form" demands, between the claims of universality and those of individuality. On the contrary, it is one and the same process, the living process of speech, in which individuality and universality are contained as equally justified and equally necessary aspects of the process. The universal is that through which the individual constructs the world, and the universal is

21. See Wilhelm von Humboldt, *The Diversity of Human Language-Structure and its Influence on the Mental Development of Mankind*, trans. Peter Heath, Cambridge Texts in German Philosophy (Cambridge: Cambridge Univ. Press, 1988), p. 49: "*Language*, regarded in its real nature, is an enduring thing, and at every moment a *transitory* one. Even its maintenance by writing is always just an incomplete, mummy-like preservation, only needed again in attempting thereby to picture the living utterance. In itself, it is no product [*Werk*] (*ergon*), but an activity [*Thätigkeit*] (*energeia*)."—Eds.

what constructs the world of the individual. We are not dealing with divisions within Being, with an opposition and separation of regions that meet but can never truly interact with each other.

We have here instead an interaction of forces, of impulses of movement. Every use, no matter how transient and temporary, of a linguistic form is such an impulse, which does not leave the world of linguistic forms in the same condition in which it had found it, but which affects it as a whole, which it changes, however imperceptibly, and makes receptive for future, new formations. In comparison with the traditional, basic metaphysical view, there is a complete inversion here in the relationship between the "absolute" and the "relative." According to that view the opposites that cannot be united in the realm of the finite are made to disappear as soon as they are projected into the infinite, as soon as one moves from the sphere of the conditioned to that of the unconditioned. But here the opposite proves to be the case. Life and form, continuity and individuality, diverge radically as soon as we take one of them to be absolute, as soon as we see in them different metaphysical kinds of being. But this gulf is closed if we instead put ourselves in the midst of the concrete process of formation and its dynamics, if we take the opposition of the two aspects as an opposition not of beings, but of pure functions. What seems to be a real opposition when seen from the standpoint of Being becomes merged; it becomes a correlation and cooperation, when regarded from the standpoint of activity, of intelligent creativity.

In every field it is the truly productive and, in the highest sense, creative minds that have most strongly felt this correlativity and cooperation. As far as language is concerned, there are among the great creators of language of course perhaps none who did not at times feel the given world of linguistic forms as a limitation and bond, who would not have complained, as Goethe did, that he had to ruin both life and art in this "poorest stuff."[22] But they themselves are the living and constantly renewed proof of the intellectual spontaneity of language, by again and again breaking through these barriers because none of them regards language as a finished product;

---

22. See Goethe, "Venetian Epigrams, 1790," in *Goethe's Roman Elegies and Venetian Epigrams: A Bilingual Text*, trans. L. R. Lind (Lawrence: Univ. Press of Kansas, 1974), epigram 29, pp. 95, 97. The full epigram reads as follows: "I've tried many arts: I've sketched, I've engraved in copper, / Painted in oil, and I've modeled a lot in clay, / Without understanding as yet, learned, accomplished nothing. / Only one talent I've brought near to masterhoood: / To write German. And so I botch as an unhappy poet, / I'm sorry to say, life and art with the poorest stuff." See *WA*, Abt. 1, vol. 1, p. 314.—Eds.

rather, it proves in their hands to be capable of continuing adaptation, a pure formative energy with an unlimited openness. What it is at some particular moment depends in the end upon this energy, on the expressive will and expressive power which stand behind it. Goethe himself says this in one of his youthful poems, "Sprache" [Language], which, compared to that Venetian Epigram, seems to be its opposite and palinode. "What's rich and poor! What's strong and weak! / Is the buried broken urn rich? / Is the sword in the arsenal strong? / Take them up mildly, and friendly happiness / Flows forth, Divinity, from you! / Grab hold for victory, power, the sword, / And over your neighbor, fame!"[23] The formative power of language is not to be compared to the current of a river, which crashes against and breaks on the presently given linguistic forms as against a wall; rather, it floods these forms themselves and keeps them internally mobile. In this process even what has become fixed is recast again and again so that it cannot become a completely rigid armament; on the other hand each momentary impulse, the creativity of the moment, acquires through it its continuity and constancy. This creation would have to be evanescent, would have to disappear like a breath into the air, if in the midst of its rise and development it did not meet with something that was already developed. This is not mere "matter" for it, but a product of and a witness to the same forces that brought it about. In this way the individual, temporally bound speech act flows into the great riverbed of language; but it does not become completely lost in it. Rather, the stronger its individuality, the more it is preserved and the more it reproduces itself so that the impulse which it contains is not exhausted in a momentary form, but influences it further and further so as to affect the flow of the whole, its intensity, its direction, its dynamics, and its rhythm.

It is only by such dynamic comparisons, not in static images, that it is possible to describe form as form-that-is-becoming: γένεσις εἰς οὐσίαν. Just as scholastic metaphysics coined the concepts of *natura naturata* and *natura naturans*, so the philosophy of symbolic forms must distinguish between *forma formans* and *forma formata*.[24] The interplay between both is

23. See Goethe, "Sprache," *WA*, Abt. 1, vol. 2, p. 256: "Was reich und arm! Was stark und schwach! / Ist reich vergrabner Urne Bauch? / Ist stark das Schwert im Arsenal? / Greif milde drein, und freundlich Glück / Fliesst, Gottheit, vor dir aus! / Fass an zum Siege, Macht, das Schwert, / Und über Nachbarn Ruhm!" Cassirer gives "Bruch" (broken) instead of "Bauch" (belly).—Eds.

24. Cassirer makes this distinction again in his essay "Form und Technik," in Leo Kestenburg, ed., *Kunst und Technik* (Berlin: Wegweiser Verlag, 1930), p. 19.—Eds.

what constitutes the swing of the pendulum of intellectual life itself. The *forma formans* that becomes *forma formata*, which it must become for the sake of its own self-preservation without ever becoming reduced to it, retains the power to regain itself from it, to be born again as *forma formans*—this is what is distinctive of the development of geist and culture. Contained in this are all those processes that Simmel refers to by the expression the "turn to the idea." He himself thereby conceives the idea as something opposed to life in a sphere which is, if not adversarial at least distant from it, as fundamentally transcendent, to which a bridge can be found only by a turning away, a turning back by life, in a particular "rotation of the axis of life." For everything ideal—the ideal that we call art or religion, no less than that which we call by the names "knowledge" or "truth"—represents an individual objective content of its own and thereby belongs to the level of logical, autonomous—no longer vital—meaning.[25] But how could life "turn to" this objective content if the relationship and tension, the "intention," toward it did not already originally lie enclosed within it, indeed if this very intention were not an aspect of it, its being, and its final fulfillment? So, if we see it in the mirror of the "symbolic forms," the "turn to the idea" cannot be described as life bidding itself farewell in order to go forth into something foreign and distant from itself; rather, life must be seen as returning to itself, it "comes to itself" in the medium of the symbolic forms. It possesses and grasps itself in the imprint of form as the infinite possibility of formation, as the will to form and power to form. Even life's limitation becomes its own act; what from outside seems to be its fate, its necessity, proves to be a witness to its freedom and self-formation.

We have so far sought to expose and characterize this basic situation with the example of language, but it emerges just as distinctly and in the same paradigmatic sharpness in the shaping of every other "symbolic form." For instance, if we consider the form of myth, then we can only understand myth's objective "meaning" and objective forming activity not by just conceiving it as a form of perception or thought, but by conceiving it as an original "form of life." Wherever specifically human existence and life is apprehended, we already find it wrapped up in the primordial forms of myth. It does not "have" these as objects; rather, it *is* in them, has entered into them and is interwoven with them. This holds for the details of myth as well as for myth as a whole. The specific nature, coloration, and tone of

---

25. Simmel, "Die Transzendenz des Lebens," p. 24 (Cf. above p. 9).—Cassirer. Simmel, "The Transcendent Character of Life," p. 372.—Eds.

the feeling of life define the character of the mythical world of images, define the form assumed by its gods and demons.[26] The further back we go, the more we seem to approach the truly primordial level of myth, the more clearly this "closeness to life" becomes. But in the higher and highest forms of religion this immediate closeness to life has given way to another relationship. Here we arrive at a form of the divine in which the divine appears to be raised above all life and all Being. But no matter how this transcendence, which the divine in itself is supposed to have, is conceived, another factor emerges as soon as we grasp its appearance, its revelation within the human world. This process again reveals to us the same polarity that we found in the world of language. Every vision of the divine, no matter whether it is of the most personal and individual kind, is referred at the instant of its expression and communication to a field of existing forms of religious expression and is bound to them. But the highest religious conceptions are able in one and the same act to enter into this bond and also to overcome it. They both destroy and create forms; they enter into the conditioned language of religious forms by internally breaking away from it and exposing its contingent nature. All truly religious and prophetic spirits appear to the world of these forms to have such a Janus face. They break up the *forma formata*, but by their readiness to destroy and by the act of destruction itself they open up again the way to *forma formans*. Here we find the same rhythm, the same characteristic swing of the pendulum, but once again there is no "over here" and "over there," no reaching over from one area into another, to a completely different one wholly beyond the first, but only the mutual affection of forces upon one another, putting them into a virtual but quite delicate balance.

The same basic relationship is represented again as soon as we consider the inner structure of the theoretical world. We seem here, if anywhere, to have reached the point at which, instead of a mere delicate balance, a rigid one has been achieved. We stand, then, on the ground of the "logical" as such, and this is defined by its unyielding necessity, by its absolute identity, in Platonic terms: by the "ever self-consistent and invariable."[27] Yet this unconditioned constancy and identity holds only if we consider pure logical form *in abstracto*, if we separate it from all its intertwining with the

26. Cf. on this esp. [*PSF*] vol. 2, pp. 175ff.—Cassirer. In referring to earlier volumes of his *PSF*, Cassirer made it his practice throughout volumes 2 and 3 to give the citation by volume number and page, without providing any further details.—Eds.

27. See Plato's description of the divine, in *Phaedo* 80B1f.: ἀεὶ ὡςαύτως κατὰ ταὐτὰ ἔχοντι ἑαυτῷ ὁμοιότατον. *Collected Dialogues*, p. 63.—Eds.

world of becoming and with all the "applications" that it undergoes. If on the other hand we look at this and consider the idea not as such but as the "participation" of the appearance in the idea, then here too we are quickly presented with another picture. This participation is not attained by the "material" of sensation being taken up into and determined according to a system of completely finished theoretical forms. With Kant it seems again and again as though, according to the organization and architectonic division of the *Critique of Pure Reason*, that theoretical knowledge of nature is built up when the "given" of sensation enters into the a priori forms of pure intuition and the pure understanding through a specific place of admission, which has been ready and waiting from the beginning. If one wants to see this as anything more than a methodological abstraction, if one believes that the elements which have here been separated in analysis must also be given as separable parts of the knowing process, then this conception has been progressively refuted in the course of the development of our theoretical knowledge since Kant. This development proves ever more clearly that the purely theoretical means of thought in no way endure as something external, as merely opposed to the material of experience that these are supposed to enter into and organize. Here too we can recognize the means of thought and their theoretical significance only in theoretical thought's living function, only in its work and in its achievements. By their act of determining something these means attain their own complete determination. Since this act never comes to an end, this determination can also never be totally completed and can never be regarded as incapable of further modifications.

The theoretical form also proves to be capable of an unlimited evolution—and this sacrifice of finality in no way defeats its universality. For the "apriority" of the theoretical form is safeguarded in its evolution and transformation; in fact, its full significance and true meaning emerge in this way. The concepts and propositions that the unity of our theoretical knowledge of nature, its divisions and systematic structure, are based upon, are never taken simply from experience. They are logically prior to it in the sense that they represent the line or direction for thought. They set the goal for it, and they help to prepare the way that leads to this goal. The way is not prescribed from the beginning, and no markings exist; clearing the way is the true task of theoretical thought and it is in this that the achievement of the a priori consists. Theoretical form can only unfold in constant contact with the empirical world of "facts" and in the constant reactions that it experiences in this way; only thus can it unlock the richness of its fashioning power, its inner "possibilities." It gives forth its riches insofar as it is required to do so by the opposite side; but the thing that poses the demands is not at the same time what holds the foundation of theoretical form together. This mutability of the theoretical form has come to be recognized in the history of exact science since theoretical mathematics has abandoned the idea of the "singularity" of Euclidean geometry and theoretical physics the "singularity" of classical mechanics. This abandonment has frequently been condemned as a skeptical resignation. In truth, however, it in no way denies the systematic unity or even the systematic completeness of theoretical knowledge; rather, it recognizes that the path to this unity is not a simple one, but highly complex. This becomes most apparent if we consider the fundamentally new relationship that has been created in modern physics between observation and measurement.

In the worldview of the older physics these functions appear to be coupled to each other, but both of them nonetheless possess a relatively independent meaning, and the achievements of the one can be separated from the other. The "axioms" of measurement can be formulated in completely distinct ways, independent of the "facts" of observation, and they appear to be the very thing that distinguishes the pure "form" of experience from its mere content, from particular physical objects and events, which are subject to measurement. Every individual measurement is subject to a universally valid metrics, the metrics of Euclidean space, and this is what provides the firm housing, the theoretical scaffolding for all physical experience. Individual observations formed in thought are explained and conceptually grasped only by first being drawn within the previously determined schema of space. But this, so to speak, substantive character of space, as some uniform substratum for all material phenomena, is lost in modern relativistic physics. In it, the concept of the metric field takes the place of a single "absolute" space. This does not possess at all the same independence from matter; instead, it is defined and constituted by it. The "form" and "content" of physical experience, "measurement" and "observation," the objects "in" space and "in" time, and time and space themselves now grow into one another in a completely new way. Each of these two aspects proves to be definable only in terms of and through the other. The "metric field" stands independently of the material one that the world takes up.[28] The

---

28. For details see, e.g., Weyl, *Raum Zeit Materie*, 4th ed., §12, §27; cf. also above p. . . .—Cassirer. Hermann Weyl, *Space-Time-Matter*, trans. Henry L. Brose (New York: Dover Books, 1951), §12, §27, pp. 95ff., 218ff. Cassirer's manuscript provides no page number. *PSF*,

form as "pure" form is not thereby eliminated, but it no longer possesses the uniformity and rigidity that were attributed to it in the system of classical physics. It now has a finer knit and is more differentiated; it has become infinitely more supple. Every point in physical space can now have "its" metric form without these infinite determinations disintegrating, without the possibility being eliminated that in their construction and in their individuality they could come together in a lawful unity. Thus we see that from the viewpoint of theoretical thought, exact form too is able to fulfill its task all the better and with more assurance the less it is understood as a fixed demarcation, the greater and freer it is to display its mobility and potentiality for giving shape.

Yet in showing this "principle of movement," which resides in every form as such, the objection that the metaphysics of life raises against the world of form and causes it to question its value is in no way appeased or countered. The question appears in the end to consist not in whether form is capable of movement but whether the kind of mobility that takes place in and through form is up to the pure mobility of life and can accord with it. Does the turn to form mean an intensification of this pure motility of life, or does it not, rather, really mean its slackening and degeneration? Is the "turn to the idea," even if it seems to be a continuation of the process of life, the completion of this process or is it not its falling off? All romantic philosophy has frequently opted for this latter alternative. It repeats variations on Byron's *Manfred*: "The Tree of Knowledge is not that of Life."[29] It does not take knowledge only in the limited, narrow sense of theoretical "scientific" truth, but the whole broad sphere of consciousness, of *cogitatio* in general. Where the first ray of this "consciousness" lights up, there its innermost power arises, foreign to life and opposed to its innermost tendency. In modern metaphysics this romantic thesis of the unbridgeable gulf between the creative ground and the world of *cogitatio*, between "life" and "geist," has found no more radical defender, no one who has as sharply stressed this position, than Ludwig Klages.

His complete theoretical doctrine of "consciousness" is concentrated into a proof of this, its life-destroying significance. According to him, life can

---

vol. 3, p. 354, n. 37, cites some of the same passages from Weyl's *Space-Time-Matter* on the group theory of "space metrics."—Eds.

29. Lord Byron, "Manfred, A Dramatical Poem," *The Works of Lord Byron*, ed. Ernest Hartley Coleridge (London, 1905), vol. 5, act 1, scene 1, p. 85: "But Grief should be the Instructor of the wise; / Sorrow is Knowledge: they who know the most / Must mourn the deepest o'er the fatal truth, / The Tree of Knowledge is not that of Life."—Eds.

still find a way back to itself only in ecstasy, in the turn away from consciousness and in extinguishing it. It is not, as one might believe, the human mind which liberates itself in this way, but the soul, and it does not liberate itself from the body, but from the mind or intellect. This is the struggle that runs through all existence and the whole history of mankind: the struggle between life as the all-pervasive, truly creative, primordial, cosmic potentiality, and a power outside space and time which opposes this reality, as it is bound to space and time. This power presumes itself to be greater than this reality, and yet in this detachment it proves in the end to be impotent and incapable of any genuine productive energy. Geist or intellect, the origin of all judging consciousness and all goal-seeking willing, the creator of "culture," is transformed in this creativity into a curse on mankind, setting man off and isolating him in the middle of the all-encompassing stream of life, that is, creating an independent individual ego, cut off from the deepest unities of the cosmos, a "self," or a "person." "While every non-human creature, although itself unique and with its own inner life, pulses in the rhythm of cosmic life, man has separated from this the law of mind. What for it, as the underpinning of ego-consciousness, seems to be the superiority of predicative, calculative thought over the world, to the metaphysician, if he enters into it deeply enough, appears in the light of the subjugation of life under the yoke of concepts!"[30]

This is the judgment passed on the world of intellectual forms, which is recognized to be a world without essence. To the primordial ground of life it appears not only to be something "other" and in principle "transcendent" but also to be the absolutely negative. If we are to understand this doctrine, we must take it in terms of its own immanent presuppositions, we must return to the primary phenomenon that is its starting point and in which it is rooted, both systematically and psychologically. This primary phenomenon is the pure experience of expression. In the entire history of metaphysics there is perhaps no doctrine that is as strongly oriented toward this one side, that has such a thoroughly "physiognomic" character as does the view of Klages. The personal gift of grasping the totality of reality in expressive characters and of being able to re-create it again as a unique whole has led here to a philosophical theory whose starting point is not "Being," not some objective determination, but a pure function of expression as such. What Klages recognizes as ὄντως ὄν, as the true and original

30. Ludwig Klages, *Vom kosmogonischen Eros* (Munich: [Georg Müller,] 1922), p. 45.—Cassirer.

reality, is manifested in and exhausted by this single basic function. In accordance with this, the doctrine of the "reality of the images" is one of the most important features of his metaphysics and perhaps provides its systematic central issue. Here the being of the image is not at all secondary and derived, something merely "subjective" as compared to the objectivity of things and objective being; it is, rather, the actual root, truly original Being. Again and again he proclaims the predominance of intuitive inwardness over the mere capacity to perceive impressions, the primacy of the "demonically-living reality of the images" over the mechanical motion of the world of things.[31]

With this basic conception Klages' doctrine is able as almost no other to do justice to the true significance of myth. It does not seek to "think" the nature of myth from outside, but to enter into its characteristic and specific way of seeing things. By virtue of this viewpoint, however, it is forced from the outset to remain within the sphere of mythical vision. Just as for Bachofen myth is not fiction or invention, but an organ for the discovery of the historical world and of historical reality, so it becomes here an organ of metaphysical knowledge. For myth, the image is never something merely mediated, never a mere "sign" or "allegory"; the essence itself of a thing is contained in it. As an image, or as expressive, the phenomenon is not merely a representation designating an object separated from it; we are seized by a demonic, living presence right before us. Klages' doctrine seeks to provide a kind of restitution and rehabilitation of this basic attitude, but it, of course, becomes its metaphysical hypostasis. From this hypostasis, from this elevation of the world of expression to the position of the sole reality, it now immediately follows that anything that goes beyond this world, that belongs not to the dimension of pure expression but to that of "representation" or "signification," must pale into insignificance and become a mere schema. Even perception, if it is understood as anything but a purely expressive experience, if it is directed to something objective or thing-like, is subject to this same verdict. Where we see the world in terms of things and divide it up accordingly, we have already destroyed its immediate, living reality. The distance becomes even greater, the split becomes even more incurable if thought moves to the region of "pure" forms in which it can only grasp itself and regard itself as in a mirror instead of what truly exists, the reality of life. Here, where the pure "energy" of thought

---

31. Klages, *Vom kosmogonischen Eros*, p. 94; on the doctrine of the "reality of the images" cf. esp. pp. 74ff.—Cassirer.

seems to have climbed to the highest level, the bond that ties the world of man to the cosmos is completely cut off. Man has become "autonomous," but the law that he has now haughtily erected and that he seeks more and more to apply to everything vital, is empty and lifeless, is deeply alienated from everything that gives reality its content and value.

If this view, this indictment of the "intellect" and the world of intellectual forms as it is raised here, is to be justified, then there seems to be only one way for this justification to take place. It is not sufficient to conceive of the "intellect" as a mere abstraction; rather, its concrete self-development, all of its phenomena and manifestations must be felt and then understood. For all of them, for language and for myth, for art and for theoretical knowledge, for religion as well as for morality, in short, for the whole sphere of consciousness, the *cogitatio*, we require proof of the basic thesis, the thesis of the absolute negativity of the intellect. Klages' own argumentation does not take this long and toilsome course; rather, it focuses from the very beginning on a particular feature, a particular aspect of the inellect that must serve as the representative of the whole. Wherever Klages' argument tries to describe "consciousness," to show its essential nature and so to expose it, it is always taken not so much as something "speculative" but as something "technical." Its aim does not consist in the pure observation of the world but in its domination and subjugation, and no matter how purely "theoretical" its achievements may seem to be, they are all directed to this goal. Bacon's phrase *scientia propter potentiam*[32] appears in this approach to be extended to the whole domain of *cogitatio*. What we call the "understanding," "will," or "culture," these are only names for humankind's unrestrained drive to dominate, only names for that "calculating will to appropriate," which separates itself from the inexhaustible fullness of life in order to subjugate it all the better and make it obedient to man's will. Man has clashed with the planet that bore and nourished him, in fact, with the course of all creation, because he is possessed by this vampire, this power that destroys the soul.[33]

But as searing and convincing as this condemnation of human culture is,

---

32. See Francis Bacon, *Novum Organon* (1620), *The Philosophical Works of Francis Bacon*, 14 vols., ed. James Spedding et al. (London: Longman, 1858), vol. 1, p. 157, aphorism 3: "*Scientia et potentia humana in idem coincidunt, quia ignoratio causæ destituit effectum*" (Knowledge and human capabilities complement one another insofar as a lack of knowledge of the cause also misses the effect).—Eds.

33. Ludwig Klages, *Mensch und Erde: Fünf Abhandlungen* (Munich: Georg Müller Verlag, 1920), pp. 40ff.; cf. esp. the essay "Bewusstsein und Leben" [1915], pp. 49ff.—Cassirer.

if we understand by culture nothing but an aggregate, the constantly renewed accumulation of "goods," the question still remains open whether this denigration of cultural *inheritance* has actually found the center of its target, whether its true significance has been refuted. This question could be affirmed only if we were from the outset to conceive of the significance of culture and its historical development the way that the metaphysics of life understands and defines it. Klages' doctrine provides the consistent systematic and historical conclusion for a view whose roots go back to Schopenhauer and Nietzsche. Here is where this conception of geist arises, this view of the "intellect," which makes it the complete slave of the will. For Schopenhauer this servitude is not yet unlimited or unconditioned; even though the intellect, as far as its origin and development are concerned, is the will's creation, it is able to escape these chains, to break free from the will's dominance, to recognize it as "blind will" and to negate it. In this turnabout we find the true activity of geist; in it are rooted art, pure knowledge, and religion. For Nietzsche these activities have also lost the illusion of independence with which they regale themselves; they are nothing but mere disguises, changing masks behind which the all-powerful, all-prevailing "Will to Power" hides itself.[34] Once this unmasking, this "exposure" of geist has been carried out, the next step was to demand its complete devaluation and rejection. It is futile to wish to dispute the outcome, the consequence of this development, if we accept its premises. It is not the inferences that are drawn here, but the concept of geist that is presupposed against which an objection can be made. Does this concept refer to something factually real, to an independent power, or does it perhaps refer to a mere idol, a delusion—a nightmare—that the metaphysics of life and the will have themselves created? Is this nightmare perhaps only the dark shadow that this metaphysics casts—a shadow that disappears if instead of seeing in geist a foreign and transcendent, demonic power of fate that breaks into the world of life, we take it in terms of its pure phenomena, if we take it in its "acts and sufferings."[35]

34. On the "masks" of the Will to Power, see aphorism 774 of Nietzsche's *The Will to Power*, trans. R. J. Hollingdale and Walter Kaufmann (New York: Vintage Books, 1968), p. 406. See aphorism 338: "Die maskirten Arten des Willens zur Macht," in Nietzsche, *Der Wille zur Macht: Versuch einer Umwerthung aller Werthe, Nietzsches Werke* (Leipzig: C. G. Naumann, 1901), Abt. 2, vol. 15, pp. 360f.—Eds.

35. In German: "Taten und Leiden." See Goethe, *The Theory of Color, Goethe's Collected Works*, vol. 12, *Scientific Studies*, ed. and trans. Douglas Miller (New York: Suhrkamp, 1988), p. 158: "Colors are the deeds of light, what it does and what it endures." See *WA*, Abt. 2, vol. 1, p. ix.—Eds.

The philosophy of symbolic forms has sought from the beginning to establish the path that leads through the concrete productions of geist. By taking this path, the philosophy of symbolic forms finds that it meets with geist everywhere as not the "Will to Power," but as the "Will to Formation." It is not the naked domination of the world, but its formation that language, art, knowledge, and religion are struggling with. In all of them we can, of course, find a phase in which they seem bound as if by magic to the guidance of emotion and the drive of need and will. The "symbolic forms" are used like powers and means of magic to give man the "omnipotence of the will," and they confirm this omnipotence to man again and again. But all this is just the beginning of the story, not the end. Even in myth new forces start to become apparent which turn against the worldview of magic and finally lift it off its hinges. Even in myth man gains distance from the world of things in order to live in a world of pure forms; the mythic world of practical activity gradually gives way to the pure world of mythic perception.[36]

This shift from the practice of magic, as a means to influence things, to the contemplation of things occurs in language, in the fine arts, and in knowledge. They all attain to their specific content by first breaking through the boundaries of the merely "useful," which is characterized by the "struggle for existence." They must wrestle free of the means-ends relationship in order to arrive at their own purpose—the unity and completeness of their form—which is itself no longer merely purposive, but which appears as a "purposiveness without purpose."[37] Understood in this way, a pure view of reality, as it is achieved in every one of the individual symbolic forms, as well as in their totality, can never be regarded as coercion directed against this reality. For the ray of consciousness that here falls upon Being and seeks to illuminate and penetrate it, no longer belongs either to the world of things or to a practical context. This purely ideal ray leaves unaffected the "existence," the mere content, of whatever it touches. Consciousness so conceived goes beyond the primordial ground of "life," but life is thereby neither destroyed nor violated. In the sphere of intellectual consciousness which now arises, life is visible to itself; to use Fichte's

36. Cf. here esp. [*PSF*] vol. 2, pp. 199ff.—Cassirer.

37. See Kant, *Kritik der Urtheilskraft, Immanuel Kants Werke*, ed. Ernst Cassirer, 10 vols. (Berlin: Bruno Cassirer, 1912–1922), vol. 5, §17, p. 306. Hereafter cited using the abbreviation *Werke*. *The Critique of Judgment*, trans. Werner S. Pluhar (Indianapolis: Hackett, 1987), p. 84: "Beauty is an object's form of purposiveness insofar as it is perceived in the object without the presentation of a purpose."—Eds.

expression, it has become pure "seeing."[38] In this form of seeing, Θεωρία in its most universal and all-encompassing sense, geist no longer lives off the marrow of the object, but rather from its own substance; it becomes "thinking of thinking," νόησις νοήσεως.[39]

Of course, true theory does not mean the mere observation of things or simple passive submission to them, but rather a highly active achievement. Yet precisely as an energy, as action, this seeing goes beyond mere "practice." For this difference, however, the metaphysics of life has no category, in Klages as little as in Bergson; they make no distinction between action and practice. In this way Klages is the true Romantic, minimizing the value of action and wanting to return to pure receptivity and passivity. In Klages' doctrine Friedrich Schlegel's thesis of the divinity of inaction, of its "divine passivity," has been resurrected.[40] "Among the Indo-Germanic languages," Klages writes, "there is hardly one which does not describe the depth and power of feelings as befalling, suffering, or falling victim to it! 'Pathos' (πάθος), 'passion' (*passio*), 'affection': three ways of being 'affected' as the highest measure of feeling coming from the depths of the soul! If only the obvious question had been raised, what is it actually that does the suffering and what is it that does the affecting, then the answer could not have been overlooked: our ego is passive, suffering, affected and it falls victim to the victorious power of life."[41] Metaphysics must extricate itself from the activity of mere thought; it must learn again to be suffering, receptive, "pathetic," if it is to grasp and relive the world in pure feeling instead of construing it in concepts. Yet in this drive to negate thought and to extinguish the self a secret presupposition is preserved which no mysti-

38. See Fichte, "System der Sittenlehre," in Johann Gottlieb Fichte, *Nachgelassene Werke*, ed. J. H. Fichte, 3 vols. (Bonn: Adolph Marcus, 1835), vol. 3, p. 17: "Seeing is immediate life which is creative through itself."—Eds.

39. See Aristotle *Metaphysics* 1074b35. *The Complete Works of Aristotle*, 2 vols., rev. Oxford trans., ed. Jonathan Barnes, Bollingen Series 71 (Princeton: Princeton Univ. Press, 1984), vol. 2, p. 1698.—Eds.

40. See Friedrich Schlegel's "An Idyll of Idleness," in *Lucinde and the Fragments*, trans. Peter Firchow (Minneapolis: Univ. of Minnesota Press, 1971), pp. 65–66: "Only calmly and gently, in the sacred tranquillity of true passivity, can one remember one's whole ego and contemplate the world and life.... And yet talking and ordering are only secondary matters in all the arts and sciences: the essence is thinking and imagining, and these are possible only in passivity.... The more divine a man or a work of man is, the more it resembles a plant; of all forms of nature, this form is the most moral and the most beautiful. And so the highest, most perfect mode of life would actually be nothing more than *pure vegetating*." Schlegel, *Lucinde: Ein Roman, Erster Theil* (Berlin, 1799).—Eds.

41. Klages, *Vom kosmogonischen Eros*, pp. 46f.—Cassirer.

cism can completely dispense with: the presupposition—to speak with Meister Eckhart—that a "spark" of the self remains which is aware of this dissolution.[42]

When the god that the mystic receives and suffers, liberates the mystic world from the world of forms, he then again and again in some way falls prey to that world as soon as he tries to see this god. There is no seeing that is merely receptivity, that does not also include a formative function. Even myth, no matter how far back we trace it and no matter how "overwhelming" feelings predominate in it, is still a kind of configuration of reality. As the expressivity of the world, it necessarily involves its metamorphosis, its transformation into an image. This image is never simply a "piece" of reality, as it appears in Klages' realistic conception of the "reality of the images." It is not merely there, then simply to pass over into the subject, as, for example, in Epicurus' theory of perception in which the images, the εἴδωλα[43] of things, are supposed to penetrate into the perceiver. Rather, it demands the living participation, the complicity of the energies of the perceiver "for" which it is to become an image. Without this participation we could at best make understandable the image's presence to thought but not the act of representation, the function of making it present. The image always refers us, by its constitutive meaning, to the "imagination," and if we trace this back to its root, it proves to be never a reproductive, but a productive function. We do not need to establish this here or go through it all in detail. It is this very achievement of the "productive imagination" that we meet with everywhere in the construction of the particular worlds of form and which is the unifying ideal thread that ties them all together. Life taken in itself does not already contain in its womb the images of things, which the ego then only has to receive passively from it. No matter how we regard it or proclaim it as the original source of all reality, life in itself is never the source of the symbols in which this reality is first comprehended and understood, in which it "speaks to us."

If we eradicate the opposite pole, from which the symbols stem, then we

---

42. Meister Eckhart often speaks of a "spark" or *"scintilla,"* which is the ground of freedom in the soul. See, e.g., *Meister Eckhart: A Modern Translation*, trans. and ed. R. B. Blakney (New York: Harper & Row, 1957), sermon 24, p. 210: "I have said that there is one agent alone in the soul that is free. Sometimes I have called it the tabernacle of the Spirit. Other times I have called it the Light of the Spirit and again, a spark." See also *PSF*, vol. 2, pp. 250–253, where Cassirer discusses Meister Eckhart's teachings.—Eds.

43. See Epicurus' first letter to Herodotus, in *The Philosophy of Epicurus*, trans. George K. Strodach (Chicago: Northwestern Univ. Press, 1963), 46a, 47a, 48, and 50 (pp. 118–120).—Eds.

have taken the "soul" out of reality from a different direction insofar as we have robbed it of its essential means to manifest and reveal itself, and we have, so to speak, pushed ourselves back into the night of eternal stillness. Reality can only be delivered from this darkness by the pure energies of geist, by a kind of creative work. Now definite, specific, and, hence, limited configurations arise from this undifferentiated and infinite primordial ground. But they do not stand in mere opposition to it, in a purely negative and negating relationship, insofar as one now regards them from the standpoint of *forma formans* instead of from that of *forma formata*. The infinity which is denied to the finished configuration lives in the pure process of configuration. This does not become solidified in any individual creation, because it is the eternally productive act. The law of meaning to which it is subject and by virtue of which it is continually reborn—not what is created from it—provides its true content. If this law were completely antagonistic to life, it would at the same time have to destroy its own essence, for it exists and has application only insofar as it is active, and it cannot become active in any way except by entering and by constantly resubmerging itself into the living world. Always changing, but ever itself, near and far and far and near,[44] geist in all of its productivity always stands opposed to life without ever turning against it, without ever being antagonistic toward it. Without this correlative relationship, as it is primarily found revealed in every artistic creation and as it is here constantly testified to, the world of cultural forms would only be a world of ghosts; language and knowledge, poetry and the plastic arts would amount to nothing but empty phantasmagoria.

The metaphysics of life does not, of course, shrink from this final consequence, but it must thereby, at least in this one point, itself enter into this sphere that it would close off for us. The metaphysics of life must make use of the intellect's administration of judgments, which it rejects, and in doing so it indirectly accepts the use of judgment. The acceptance and recognition of such judgments take place whenever such a metaphysics does not merely perceive and interpret but makes evaluations. Klages' philosophical doctrine throughout, in its origin and in its tendency, is not so much a doctrine of Being as a doctrine of value. It does not describe the world of nature and the world of geist themselves pure and simple; rather,

---

44. See Goethe's poem "Parabasis" (1820), trans. Christopher Middleton, in *Goethe's Collected Works*, vol. 1, ed. Christopher Middleton, various translators (Boston: Suhrkamp/Insel, 1983), p. 155: "Self-insistent, always changing, / Near and far and far and near, / Birth of shapes, their rearranging—/ Wonder of wonders, I am here." *WA*, Abt. 1, vol. 3, p. 84.—Eds.

it judges them and this judgment is not a purely logical act, not an act of "pure thought." It measures the world instead by reference to certain demands that are placed upon it. No proposition of this doctrine is understandable or provable if we do not accept the system of values upon which it is based and which it everywhere implicitly presupposes. True philosophy is again supposed to become prophecy, to advocate the transvaluation of those values that have left their mark on "culture": the belief in the self-sufficient power of geist, its autonomy, and "progress." A new order of values is supposed to take the place of the old crumbling one. But we can and must now ask if the value of life as something pure adheres immanently in life itself, or does it not from the beginning belong to a different dimension? Is it contained in the pure being of life, or is it not constituted only by the erection of a norm that we establish over this being and on which it is measured? The meaning of this norm, the true principle establishing norms, can in the last analysis be found only in the realm of geist.

At the beginning of the history of idealism in the modern era stands the deep insight of Nicholas of Cusa, according to which God is called the power which "gives being," while the human mind is the power which lends and justifies values. The origin of all values does not lie outside the mind but rather in it, for it is within it that we find the principle of the measure, the *aestimatio* and *mensuratio*, upon which rests the distinction between "good" and "evil," value and disvalue.[45] If this is the case, then the principle of the devaluation of the mind, no matter from what standpoint or authority this is attempted or carried out, has from the outset a definite limit set to it. Every purely negative evaluation of the mind also affirms it in one of its highest, truly positive achievements. It remains an internal contradiction to completely deny the reality of value to the function upon which the "possibility" of all values rests. Even if the entire sphere of the

45. See my *Individuum und Kosmos in der Philosophie der Renaissance*, Studien der Bibliothek Warburg[, Heft] X, Leipzig 1927, pp. 46ff.—Cassirer. Cassirer, *The Individual and the Cosmos in Renaissance Philosophy*, pp. 44ff. This passage is translated in Cassirer's *The Individual and the Cosmos in Renaissance Philosophy*, without the Latin text: "For although the human intellect does not give being to the value, there would nevertheless be no distinctions in value without it. Thus, if one leaves the intellect aside, one cannot know whether value exists. Without the power of judgment and of comparison every evaluation ceases to exist, and with it value would also cease. Wherewith we see how precious is the mind, for without it, everything in creation would be without value. When God wanted to give value to his work, he had to create, besides the other things, the intellectual nature." Cassirer gives the source as *De ludo globi*, lib. II, fol. 236f. The reference should read "167b." Cassirer also refers the reader to *Das Erkenntnisproblem*, vol. 1, p. 58 n, where the Latin text is reproduced.—Eds.

intellect were conceived as something negative, even if all its activities were denied and rejected, the mere assigning of this negative meaning is itself a new act that holds us firmly in the sphere of geist that we had hoped to flee. For only geist is able to do the "impossible"; only it can make distinctions, choose, and judge.[46] This "judging" of course is—and herein lies perhaps its true depth and its final mystery—such that it is within itself capable of turning around, that as the directive principle it does not make an exception of itself, but rather that it is able to turn against itself.

This turnabout, this "reflection," entails no break within geist itself; rather, it is the form in which it proves itself and reconfirms itself, something that is characteristic of and typical of it alone. So what threatens constantly to tear it asunder is also what always brings it back to itself; this being two-in-one is its true fate and represents its actual achievement. Life as such knows no such turning back upon itself, no such reaffirmation. Of course, life does not appear to require it as long as it remains within itself in an unbroken unity, in which it rests "blissfully in itself." Yet even this peace is not bliss in the full sense; it becomes such only for the eye of the mind that is directed toward it and turns back to see it. To pronounce something blissful or to damn it is only possible for something that is capable of negating itself, for this act of self-negation always also represents an act of self-assertion.

46. See Goethe's poem of the early 1780s "The Godlike," trans. Vernon Watkins in *Goethe's Collected Works*, vol. 1, pp. 78–83: "Yet man alone can / achieve the impossible: / He distinguishes, / Chooses and judges; / He can give lasting / life to the moment." *WA*, Abt. 1, vol. 2, p. 84.—Eds.

Chapter Two

The Problem of the Symbol as the Fundamental Problem of Philosophical Anthropology

1. [The Problem of Philosophical Anthropology]

THE problem of a "philosophical anthropology" does not stand outside the purview of critical philosophy and even less in systematic opposition to it. If we need any historical proof of this, it can be found in the fact that it is none other than Kant himself who grasped this problem in all its significance and who sought to construct a system of anthropology upon a broader and more fundamental basis than the psychological opinions of the eighteenth century were able to provide. As far as its importance as an academic discipline is concerned, anthropology is a high point, a topic for which Kant showed a particular preference and to which he returned again and again. In fact, there is a period in which this topic became the actual center of Kant's thought, during which he upheld the view that, at least from the standpoint of pedagogy and didactics, anthropology is primary in the system of philosophy. During this period Kant demanded that ethics—which he later so sharply and radically contrasted to anthropology—must begin by historically and philosophically considering what actually occurs before it moves on to indicate what should be. He wants "to show what the method is according to which we must study *mankind*, not merely those men, misshapen by the coincidental changing form that they received by chance, something about which even philosophers have almost always been mistaken; rather, the *nature* of man, which is always constant, and through this constancy has its proper place in the creation." "This method of social investigation," he adds, "is a wonderful discovery of our own times and is, if one considers it in its full plan, something which was completely unknown to the ancients."[1]

This "full plan" was not, of course, no matter how clearly Kant conceived it and no matter how he held to it through all the different periods of his thought, ever carried out or brought to completion in the system of transcendental philosophy itself. For this system's fundamental tendency is oriented toward the question of *quid juris*, not that of *quid facti*. Its central problem lies in the "objective," not in the "subjective" deduction, in the question of the nature and foundational principle of particular areas of meaning which, as is emphasized over and over, in no way is to be confused with the question of their subjective representation in "consciousness," but something methodologically strictly differentiated from it. This difference is already sharply made in the preface to the *Critique of Pure Reason*. Consideration of the pure concepts of the understanding, Kant indicates, has two sides to it: one relates to the objects of pure understanding and seeks to explicate the objective validity of its concepts a priori; the other is directed toward the pure understanding "itself, its possibility and the cognitive faculties upon which it rests; and so deals with it in its subjective aspect. Although this latter exposition is of great importance for my chief purpose, it does not form an essential part of it. For the chief question is always simply this—what and how much can the understanding and reason know apart from all experience? not:—how is the faculty of thought itself possible? The latter is, as it were, the search for the cause of a given effect, and to that extent is somewhat hypothetical in character (though ... it is not really so); and I would appear to be taking the liberty simply of expressing an opinion, in which case the reader would be free to express a different opinion. For this reason I must forestall the reader's criticism by pointing out that the objective deduction with which I am here chiefly concerned retains its full force even if my subjective deduction should fail to produce that complete conviction for which I would hope."[2]

When Kant in this passage lets fall one of the threads in his investigation that he himself had taken up, one would expect that in the following period someone would take it up again. It seemed in fact as though no other period before Kant's time was as suited to grasp the basic problems of

1. Kant, "Nachricht von der Einrichtung seiner Vorlesungen in dem Winterhalbenjahre 1765–66," *Werke*, ed. [Ernst] Cassirer, vol. 2, p. 326.—Cassirer.

2. Kant, *Kritik der reinen Vernunft, Werke*, vol. 3, p. 10 (A xvii). Kant, *Critique of Pure Reason*, trans. Norman Kemp Smith (New York: St. Martin's Press, 1965), p. 12.—Eds.

philosophical anthropology or to tackle them with new means. For this period of thought had access to the tremendous material that comparative morphology and human developmental history had worked out. Only now, when the question was raised about "mankind's place in creation," did it seem as though it was possible to move on all sides with the certitude of a firm, empirical foundation under foot. The question, as Kant put it, now appeared to need rephrasing and a definite reformulation. Even when Kant asked about the nature of mankind, he was thinking of something stationary, not its changing nature, and this latter is conceived in this sense not as some mere empirical constancy, but as an ideal determination, an ideal essence. Kant's goal is to know[3] "what perfection of mankind is appropriate to the state of *naiveté* and which in the state of *wise* simplicity, and what, on the other hand, are the guidelines for his behavior when man, in striving to go beyond both of these limits, to attain the highest level of physical or moral excellence, but deviates more or less from both."[4] This way of stating the question, which so typically breathes the spirit of the eighteenth century, appears to have been overcome and dismissed in the nineteenth century, the era of strict "Positivism." From then on, the "nature" of man means nothing ideal, but something purely factual, and this can be determined nowhere with as much certitude and exactitude as in the investigation of purely physical organization. The leading idea of this research is provided, however, by the principle of continuity and the constant evolution of natural forms. The more consistently this principle is followed, the more unhesitatingly it is extended to all phenomena of human existence and action, and the more clearly these phenomena are conceptually grasped. Their "explanation" appeared to be able to imply nothing other than their subsumption under the general causal structure of becoming and the establishment of their place within this structure. In addition, all questions of sense and meaning had to be brought under this point of view, if they were to be stripped of their metaphysical shell and be raised to the status of rigorous scientific questions.

The goal of philosophical anthropology, as Kant saw it, was thereby pushed into the distance; it seemed now to turn out to be a mere intellectual utopia. Until rather recently it seemed as though this decision was the last word of wisdom, as if anthropology had in accordance with Comte's law of

3. *Marginal note in pencil:* N.b. Pp. 105–151 taken to Berlin on 23.XII (for Bergson lecture!).—Eds.

4. Kant, "Nachricht von der Einrichtung seiner Vorlesungen 1765–1766," *Werke*, Cassirer, vol. 2, p. 326.—Cassirer.

three phases[5] finally left its "speculative" epoch and entered the "positive" one for good. But now the signs are increasing in number that, if we look at the recent developments in philosophy, the methodology of anthropology as it has been shaped under the influence of the idea of evolution and the great evolutionary systems, particularly Herbert Spencer's, no longer stands unquestioned and unshaken. It is the later works of Scheler and those of the thinkers near to him that most clearly show this change. The question of the "particular position of mankind" is again being raised in a totally different sense than in the formal view of natural science and such a scientific theory of development. Anthropology is again understood not just as a necessary and integrating component part of empirical research into nature but also as pure "research into essences." While remaining so close to and necessarily a part of natural philosophy, it has become nonetheless an important and essential factor in the construction of a "philosophy of meaning."

"Philosophical anthropology" is supposed now to unfold in two directions and extend into a kind of twofold dimension in which it conceives man not only as subject-object of nature, but as subject-object of culture. "The level, on which man must always strive upward anew, with great effort and with sacrifices of all kinds"—so he emphasizes—"the level of intelligent activity, creative work, the level of his triumphs and defeats, intersects with the level of his bodily existence. Hence, the struggle for existence, without which man is not man, also has significance for philosophical method; it reveals the Janus face of this creature, the necessity for knowledge that does not just reconcile or mediate this twofold aspect of his existence, but conceives it in terms of *one* fundamental position."[6]

If we understand the task of philosophical anthropology in this sense, then the questions it deals with closely approach our own problem. In fact, we can now predict that the fundamental answer to the question of the

---

5. See *Auguste Comte and Positivism*, ed. Gertrude Lenzer (New York: Harper & Row, 1975), p. 29: "From the nature of the human intellect, each branch of knowledge, in its development, is necessarily obliged to pass through three different theoretical states: the theological or fictitious state; the metaphysical or abstract state; and, lastly, the scientific or positive state." Comte, *Système de politique positive ou Traité de Sociologie* (Paris: chez l'auteur et chez Carilian-Goeury & Vor Dalmont, 1854), vol. 4, appendice général, p. 77.—Eds.

6. Helmuth Plessner, *Die Stufen des Organischen und der Mensch. Einleitung in die philosophische Anthropologie* (Berlin: [Walter de Gruyter,] 1928), p. 32. Only a brief sketch of Scheler's long-awaited and announced philosophical anthropology is available at the time of the writing of this chapter. It was published under the title: "Die Sonderstellung des Menschen" in the collection edited by Hermann Keyserling entitled *Mensch und Erde* (Darmstadt[: Otto Reichl Verlag,] 1927), pp. 161ff. [161–254].—Cassirer.

"essential concept" of mankind which it seeks can come only from a philosophy of "symbolic forms." For these forms indicate to us the level of intelligence in human action, and they contain the universal defining elements of this level. In the medium of language and art, in myth and theoretical knowledge, that turnabout or intellectual revolution takes place which permits mankind to set the world aside in order to draw it closer. By virtue of these "forms" mankind attains proximity to the world and a distance from it which no other creature possesses. If we are to identify this process of delimitation, to draw a line of demarcation between mankind and the totality of the world of living things, this can occur only by taking the concept and structure of this configuration as a starting point, and by trying to grasp not so much its development as its content. No metaphysics and no empirical fact will ever be in a position to illuminate the "origin" of this configuration in the sense that it puts us back at the temporal starting point, that it permits us immediately to eavesdrop on its beginning. We can never penetrate back to the point at which the first ray of intellectual consciousness broke out of the world of life; we cannot put our finger on the place at which language or myth, art or knowledge "arose." For we know them all only as something already existing, as closed forms in which each particular carries the whole and is carried by it, and in which we therefore cannot indicate what is "earlier" or "later," temporally "first" or "second." All that remains open to us is the return from relatively complex to relatively simpler configurations of a particular form-world, yet in every such simple configuration, the law of the formation of the whole is already present and in effect. Every analysis that assumes it is possible to "explain" this whole by dissolving it, so to speak, into its atoms of meaning thereby commits a fundamental error. The very concept of an atom of meaning contains an internal contradiction. We can only oppose *totalities* of meaning to one another, in order to become aware of the specific intellectual norm that governs them, but we cannot trace the formative principle under which they stand to something itself not yet formed, so as to let it "develop" out of some as yet unformed "matter." A strictly naturalistic anthropology must undertake this attempt again and again, for its "possibility" depends upon the success of this attempt. But this attempt always turns out in the end to be circular; in the end one can "develop" out of elements nothing other than what had been already implicitly attributed to them, no matter how concealed this tacit assumption has been. The path that all such attempts must take and that alone promises to lead to the goal already has been shown with exemplary precision and clarity by Darwin.

Darwin's work *The Expression of the Emotions in Man and Animals*[7] is just as epoch-making and methodologically foundational for its field as was his work on the origin of species.[8] With an ingenious eye for what is important Darwin grasped the very point at which the world of "natural" being changes into that of "intelligent" being and at which therefore, if at all, the continuity between them both seems to be immediately exhibited. The phenomenon of expression seems to be a genuine primary phenomenon of life that extends down to its lowest grades and levels. Even the plant kingdom seems to participate in a way in this phenomenon. The plant seems, as Scheler puts it, to possess a certain "physiognomic of its inner states" (weak, strong, luxuriant, sparse, and so on).[9] Hence, if it is possible to grasp the process of expression simply as a process of life and thus describe it in purely biological categories, then the way has been cleared which promises in principle to lead in an unbroken and continuous progression from a purely natural existence to the highest intellectual productions. The problem appears to have been solved the moment that we succeed in reducing language to a purely expressive function and can prove that this latter itself, as far as its "principle of movement" is concerned, is a product of purely vital processes, the final point in a course of development which is subject to no other law than that of "natural selection," biological adaptation.

The procedure that Darwin suggests for this is well known. It consists in interpreting the act of expression so that it is merely a residue of a goal-directed action.[10] The clenched fist is nothing other than the weakening of a "real" attack; the showing of one's teeth as an expression of anger and rage goes back to an epoch in which the teeth, especially the sharp canine tooth,[11] were still used as real organs for fighting, as means of attacking and destroying an opponent. Once mimetic expression is recognized in this way as a direct continuation and kind of sublimation of certain acts of life, which are subject to the principle of utility, then we need only to make a

7. Charles Darwin, *The Expression of Emotion in Animals* (New York: D. Appleton, 1873). Cassirer cites this work from the German trans. *Der Ausdruck der Gemüthsbewegungen bei dem Menschen und den Thieren*, vol. 7 of *Ch. Darwin's gesammelte Werke*, trans. J. Victor Carus (Stuttgart: E. Schweizerbart, 1877).—Eds.

8. Charles Darwin, *On The Origin of Species by Means of Natural Selection* (London: John Murray, 1859).—Eds.

9. Scheler, above ["Die Sonderstellung des Menschen"], p. 169.—Cassirer.

10. See "Uncovering the Canine Tooth on One Side," in Darwin, *The Expression of Emotion in Animals*, pp. 249–253.—Eds.

11. Ibid.—Eds.

second step in order to include language completely within this kind of explanation, by treating it as a sublimation of the expressive function. Wundt's work on language still attempts to follow this course. The "developmental theory" of language that Wundt upholds[12] rests on the assumption that the entire intellectual content of language stems originally from the expressive function, that it is nothing but systematized and regulated expressive movement. With that, the circle seems to be closed; the world of culture, the prototype of which is language, has been taken up into nature and explained by means of the same principle as nature. All purely "monistic" means of explanation meet in the end at the same place. Considered methodologically, they are attempts to understand the pure contents of meaning by making them arise from natural existence, by taking phenomena that at first glance appear to belong to a different dimension and relocating them in the dimension of events.

The thing that repeatedly leads to attempts of this sort and provides them with formal justification and intellectual support is the circumstance that within the world of processes there are in fact no "jumps," no breaks in the continuity of becoming. Every phase of becoming taken as such flows imperceptibly into the next. But this temporal interlocking of the phases of processes does not exclude the sharp distinction, the opposition of the ideal contents, that are found in the process of becoming. No matter how the question of the becoming of natural forms is answered, the field of intellectual becoming follows not the law of evolution, but the law of mutation. Here there is not simply wave after wave in a uniform flow; rather, here one clear and distinct configuration confronts the next. Even when a new configuration immediately follows upon the earlier ones it is not simply their result, but represents something unique and independent. No matter how closely they make contact with what comes before them, so that there are no "gaps" between them and their antecedents, they neither arise from these antecedents, nor can they be explained by reference to them nor inferred from them: "All that is noble the gods freely send down from above."[13] Each of the preceding analyses of particular symbolic forms has

12. Wilhelm Wundt, *Völkerpsychologie*, vol. 1, *Die Sprache*, 2d ed. (Leipzig: Engelmann, 1904), pp. 37–135; *PSF*, vol. 1, pp. 177ff.—Eds.

13. "Alles Höchste, es kommt frei von den Göttern herab." From Schiller's poem "Das Glück," in *Musenalmanach für das Jahr 1799*, trans. as "Fortune," in *The Poems of Friedrich von Schiller* (Chicago: M. A. Donahue, n.d.), p. 241. Friedrich Schiller, *Sämtliche Werke*, Säkular-Ausgabe, 16 vols., ed. Eduard von der Hellen (Stuttgart and Berlin: J. G. Cotta, 1904), vol. 1, p. 121.—Eds.

introduced us to this characteristic double determination. The question was not how they arose but their content; even where the analysis attempted to investigate the makeup of this content, to discriminate between different "levels" in it, the guiding interest was not genetic-historical, but purely phenomenological. But even within this phenomenological analysis of the individual forms we see again and again how inseparably the purely "intellectual" contents are interwoven with the "vital" ones and how greatly their structure is governed by vital tendencies. A world shaped by myth could not be grasped if we conceive it exclusively as a form of thought or if we take it purely as a form of life; only the interconnection of both these determinations can provide its true constituent principle. In the same way we found in the organization of language how thought expressed in language, *logos* itself, arises in the field of human action and reflects the different aspects and directions of action so that "theoretical" meaning appears to be anchored and rooted originally in "practical" meaning.[14] But no matter how closely these two spheres approach each other, they never merge into each other. The theoretical element of "seeing" did not result from a decline in the element of action; rather, it was the other way around: action separated more and more from its original basis in life, from its merely "vital" direction, as it became mixed with intellectual forms.

This is perhaps nowhere so obvious as in the area of "technical" effort itself. It appears everywhere to be subject in the highest degree to the notion of mere utility; it seems to have given in to it completely, once and for all. Yet the basic medium of technology, by virtue of which mankind is connected to the being of nature and through which it appears to bind mankind to it, is actually the beginning of the self-liberation of the mind. For, with tools, the immediate grasping of an object is replaced by a mediated relation. The goals of the will and desire move off now into the distance. Now, instead of being driven to them as if by an instinctive compulsion wrought by some overwhelming power of nature which mankind cannot oppose, technology sees them through a kind of refracting medium. Tools can arise only where the mind has become capable of conceiving of a "possible" object instead of giving itself over directly to a real one and losing itself in it. A consciousness of this new attitude and reality is expressed in the fact that tools are not only created and made use of, but they also are worshiped. In this worship, which proves to be one of the fundamental tendencies of the mythic worldview, the tool is raised

14. For details see esp. [*PSF*] vol. 1, pp. 249ff.; vol. 2: 184ff.; 199ff.—Cassirer.

above what it immediately is and does and is regarded as an intelligent force. This way of regarding tools, this transformation and projection into the ideal, then becomes the seed and starting point of a new total view which mankind attains of the world and itself.[15]

Even this single example shows how the analysis of the particular symbolic forms can help us in the attempt to create a philosophical anthropology. In fact, there is no other means by which to distinguish the specifically human world from the world of natural forms or to uncover what it is than by studying it within this medium. When it is passed over or not fully recognized for what it is, we are left with no sure way of distinguishing in principle between them. The most obvious and, so to speak, least suspicious way to make this distinction appears to be to limit oneself to particular, purely objective criteria, that is, to what can be shown directly to be physical characteristics. If we proceed from the presupposition that nature has neither a kernel nor a shell, that it is rather "all things at once,"[16] then for every "internal" difference we will also have to find an "external" one as its necessary correlate. Only with this do we seem now to have a secure guideline for the investigation and to call up the dangers of "subjectivism."

Uexküll built his *Theoretical Biology*[17] on this methodological basis. The basic thought behind this biology consists in the claim that access to the different worlds of the individual forms of life can be had only through study of their "organization." If we submerge ourselves in the anatomical structure of a living creature and at the same time make as clear as possible to ourselves the extent of the achievements that this structure brings about, we thereby have delimited the field of its existence and its activities. This organization itself creates the environment of a living thing so that it is in no case a constant but, rather, different for every creature, since it varies with their organizations. Just as environmental factors are objective, so too we must take as objective the effects called forth by them in the nervous system. They too can only be determined by reference to the body's structure, and from the outset they are seen and regulated through it. Now the

15. For details on this see esp. [*PSF*] vol. 2, pp. 161ff.—Cassirer.

16. See Goethe's poem "True Enough: To the Physicist" (1820), trans. Michael Hamburger, in *Goethe's Collected Works*, vol. 1, ed. Christopher Middleton, various translators (Boston: Suhrkamp/Insel, 1983), pp. 236–237: "Nature has neither core / Nor outer rind, / Being all things at once." See "Allerdings. Dem Physiker," *WA*, Abt. 1, vol. 3, p. 105: "Alles ist sie mit einem male."—Eds.

17. Uexküll, *Theoretical Biology*, trans. Doris L. Mackinnon (New York: Harcourt, Brace, 1926).—Eds.

totality of these effects is what we designate as the "inner world" of a living creature, so that—as Uexküll emphasizes—even establishing the existence of this inner world is "the unspoiled fruit of objective research," which "should not be clouded by psychological speculation. . . . Over the inner world and the surrounding world stands the creature's organization, governing everything. Research into the organization can . . . alone provide the healthy and secure foundation for biology. . . . If the configuration of this organization becomes the center of research for every species of animal, then every newly discovered fact finds its appropriate place at which it then gains its meaning and significance."[18]

We do not deny the usefulness of this approach to research nor diminish the far-reaching results that it has achieved for biology. Nevertheless, it can take us no further as soon as we turn to the basic problem of "philosophical anthropology." The concept of mankind is defined for it not by any specific, identifiable structural features, but through the comprehensive totality of mankind's achievements. The totality of these achievements can in no way simply be read off from mankind's "organization," such as from the organization of the brain and the nervous system. Uexküll conducted his research primarily in the area of the lower animals, and from the results that he attained he inferred the general schema that he termed the "functional circle" [*Funktionskreis*] of living creatures. The "surrounding world" [*Umwelt*] or environment of every animal cannot, in general, be defined by *our* concepts of "objects" and "characteristics"; rather, it stems from the whole of its organization and corresponds in every feature to this whole. In the world of the earthworm, there are only earthworm things; in the world of the dragonfly, only dragonfly things. Considered closely, this surrounding world falls into two parts: a receptor world [*Merkwelt*], which embraces the stimuli of the things in the surrounding world, and an effector world [*Wirkungswelt*], which consists of the sensitive areas of the effectors, of the creature's effector organs. "The common stimuli sent out by an object in an animal's environment provide it with a cue. In this way characteristics of the object which exercise a stimulus become *carriers of cues* for the animal, while those features of the object which serve as a target become *carriers of effects. In a given object the carriers of cues and carriers of effects are one and the same*: this permits us to give a brief expression to the astonishing fact, that all animals are adapted to the objects in their environment."[19] The animal

18. Jakob von Uexküll, *Umwelt und Innenwelt der Tiere* [2d ed.] (Berlin: [Julius Springer,] 1921), p. 5.—Cassirer.

19. von Uexküll, [*Umwelt und Innenwelt der Tiere*,] pp. 45f.—Cassirer.

thereby notices no object unless it is one that enters in some way into the sphere of its activity. The direction of this action and its specific "interest" is what determines the kind of things that are given for it, its "objects." The closed nature of this "functional circle," this interrelation of "noticing" and "effecting," appears to loosen up the more we approach the human world until finally, in this world, even the bond that otherwise everywhere defines the unity of the organism seems to be broken.

Mankind steps out of the sphere of mere noticing and simple effecting—at first only hesitatingly and unconsciously, but then more and more clearly and resolutely—in order to conquer a new realm, the realm of "observation." The stronger this new power of observation becomes, the more that mankind finds itself removed from the play of "action" and "reaction," as it otherwise holds sway in the organic world. To the extent that the animal has its own surrounding world and so orders it through different, discrete determinations, both the existence of this world as well as the divisions in it depend upon the dynamics of the animal's physical drives. These drives alone ignite the torch by whose light the animal is able to distinguish specific configurations in the world surrounding it. Only as long as it is immediately effective does the possibility of "attentiveness," of being watchful for external stimuli, exist for the animal. Hence, as Uexküll's experiments show us, the "receptor world" of the animal is completely different for an animal that is satiated than for one that is hungry.[20] The instinct to eat, after it rises or fades away, gives this world a completely different face. It is the quality, the differentiation of the specific drives, on which rests the division of the surrounding world into particular circles of existence. With most animals a plurality of "functional spheres" can be distinguished which can be designated as the spheres of prey, of the enemy, of sexuality, of the medium.[21] The contents of these spheres have different effects on the animal and elicit various, differently directed movements. "The animal's plan of action," as Plessner summarizes Uexküll's findings, "is the net in which it catches the world. A very primitive primacy of the practical governs all, for the receptor sphere [*Merksphäre*] configures the

---

20. Uexküll's *Theoretical Biology*, p. 51: "There can be no doubt that the completely different behaviour of animals in the states of hunger and satiety, is referable to change in the irritability of the central organs belonging to the food-circle. For a newly-fed shark a dead sardine simply is not there, because in this condition the shark's 'stimulus threshold' is too high. But hunger lowers the stimulus threshold, and then the sardine appears in the sensed-world of the shark."—Eds.

21. Cf. von Uexküll, [*Umwelt und Innenwelt der Tiere,*] p. 46.—Cassirer.

content and form of the categories in which it places them in the service of the search for food, of defense, of mating, of laying eggs, and so on. If some datum appears in the receptor sphere, it presents itself as a signal, never as an object."[22] This iron ring connecting the "receptor system" with the "effector system" in the animal and which at every moment joins and fits them together appears to be broken as soon as we enter the world of specifically human consciousness and specifically human ways of fashioning this world.

With this break mankind appears of course to be cast out of the paradise of organic existence so typical of the simple forms of life, which seems to surround and shelter them with loving care. In his description of *Paramaecium candatum*, a species of infusoria, Uexküll says that, by comparison, this animal rests more peacefully in its environment than does the child in its cradle. "It is surrounded everywhere by the same helpful stimuli, which protect it from false movements and lead it again and again to the sources of its nourishment and well-being. Paramaecium is so embedded in the world, everything must work out to its benefit. The animal and environment together form a closed purposive organization."[23] Mankind goes without such security and such protection as soon as it ceases simply to live in its environment and begins to build up this environment itself, as soon as it brings forth this environment from its own intellectual activity. But by partaking of the protection of purely organic existence, man has at the same time liberated himself from the compulsions of this existence. Now man comprehends a world of objects not just according to how they effect him and what they accomplish for his vital interests but according to what they are and mean in themselves. His "noticing" becomes detached from dependence on his actions and sufferings; he becomes "free of all interests."[24]

Kant showed us this basic feature of pure observation as it is found within the world of aesthetic objects where it does emerge in its highest power and sublimation. It is in no way limited to this sphere, but rather proves to be distinctive of and decisive for every form of "seeing" and "picturing," for every creation and grasping of worlds of form and of

22. Plessner, *Die Stufen des Organischen und der Mensch*, p. 246.—Cassirer.

23. von Uexküll, [*Umwelt und Innenwelt der Tiere*,] p. 41.—Cassirer.

24. Reference to Kant's doctrine of the judgment of taste. See *Kritik der Urtheilskraft, Werke*, vol. 5, §2, pp. 272f. Kant, *The Critique of Judgment*, "The Liking that Determines a Judgment of Taste is Devoid of All Interest," trans. Werner S. Pluhar (Indianapolis: Hackett, 1987), pp. 45–46.—Eds.

values in these worlds. The turn to form, as it is found not only in art, but in language, myth, or theoretical knowledge as well, is always a kind of retuning that the subject undergoes in itself, in the totality of its sensitivity to and attitudes toward life. This turnabout, this μετανοεῖν,[25] provides the beginning and the presupposition of every kind of *noesis*. The simplest and most pregnant definition that a philosophically oriented "anthropology" is capable of giving for mankind would therefore perhaps be that mankind is "capable of form." *Capaso formae*: this is how, borrowing a scholastic term, mankind can be briefly and sharply defined. Man's characteristic attitude toward the world and the way he regards objects lies contained herein. Schiller spoke of this basic relationship by terming it "the first liberal relation which man establishes with the universe around him. If desire seizes directly upon its object, contemplation removes its object to a distance, and makes it into a true and inalienable possession by putting it beyond the reach of passion. The necessity of nature, which in the stage of mere sensation ruled him with undivided authority, begins at the stage of reflection to relax its hold upon him. In his senses there results a momentary peace; time itself, the eternally moving, stands still; and, as the divergent rays of consciousness converge, there is reflected against a background of transience an image of the infinite, namely *form*."[26] These lines taken from Schiller's *On the Aesthetic Education of Man* are to be taken in the sense of a specific aesthetically oriented Humanism. Schiller wishes to distinguish the "aesthetic state" of mankind from its "first physical state." But the significance of these lines goes far beyond this goal; this passage is applicable to every kind of "reflection" and to every world of form that is disclosed in and through such reflection.

If we consider this basic relationship more closely, then we lose all hope of ever grasping these worlds of form and the law to which each of them is subject by investigating the causal conditions of their development, their temporal rise. For no matter how successful we are in moving the world of thought in the direction of natural existence, the difference between them still remains, in principle, irrevocable. The transition from the one to the other is always a kind of μετάβασις εἰς ἄλλο γένος.[27] Whenever we

25. "change of mind."

26. Friedrich Schiller, *On the Aesthetic Education of Man: In a Series of Letters*, ed. and trans. E. M. Wilkinson and L. A. Willoughby (Oxford: Clarendon Press, 1967), letter 25, p. 183. Schiller, *Ueber die ästhetische Erziehung des Menschen in einer Reihe von Briefen, Sämtliche Werke*, vol. 12, p. 99.—Eds.

27. "transition to another genus." This "switching of categories" was conceived as an

compare the world of "theoretical observation" with that of organic events and activity, the former always has an additional, completely primitive and original motif. Yet as little as the world of the mind can be "derived" from nature in the sense of an evolutionistic metaphysics, knowledge of the mind appears nonetheless to be bound in a completely different, even antithetical, methodological sense to knowledge of nature. It is not so much the continuity that we find between them as, rather, the contrast which appears to open up the actual essence of them both to us. Neither of these two worlds becomes truly transparent to us as long as we only consider them by themselves in terms of their own structural principles. We must instead contrast them with each other, we must, so to speak, let the one be reflected in the other in order to attain an image of them in such "repeated mirroring."[28] If we were able to go back to a level of existence that remains prior to that great process of transformation that takes place in each of the individual symbolic forms, then the secret of these forms would finally be open to us. We would no longer only be caught up in them but would also stand above them; in the midst of their activities we would be conscious of their limits. The intellect does not grasp itself as long as it remains isolated in itself. It acquires its highest knowledge of itself only when it goes beyond the form of thought which is in accordance with it—when it overreaches all its "discursive" logical forms and attains the sphere of pure intuition. As little as it is able to redeem this sphere by itself, it can nonetheless recognize it as in principle something "other" than itself, and by virtue of this recognition it now understands itself, its mediated and conditioned character.

We have here described the path taken by Bergson's metaphysics, a metaphysics which by its own definition declares that it aims to provide a kind of knowledge that goes beyond every type of mediacy, beyond mere "symbolism."[29] Bergson's concept of "creative evolution" follows not the

---

error in argumentation in Aristotle *Posterior Analytics* 1.7.75a38–40. Cassirer refers to it here and in many other places throughout his writings in a positive way, as a kind of gestalt switch.—Eds.

28. A reference to Goethe, "Wiederholte Spiegelungen," *WA*, Abt. 1, vol. 42.2, pp. 56–57.—Eds.

29. Cf. on this the Introduction esp. pp. -ff.—Cassirer. Here "Introduction" probably means the introduction to *PSF*, vol. 3, where Bergson's definition of metaphysics is quoted: "the science that aspires to dispense with symbols" (p. 36). Bergson, *Introduction to Metaphysics*, auth. trans. T. E. Hulme (New York: Macmillan, 1955 [1912]), p. 24. Hulme translates the verb *prétend* as "claims," whereas Ralph Manheim chooses "aspires' to render Cassirer's *Anspruch erheben*. Manheim is taking liberties with this definition, for "aspiring" to dispense with symbols is a much weaker claim than Bergson makes. Bergson says that metaphysics

guiding notion of continuity, but that of difference, the fundamental "discretion" of areas of life. None of the steps that it embraces under the names of *torpeur, intelligence, instinct*[30] can be traced to the other. Each represents, in comparison with the other, a specific and new total direction of the "will to life." The basic error which has governed all philosophy since Aristotle—Bergson explicitly declares—consists in the fact that philosophers saw in vegetative life, animal instinct, and the life of reason one and the same developmental tendency, whereas in truth they are three divergent directions, whose oppositions become all the more obvious the further that development progresses. "The difference between them is not a difference of intensity, nor, more generally, of degree, but of kind."[31] Here we come to a point at which the metaphysics of life, as Bergson develops it, arrives at results that appear to agree with our fundamental inferences from the analysis of the symbolic forms, hence, from a pure philosophy of mind. It also draws the line that divides "life" and "mind" in the sharpest way—the "that" of this distinction is clearly worked out, however one may in the last analysis judge its correctness and value. From this viewpoint there now arises a new question if we remain within the presuppositions of Bergson's doctrine. Life as such, as absolute Being, may also be divided; it may break apart into the three completely divergent directions of vegetative dullness, animal instinct, and human intellect—but it is never enough for a metaphysics of life simply to register and describe this separation. A metaphysics, a philosophy of life is subject to a new demand for unity. The divisions in being cannot lead to an absolute division in knowledge if, on the other hand, this knowledge is to achieve its goal: giving knowledge of being. The plurality of the three areas of life—*torpeur, instinct, intelligence*—does not explain how it is possible that the last level is not only really distinguished from the first two, but also recognizes ideally that it is separated from them. This "grasping" of itself and its own conditioned nature

---

"claims" to *accomplish* the task. Cassirer's rendering in German is correct, as is Hulme's English version. Henri Bergson, *Introduction à la métaphysique*, first published in the *Revue de Métaphysique et de Morale* 11 (1903): 1–36, esp. p. 4: "La métaphysique est donc la science qui prétend se passer des symboles."—Eds.

30. See Bergson, *Creative Evolution*, auth. trans. Arthur Mitchell (New York: Henry Holt, 1911), p. 98. The title of chap. 2 is "The Divergent Directions of the Evolution of Life—Torpor, Intelligence, Instinct." Bergson, *L'évolution créatrice*, 2d ed. (Paris: Félix Alcan, 1907).—Eds.

31. Henri Bergson, *L'évolution créatrice*, Chap. 2, 2ᵉ édition Paris 1907, pp. 146f.—Cassirer. Bergson, *Creative Evolution*, chap. 2, p. 135. Cassirer translates this passage into German himself; the English translation follows his rendering.—Eds.

is itself once again a "reaching out" and "overreaching": a vision of the totality of life from the "standpoint" of intelligence.

How are such an overview of the whole and a review of it possible when in reality "intelligence" is nothing other than what it seems to be for Bergson: a part of everything, which never is equal to the whole, a mere effect which can never express its cause, a "lantern that is made in a cellar instead of a sun that lights the world"?[32] This is the essential, truly critical question for Bergson's methodology. He is himself clearly conscious of the fact that a rational answer to this question is not possible within his system. The only thing that is capable of providing us with an answer is not an insight of the understanding, but a decision of the will. The Gordian knot cannot be untied—it can only be cut apart. Our thought must decide to risk the leap, a leap into an area that is dark and inaccessible to it. Reason will never, by considering its own powers, be able to expand these powers. Intelligence may ever so sharply observe and analyze its own mechanism— never will it in this way be able to transcend it. It hereby becomes more and more tangled in its own nets—it attains to ever more complicated constructions, but it never achieves anything that is superior or even different from it. "You must take things by storm: you must thrust intelligence outside itself by an act of will."[33]

The "philosophy of symbolic forms," no matter how much it recognizes the specific difference between the world of "geist" and the world of "life" or how sharply it emphasizes it, is, of course, denied this kind of solution to the problem. It cannot simply give itself over to irrationalism; it cannot attempt to drive the intellect beyond itself by means of a decree of the will; it cannot exchange the mediacy of analysis for the immediacy of intuition. For all this is denied it by the methodological rule to which it ascribed from the beginning. This method restricts it to the limits of immanence. "Immanence" does not, of course, mean to remain fixed in the confines of any particular form—such as the theoretical, scientific form; rather, this term is understood to mean the totality of possible ways of giving form or meaning. If we define the world of geist by means of this totality, then the

32. Cf. [Bergson], *L'évolution créatrice*, Introduction, page III.—Cassirer. Cassirer translates this passage into German himself; the English translation follows his rendering. Bergson, *Creative Evolution*, p. x: "And lo! forgetting what it has just told us, it makes this lantern glimmering in a tunnel into a Sun which can illuminate the world."—Eds.

33. *L'évolution créatrice*, p. 211.—Cassirer. Bergson, *Creative Evolution*, p. 193. Unlike Cassirer's previous quotations from Bergson, this is given in French: "Il faut brusquer les choses, et, par un acte de volonté, pousser l'intelligence hors de chez elle."—Eds.

"Archimedean point" of certitude that we are seeking can never be given to us from outside of it, but must always be sought within it. The mind cannot peel off, like snakeskins, the forms in which it lives and exists, in which it not only thinks but also feels and perceives, sees and gives shape to things. It cannot, by a kind of organic metamorphosis, enter into another level of essence and life different from the one it is in. Yet as little as the mind can ever in reality alienate itself from its basic form, so neither is it on the other hand ever completely bound to this basic form; it is not confined to this as by prison walls. This is the mind's peculiar nature and its privilege; it not only "exists" in particular forms, it at the same time knows about this, its determination. If any knowledge does not come to us by intuition, it is this. Rather, such knowledge demands the mustering and greatest exertion of all the mind's "reflective" powers. Immediacy itself, insofar as there is any, can never be immediately grasped or experienced. Our approach to it is itself something thoroughly mediated, insofar as it is a kind of reduction. If we look closely, we see that it was only by means of such a progressive "reduction" that it was possible for Bergson to sketch his picture of nature and life, that he himself held up a kind of mirror for intelligence. The strength of his metaphysics is derived from a specific fundamental power of "intelligence" from which it constantly draws. "Intelligence" is the mind's capacity to take everything it creates, what it brings forth from its womb, and assume a negative attitude toward it. It does not simply "exist" in its products but rather asks about what is beyond them and even asks this in order to turn against and oppose them. We cannot and do not want to deny this, but after all we have met with before, we must look in a different direction for an answer.

We have so far tried to show how the individual symbolic forms—language, myth, theoretical knowledge—are aspects in the structure of the intelligent organization of reality. Each of them presented us with an independent, architectonic principle, an ideal "structure," or, better—since we are here never dealing with describing purely static relationships, but rather with exposing dynamic processes—a characteristic way of "structuring" itself. In presenting this process we found ourselves confronted again and again with a particular methodological limitation. We could never succeed in exposing a level of "experience" or "immediate experiencing" on which the different form-giving forces come to bear and on which they can carry out their efforts as if it were a kind of raw matter. Instead, we again and again had to reject this interpretation—the interpretation that the process of "symbolic formation" only offers a reconfiguration of a given world of sensations or of perception that is finished and at hand—as if we merely added to this basic and original layer a kind of ideal "superstructure."[34] We saw that instead the particular intellectual viewpoint itself already determined the content of perception as such—that neither can be separated or isolated from the other. Each of the different kinds of "seeing" define by themselves their own order of the "seen," whereby the seen and the viewpoint, the perceived and the ideated, the "present" and the "representative" can always only be shown as one in the other, in correlative connection, interwoven with one another.

But a new outlook appears to open up to us as soon as we expand the circle in which we have previously conducted our investigation. Observation of the realm of natural forms promises to provide us with what the observation of intellectual forms failed, and had to fail, to provide. For here, so it seems, the distinction is provided by reality itself, which our philosophy, "thought's art of making distinctions," is never able to make with any real sharpness. If the experiential world of other organisms were open to us, if we were able to have them open to our view as are our own phenomena of consciousness, then we would find in them a pre-mythical, a pre-linguistic, a pre-theoretical world, and we could then find in this something truly immediate by which we could finally measure everything absolutely and so decipher all these forms of mediation. Outside all these refracting media in which our intellectual existence holds us captive we would then stand eye to eye with life itself in its absolute character and immeasurable variety. Only then, to use a metaphor, could we compare with certainty the genuine and original metal of reality to the subsequent minting that it underwent in thought.

Only one, albeit decisive, methodological question arises here: by what means are we to attain this "transposition" into another reality of experience different from our own? It is obvious how uncertain, how slippery, here every logical deduction, every mere analogical inference would be, but

---

34. See the Introduction to Karl Marx, "Towards a Critique of Political Economy," in *Capital and Other Writings*, ed. Max Eastman (New York: Modern Library, 1932), p. 10: "In the social production of their subsistence men enter into determined and necessary relations with each other which are independent of their wills—production—relations which correspond to a definite stage of development of their material productive forces. The sum of these production-relations forms the economic structure of society, the real basis upon which a juridical and political superstructure arises, and to which definite social forms of consciousness correspond." Karl Marx, *Zur Kritik der politischen Ökonomie*, ed. Karl Kautsky, 2d ed. (Stuttgart, 1907), p. lv.—Eds.

at this juncture "induction" is of equally little help in taking experience and observation any further. As far as the world of other living creatures is concerned, it provides us only with the picture's frame, never with its contents. It gives us nothing other than the physical outline of the gestalt, the "organization," and by itself, using purely empirical means, it can provide us with nothing more. Should we now, when the empirical fails us, call upon fantasy—should we, since the logic of our concepts and the method of observation can help us no further, give ourselves over to an aesthetic form of "empathy"? Empirical science will always object most sharply to such an approach. To portray and deck out the "inner world" of animals with qualities of feeling that we can neither prove nor deny, as Uexküll declares, cannot be "the occupation of serious researchers."[35] A critically inclined philosophy cannot afford simply to dismiss this objection of the strict empiricist. However, the radical claim of "behaviorism," according to which all animal existence is confined to what is accessible to us in external animal behavior, also cannot do justice to the problem that confronts us here. Here too a thesis about method is turned into a dogmatic claim. This latter can only be set out by twisting and denying what is in the phenomenon itself, if not "given" in it, at least as something about which we can inquire. No theory is capable of eliminating the fact that within the "natural worldview" animals are given to us, not as machines, but "animated" creatures, that they appear to us living bodies and not as moving objects. The world of the "It" does not originally consist here of something independent, but rather can only be attained by a methodological abstraction from a given world of the "You."[36]

Thus when our thought turns to this problem it appears always to become caught up in an insolvable dilemma; it appears to be necessarily brought to a point from which it is equally possible to move forward or backward. It could almost seem that the only possible escape is to make a virtue of the problem—that we practice a kind of conscious methodological asceticism and renounce the attempt not only to find a solution to the problem, but even to formulate the problem at all. We seem here, if any-

35. von Uexküll, [*Umwelt und Innenwelt der Tiere*,] p. 5.—Cassirer.

36. On all this cf. esp. above, Chap. —, pp. -ff. On the methodological criticism of "Behaviorism" cf. now particularly the discussion by Karl Bühler in his *Die Krise der Psychologie* (Jena: [Gustav Fischer,] 1927), pp. 18ff. [§3 "Der Behaviorismus und die geisteswissenschaftliche Psychologie," pp. 18–28.]—Cassirer. Cassirer's incomplete reference is probably to *PSF*, vol. 3, pt. 1, chap. 2, which concerns the phenomenon of expression (*Ausdruck*) and the primacy of the "thou" (*Du*) over the "it" (*Es*).—Eds.

where, to be at the point where thought as *intellectus ectypus* must recognize that it is not a match for thought as *intellectus archetypus*, the point at which the "adventure of reason," as Kant termed it,[37] proved to be unworkable, the attempt to have a single plan for a joint comprehensive view and interpretation of the totality of all life.

There is still another way to obtain an intellectual view of the variety of organic forms of life and the accompanying phenomena without having to decide to opt for that intellectual "taking by storm" that Bergson insists upon—without our having to demand of "intelligence" that it jump over its own limits and, as in a kind of ecstasy, take on a new form of being. We cannot exchange one form of intelligence for another; we cannot replace its "discursive" type of conceptualization with immediate vision. But within its form of the concept, within its *"discursus"* itself, we can turn it around, and by such a change in direction, if at all, we can make the world of "immediacy" visible to us. What cannot be given to us directly through metaphysical intuition or by empirical observation becomes indirectly accessible through a kind of systematic "reconstruction."[38] This provides us in general with the method by means of which we are able to expose the unique character of "subjectivity." As long as we remain in the sphere of the "objective spirit," as long as we have an eye only for the works of geist as such and seek to grasp and encompass their contents, then all our powers of observation are directed to and captivated by this. But this cannot be an unconditioned and insuperable limitation, for this is the basic characteristic of thought, that it can step back, not just from the "outer world" of physical existence, but from itself, even from what is the adequate expression of its existence. When it looks at the various ways in which it gives form and meaning to objective things, then this "looking" includes the possibility of turning itself around. The ability to assume such an intention, to be directed to or be intent upon certain objects or contents of meaning, corresponds on the other hand to the capacity for "abstraction."

---

37. See Kant, *Kritik der Urtheilskraft, Werke*, vol. 5, pp. 498f. *Critique of Judgment*, p. 305, n. 5: "A hypothesis like this [of nature as being purposively ordered] may be called a daring adventure of reason, and one that has probably entered, on occasion, even the minds of virtually all the most acute natural scientists."—Eds.

38. See Paul Natorp, *Allgemeine Psychologie nach kritischer Methode* (Tübingen: J. C. B. Mohr [Paul Siebeck], 1912), chap. 8, "Die Methode der Konstruktion" (pp. 189–213). He outlines a method that is supposed neither to explain (as in a science of laws) nor merely to describe (as in a science of facts), but to lead to a reconstruction of the immediate in consciousness.—Eds.

True intellectual self-consciousness arises only where both of these aspects condition each other and where they balance each other. The existence of self-consciousness is bound to this condition. One can say that it is nothing but the equilibrium between the "productive" and the "abstractive," the formative and the reflective powers of thought. So "intelligence," if we use this word in its broadest sense, cannot ever flee itself; it cannot shed the underlying categories by which alone there can be a cosmos of being and meaning for it. But what is given to intelligence is this: that in the midst of the application of these categories, it can turn back to their "origin," it can ask about their ground and significance. This question is the beginning of a new attitude. The application appears now as though it has been stopped, as though it has been interrupted. Intelligence is discovered through this interruption and raised to consciousness. But the act of negation contained in this is directed not so much toward the function of mind as against its initial function. The mind does not abandon its essential nature; rather, it traverses it, its essential nature, in two directions. Its discursive movement now acquires a double "sense," a positive and a negative one.[39]

While all its energies were directed toward its immediate activity, toward the construction of individual worlds of form, it now can attempt a kind of "dismantling." But this dismantling can of course never be understood in an ontological sense, but only in a purely methodological one. It does not involve getting rid of objective, intellectual creations, but only ignoring them in a specific, limited sense. We no longer expect intelligence to make a leap, a *salto mortale*. In a sense, of course, it turns against itself, yet with the intention not of negating its own essential nature, but of recognizing it. It acquires this knowledge not by just running through the individual phases of the process of construction, but by reviewing the way they correlatively link up to one another. It expands its own horizon through this review so that it is able—although only in a specific and limited sense— to bring in not simply all the forms of the mind but all the forms of life as well.

We saw how not only our world of concepts but also our whole world of

39. On this definition of the "plus-and-minus sense" of knowledge cf. esp. the basic formulations in Natorp's *Allgemeine Psychologie nach kritischer Methode*, Tübingen (J. C. B. Mohr [Paul Siebeck]) 1912, pp. 69–72, and the critical discussion of them given earlier (Book -, Chap. -).—Cassirer. The earlier discussion Cassirer mentions here is in *PSF*, vol. 3, pp. 53–57.—Eds.

sensation and world of perception are subject to characteristic conditions of form and are inseparably interwoven with them. But this positive context and cohesion also have their negative side. If we seek, even hypothetically, to abstract from their conditions, then we have entered into a world that is to be conceived differently from ours not only as regards its form but also as regards its "matter." The "reality" of this world, the kind of phenomenal "givens" in it, cannot in any way be equated with our "world of experience." Of course, we can never hope actually to make ourselves fully aware of this other reality *in concreto*, or even imagine it in all of its individual features, to be able to re-experience it directly and to describe it by virtue of this re-experiencing. Every such imaginative attempt at illustrative clarification must necessarily mislead us. By comparison, it is possible and justifiable methodologically to attempt to grasp the general structural principle under which other worlds of experience stand and to contrast this principle with the principles that determine our sensory-intellectual world. This contrast and opposition then become a new means for distinguishing and critically setting the limits between "nature" and "geist," between "life" and "consciousness," a delimitation which nevertheless remains strictly within the world of thought and utilizes only its own, immanent means.

Now, after these preliminary, general considerations we can finally show precisely the service that a systematically constructed "philosophy of symbolic forms" can provide to the foundation of a philosophical anthropology. It can be fruitful in two ways; it would, to speak with Kant, serve both as a "propaedeutic" and as a "discipline." It would prepare the ground and soil and it would at the same time prevent it from leaving this secure ground and losing itself in speculations that can be neither confirmed nor refuted by any "possible experience." However, before we begin to show in any detail the fruitfulness of the philosophy of symbolic forms for the sphere of problems that concern us here, we must express a general, methodological hesitation. Do we not, by entering into this sphere of problems, again expose ourselves to all the ambiguities and dangers of "Psychologism"? Are we not, by raising this very question, being untrue to the basic position that Kant worked out for "critical philosophy"? We can oppose this objection by pointing out that it was none other than Kant himself who, in the *Critique of Pure Reason*, showed the way of the "subjective deduction" as well as of the "objective deduction." He not only asked about the conditions of the possibility of objects of experience—experience for him is in addition "a kind of knowledge that requires the understanding"[40]—he also directed the critical question to this kind of knowledge, to "the capacity to think itself."[41] In fact, the essence of Psychologism consists in the fact not that one follows the "subjective deduction" at all, but that it is not clearly and sharply distinguished from the tasks and method of the "objective deduction." The actual and true victory over Psychologism can therefore never consist in avoiding the problems of "philosophical anthropology," but in giving these problems their proper place within the system of philosophy. Only where this place is not found, where this "transcendental topic" fails, do those shifts in limits result, those "sublimations," that have led to the conflicts between Psychologism and pure logic.[42]

Sublimations of this kind arise not only where the proper separation of problems is missed but also where their proper connection is missed as well. The critical analysis of consciousness remains incomplete and one-sided insofar as it is directed exclusively to the world of the "object" or to that of the "subject," instead of recognizing that both are related and correlatively connected to each other. It must direct itself both to the manifold modes of "appearance" as well as to the objective meaning and the contents that are grasped in these modes. A division and an ambiguity can then arise from this only if, instead of conjoining these, themselves fully justified and necessary questions, they are confused with each other and uncritically mixed together. Philosophical thought may not ignore either of these two approaches, but it is necessary that we demand that it always be aware of which one of the two it has under consideration. The analysis of the individual symbolic forms has shown us this again and again; now we must seek to understand this more deeply by trying to summarize in a systematic review what we found there and to generalize from this summary.

2. [Life and Symbolic Form]

The basis for this procedure of systematic "reconstruction" in which we, following Natorp, see the actual method of a "critical psychology" must be conceived in the broadest and most comprehensive way possible. The dan-

---

40. Kant, *Kritik der reinen Vernunft, Werke*, vol. 3, p. 18 (B xvii). *Critique of Pure Reason*, pp. 22–23.—Eds.

41. Cf. above p. -.—Cassirer. The manuscript gives no page number here. Perhaps this is a reference to p. 35 above.—Eds.

42. See Kant, *Kritik der reinen Vernunft, Werke*, vol. 3, pp. 229–236 (B 324–336). *Critique of Pure Reason*, "Note to the Amphiboly of Concepts of Reflection," pp. 281–288.—Eds.

ger of taking too narrow an approach arises in two different ways: by limiting the starting point of our questions either in an intellectualistic or in a pragmatic sense. As far as Natorp's own construction of psychology is concerned, it followed a universal plan, but the attempt to carry out this plan led only in a very specific, particular direction. Basically, Natorp begins with Kant's threefold division; the objectivity of being corresponds to an equally pure objectivity of the ought and between these two realms, between the realm of "nature" and that of "freedom," stands the world of aesthetic objects as the "third main direction in the shaping of culture."[43] In the course of pursuing this basic conception, however, we find that this shaping of culture becomes more and more closely related to the first level of objectivity and oriented almost exclusively toward it. The question is directed—at least in the presentation that Natorp gives us in his *Allgemeine Psychologie*—completely toward "nature," and it takes the concept of nature itself in the sense and characterization given to it by natural science, by the exact knowledge of nature. This, then, constitutes the prototype and paradigm for the process of objectification in general. This process consists in the progression from the concretion of "immediate" lived experience to the abstract, general, and necessary conceptions of laws. Appearances are recognized as the appearances of objects by recognizing nature as determined through a law or through a general, prevailing relation. When philosophical self-examination does not stop at this relation, but asks about the basis of its validity, about the possibility of law-concepts in general, it must of course recognize that the opposition of "law" and "individual," of "general" and "particular," of "determinate" and "indeterminate," is to be taken never as something absolute, but always as a relative opposition.[44] But as such it remains completely fundamental; the approach toward objectivity is defined in all areas as law, the turn toward subjectivity is attained by the opposite relation, the relation to the "individual case." We have attempted earlier[45] in our investigations to expound how and why this conception of the question is too narrow; we have pointed out that not all objective "configurations" can be understood in the same sense, as a "giving of laws," the sense in which, for example, for Kant the understanding appears in its categories as "giving the law to nature."[46]

43. Natorp, *Allgemeine Psychologie*, p. 127; Cf. esp. Chap. 5., §17, pp. 125–128.—Cassirer.
44. [Natorp], *Allgemeine Psychologie*, chap. 4, §4ff.—Cassirer.
45. This is probably a reference to the discussion of Natorp in *PSF*, vol. 3, pp. 55f.—Eds.
46. Kant, *Kritik der reinen Vernunft, Werke*, vol. 3, p. 627 (A 126). *Critique of Pure Reason*, p. 148: "Thus the understanding . . . is itself the lawgiver of nature."—Eds.

We find this limitation expressed in Natorp by the fact, on the side of "subjectivity," that sensation is characterized as the last, purely theoretical "element" of consciousness. Because we have to attribute to the world of the ought the aspect of striving as its subjective correlate, and because the function of imagining corresponds to the world of the aesthetic, so all pure law-concepts, in which experience represents objects to us and objective relations as its contents, refer us back to sensation. In this sense it constitutes a final "concrete" and a final "given," which itself is of course never to be immediately found, but rather inferred from objectivity by means of a method of reconstruction. "Sensation" is to be defined in terms of quantity, taken as the final individual reality, and in terms of quality, taken as the final identity, as what is qualitatively one and simple in consciousness.[47] Hence, we are not supposed to be able to ask further about what is behind this unity; the way that it is given to us and the way it presents itself to us, the way it is divided up, for example, into definite spheres of qualities is accepted as a datum. That various theoretical presuppositions enter into this "datum" itself, which a truly thorough reconstruction would have to show and make clear, is here neither recognized nor acknowledged. In truth, "simple" sensation and its analysis into different groups, into individual "spheres of meaning," are not so much a starting point as a theoretical construction, which, however one may judge its justification and its necessity, is in no case a genuine psychological element and can represent no "ne plus ultra" of analysis. The positing of "sensation" as a mere X, as something determinable prior to all determination, and the positing of the theoretical form, of law-concepts as the means and ways of giving this indeterminate some determination, these are correlative notions for Natorp. It soon becomes clear how his analysis of the purely theoretical world takes into account only a single dimension of this world and constantly moves within it.[48]

Such a limiting of the world of theoretical form also occurs in the metaphysics of life, even though its critique has a completely different sense. Here too this critique is directed toward science, especially exact natural science. It is the final and highest product of "intelligence"; for this

---

47. Cf. Natorp, *Philosophische Propädeutik: [Untersuchungen auf ihrem Grenzgebiet,]* 3rd ed. (Marburg[: N. G. Elwert,] 1909), §43.—Cassirer.

48. Cf. on this the earlier discussions: Part -, Chap. -, p. -.—Cassirer. The manuscript gives no page numbers here. Perhaps this is a reference to *PSF*, vol. 3, pp. 56–57.—Eds.

very reason, however, intelligence's fundamental limit emerges in the sharpest way within it. This limit is found in the fact that science and the intellect in general really seem to be outfitted for grasping reality only in a speculative way; both of them were originally nothing other, and nothing more, than organs of action. Their "categories" are not forms of cognition, if one understands by knowledge the true unity of "subject" and "object," a becoming one with what is known; rather, they are forms of action. Bergson's critique of intelligence is based on his pragmatic and pragmatistic definition of it. Our thought is incapable, even in its purest logical form, of grasping the true nature of life, the process of creative evolution. How could it ever be able to grasp life itself, since it was itself created by life under very definite conditions and for definite aims? As does Klages, Bergson holds that this process suffices to expose the intellect, to show that it is merely a technical tool and so to unmask it as such. "If we could rid ourselves of all pride, if, to define our species, we kept strictly to what the historic and prehistoric periods show us to be the constant characteristic of man and of intelligence, we should say not *Homo sapiens*, but *Homo faber*. In short, intelligence, considered in what seems to be its original feature, is the faculty of manufacturing artificial objects, especially tools to make tools, and of indefinitely varying the manufacture."[49]

At first glance this definition seems to agree with the results of our own analysis. [It] also directed us to that characteristic peripeteia that takes place in mankind's intellectual existence as soon as it enters into the sphere of tools and tool-thinking. This thinking appears here to be a kind of species, not a genus, an aspect of "intelligence," but not as what conditions the whole or exhausts it. The creation and use of the tool provided us with a specific form and direction of vision, of foresight. But to the contrary we did not find that every type of vision, every kind of viewpoint whatsoever, was bound to this specific kind of seeing. If it were otherwise, then all intellectual creations would in the end prove to be mere effects. For example, language and myth would be nothing other than human "inventions" to attain particular goals and whose entire significance consists in attaining this goal. Here modern irrationalism dialectically turns into its opposite. Oddly, it comes dangerously close to that rationalism of the Enlightenment period which regarded language, for example, as a purely technical prod-

---

49. Bergson, *L'évolution créatrice*, p. 151.—Cassirer. Bergson, *Creative Evolution*, p. 139.— Eds.

uct, as a system of signs that serves solely to meet the need to pass along information and aid mutual communication.

For Bergson, in fact, the categories of science are in no way genuine and true forms of knowledge; they are, rather, social forms of action. They serve to create a mediate and quite artificial connection between different subjects, but they never build a bridge from the "I" to the "You," from one center of experience to another—they then let them meet only in an external sphere, in a sphere of communal activity. Given such an interpretation, it is most important that we reinstate "intelligence" in its full concept, before we compare it with other powers of being and measure it by reference to them. We may understand it neither in a one-sided intellectualistic manner nor in a merely pragmatic sense, but must take it as the central point of unity for all varieties and directions of the giving of form. The "human world" is constituted by the whole of these ways of giving form, not by some particular one of them. We will never arrive at a description and an understanding of this world if we extract only a portion of it, if we try to read off its total meaning from a single, privileged part of it. One might see this in the domain wherein mankind appears to stand in close proximity to the purely biological sphere and quite bound to it, or we might conceive the "mind" to be something elevated above "life," the subject of pure theory—of νόησις νοήσεως—so that it appears to have broken all ties with the organic world, but this means taking the beginning or the end of the human universe, but not this universe as a whole, as our main focus. We can understand the dynamic structure of the cultural world only by reference to this main focus, only in this way can we set the correct accents of meaning and value. This world contains a closed field of energies in which all the individual forces, no matter how they appear to diverge, are nonetheless related to a common center and are united in it.

How we are to define this "center" can, after the results of our earlier investigation, no longer be open to question. We began with the view that the meaning and value of the individual symbolic forms could never be completely obtained if we were to see in each of them only a bridge between a *finished* "inner world" and a *finished* "outer world," between an "I" and a "non-I" as given and fixed starting points. They all had, rather, to be recognized as means for the *creation* of these polar opposites, as the mediums in which and only by virtue of which the "separation and sorting out of the I and the world" takes place. The actual ideal achievement that was to be accomplished here proved in each case always to be not merely the elimination of opposites but their tension. The harmony within the world of geist always appeared to be like Heraclitus' "harmony in contrariety as in the lyre and the bow."[50] In this we found the decisive feature which serves to define not so much the content of specifically human existence as its general dynamic character. The unique feature of this character cannot be represented by spatial images because these immediately reinterpret the dynamic motif we are dealing with here so as to transform it into a static aspect, because they must treat the "object" of our concern, about whose performance we are asking, as though it were already given and present at hand. Hence, that great "crisis," that great process of separation through which the world of the mind actually first comes about, cannot be clarified by means of any spatial comparisons, by references to "here" and "there," to "inside" or "outside." The language of space becomes entangled without fail in aporias and antinomies; everything that we attempt to formulate in such terms turns quickly into its opposite.

The world of geist is no more "immanent" within the world of "life" than it is "transcendent" of it; it remains as little caught up "in" it as it raises itself "above" it. This twofold nature of "inside" and "outside" or of "above" and "below" is itself not something that is already there and given. It is one of many intellectual aspects; it is only there as the "viewpoint" of the mind. Since this viewpoint is not in itself established, since every way of looking also includes in itself the possibility of turning itself around, the possibility of "reflection," this rift can arise for us, as intellectual subjects. The apparent dualism, the rupture in "existence," is in truth nothing other than the result of a necessary duality of "viewpoints." This rupture implies that life has broken away from itself, without becoming completely "beside itself," transparent to itself, an object for itself. Every symbolic form works in its own way and by its own means to bring about this turn from mere being-in-itself to being-for-itself. Through them, along with the objective configurations of culture, that characteristic mode of conscious awareness is achieved that is found in mankind. This awareness is, in the end, nothing but an expression of the fact that man has built an "opposing-world,"[51] which now is added to the surrounding world of immediate existence, that he has

---

50. Heraclitus frag. B 51 (Diels, vol. 1, p. 87; Freeman, p. 28).—Eds.

51. In German: *Gegenwelt*. See Uexküll, *Umwelt und Innenwelt der Tiere*, p. 168: "The *Gegenwelt* is that piece of represented spatial reality for higher brains."—Eds.

directly to do no longer with "things," but with "signs" that he has created, that he is not only a part of the world, but has gone on to represent and to depict this world.

At this point the results of a critically oriented and critically founded philosophy of nature connect up immediately with the results of the philosophy of symbolic forms and can provide an indirect confirmation of its basic thesis.[52] This is what philosophy of nature teaches us: that the turn toward the "objectivity of things" is the true line of demarcation between the human world and that of all other organic creatures. The animal world appears, even where it comes closest in approaching our own, always and necessarily to remain a world of "situations" that cannot be raised to an order of objects, let alone to an order of meanings and facts. The thing that gives them their certainty and completeness, their inner, organic unity, is the circumstance that all these situations are firmly connected together, that they are exactly in tune, both with each other and with the "surrounding world" in which the animal lives. So there results a strictly defined and strictly limited sequence of all the animal's expressions of life, of all that it undergoes and does.

The world of its "receptors" and its "reality" effect each other according to a fixed rhythm; every particular class of "impressions" corresponds to a particular kind and direction of action. Whatever is outside this particular circle of possible impressions and possible movements is completely barred from the animal, is not at hand for it. Every animal, as Uexküll expresses this basic relationship, carries its surrounding world with it during its entire lifetime like an impenetrable shell. "Just as the lower animals seek out the right chemical and physical stimuli, so the higher animal seeks out with its developed eye apparatus the right forms, colors and movements, that can serve its reflexes as triggers and on which it alone depends without worry and is secure, afloat in the immeasurable of the outer world. The stimuli of the environment create at the same time a firm protective wall, which enclose the animal like the walls of a house and keep it from the

52. This relationship has now emerged particularly in Plessner's presentation of "philosophical anthropology." His results are very close to my own, even though they were reached by an altogether different route. Particular attention should be drawn here to the two concluding chapters of Plessner's work (as cited above, pp. 239ff.). [See above notes 6 and 22.— Eds.] I also find myself here in fundamental agreement with Scheler's basic view in his anthropology, insofar as I have been able to study it in the short sketch, which is all that has been accessible to me.—Cassirer.

whole foreign world."[53] As little as the animal is able ever to penetrate this wall, so little is it ever able to notice it, to "have" it as an object, as an obstacle.

All its capacities to make distinctions, no matter how keenly developed they may be, are concerned only with the level of situations themselves and are incapable of adding any other new dimension to them or changing them in any fundamental way. The "stimulus" of the external world affects it by triggering a particular movement, but it does not have any independent "reality" of its own beyond this immediate efficacy. Its ability to "notice" is essentially limited to the moment of its influence: it cannot be directed and conjoined with other such moments so as to form an "objective" unity.

This becomes all the more evident the further that we descend in the order of animals. For instance, taking one of Uexküll's descriptions, if we consider the picture that he gives of the world of the pilgrim scallop, we find that if we begin with the purely objective observation of its organization, the animal has a large number of eyes that already reveal a very developed organization, possessing a retina and lenses and even indicating an apparatus of accommodation. Further consideration reveals, however, that the influences affecting these eyes do not affect or connect up with one another. Nowhere do we have the differentiation of impressions that is needed for the outline of an "image" of the outer world. Every eye makes use of the general reflex apparatus, which is set so that it springs into action from the same excitation that can come to it from any direction. Hence, if we say of higher animals that they use their eyes, we must say of the pilgrim scallop that the eyes use the animal. They serve to initiate the only free movement that the animal is capable of, namely, swimming. "A darkening of the horizon actuates the numerous, little tentacles, that surround the eye and cause them to open up so that the eye's field of vision becomes free. Thereafter the image of an approaching object is produced on the retina. The form and color of the object have no influence on the mollusk, that is, the image on the retina does not serve to cause excitement. This is different with the movement of the image. A movement of a certain speed—not too fast, not too slow—precisely the tempo that the archenemy of all mollusks,

---

53. von Uexküll, [*Umwelt und Innenwelt der Tiere*,] pp. 182, 219.—Cassirer. The sentence about the impenetrable shell is the fifteenth of Uexküll's twenty-one "principles of biology."—Eds.

the starfish Asterias, follows is the stimulus that causes excitement. At this, the tentacles surrounding the eye lose all their rigidity, the compressed water which causes it to swell is forced into the animal and the tentacles flap like long lashes at the moving object. If it is the starfish, then the receptors are excited by the slime and the tentacles are retracted. At the same time, however, the visceral ganglion receives a strong wave of movement and this reacts by moving the locomotive muscle whose quick strokes lift the mollusk up and let it powerfully swim away from the dangerous area of the enemy."[54] We have here before us a quite distinct and particular kind of "reality" which is far removed from genuine "objectivity." Instead of "objects" there are only "series of excitations," as Uexküll calls them, in the world of the pilgrim scallop. The excitation of a shadow, followed by an optical excitation of movement, which is then finally followed by a chemical excitation—this series of features is the characterization of the enemy, the starfish, and it is sufficient to set off a series of actions by which the animal is protected from harm and danger.[55]

When this variety of features does not condense into a firm, thing-like "nucleus," when it is experienced as a mere series and not related to a specific point of unity, this limitation does not then apply just to the world of objects but concerns no less than the pure world of the "I." Neither can be separated from the other; the unity of the I does not come before that of the object but rather is constituted only through it. The *Critique of Pure Reason* uses this correlation in order, with its help, to refute subjective, psychological idealism. It shows that the notion of the I as a unified subject of representations is possible only through the support that it receives from the empirical concept of substance. Only by positing something that remains fixed in space is the notion of an enduring I possible, one which remains identical with itself in all its successive states. In this way inner experience itself becomes understandable and definable only by means of "outer" experience, the experience of constant, objective unities.[56] Without consciousness of a world of objects extended in space, and especially without the experience of the relative constancy of that empirical object that we

54. Uexküll, *Umwelt und Innenwelt der Tiere*, p. 151.—Eds.

55. On all this cf. Uexküll, [*Umwelt und Innenwelt der Tiere*,] pp. 144ff.—Cassirer. The discussion of the "Pilgermuschel" or "pilgrim scallop" (also known as the "St. James' shell") is on pp. 144–152.—Eds.

56. Kant, *Kritik der reinen Vernunft*, 2nd ed, pp. 274ff.—Cassirer. Reference to the "Refutation of Idealism," *Critique of Pure Reason*, pp. 244–247. *Kritik der reinen Vernunft, Werke*, vol. 3, pp. 200–203 (B 274–279).—Eds.

call our own body, no empirical feeling of self, no experience of one's own I can develop.

Here again we see that within the animal world this presupposition is nowhere to be found in any strict sense. The lower animals in particular seem not to distinguish sharply between their "own" body and the bodies in the vicinity, the "outer world." The movements that the animal carries out are not in general given to it as "its" movements, since in the layout of the whole organization, the "receptor" apparatus is completely separated from the "motoric" one. This separation holds, Uexküll says, up to the highest invertebrates, to the arthropoda and octopoda, so that the receptor apparatus never "hears" about the activity of the motoric apparatus. Since the animals never receive back stimuli of their own movement, that peculiar reflective relationship cannot yet exist according to which every higher creature "is" a body and at the same time "has" a body of its own. The borderline between the world of one's "own" and of the "other" is still shifting; one's "own" body is not yet in any definite way set off or isolated from its surroundings. But without such an isolation of the body as a material substratum there can be no closer definition in terms of conscious awareness, no "being-for-itself."

The same fundamental limitation seems to hold for all contents that enter in any way into the "functional circle" of the animal. To the extent that these contents are present for the animal at all they are not present as constant determinations, as "things" with enduring "characteristics." Their features depend completely on the way they occur under the particular conditions in which they enter into the functional circle. The result in Volkelt's well-known experiments[57] with the round-web spider was that the spider behaved totally differently toward an insect that flew into its net in the usual way than when the same insect in an unusual fashion was put right into its lair, where the spider normally waited for its prey. The insect is not treated in both cases as the "same" object, but rather is met with completely different kinds of behavior.[58]

Volkelt's explanation for this fact is that the animal, instead of living in and with "things," lives rather with "complex qualities" and that it [is] always only a specific, quite indefinite total situation and [not] the single

---

57. See Hans Volkelt, *Über die Vorstellungen der Tiere: Ein Beitrag zur Entwicklungspsychologie* (Leipzig and Berlin: Wilhelm Engelmann, 1914), pp. 17f.—Eds.

58. Cf. above p. -.—Cassirer. The manuscript gives no page number here. Perhaps this is a reference to *PSF*, vol. 3, p. 152 n., which is about Volkelt.—Eds.

elements of the situation that define the actions of this animal. On the level of animals the totality of sensory data is not portioned off into thing-like structures, nor are these data divided up into individual atoms of meaning, into simple "sensations." Instead, a broad field of the sensory given, perhaps the whole presently given complex, is encompassed by a single quality that contains everything, but which is undifferentiated and diffuse and yet has a specific complex quality. The flow of such diffuse qualities, which can be regarded as regular and rhythmic in structure, but not as possessing the persistence and steadfastness of specific, clearly delimited spatial objects, is therefore definitive of the animal's "world of representations."[59] Instead of objects that the animal "thinks about," which it is able to "regard" as independent, it lives with sensory melodies. The landscape, for example, that the carrier pigeon sees below itself is not comparable to a map; rather, it appears to the pigeon as relatively undifferentiated and diffuse, somewhat like the way a pattern appears to us when we glance at it. "The impressions of the landscapes which follow one upon the next do not come together to form a series of discrete, well-defined images, but rather are like an optical melody.... The animals find their way from one landscape to the next with these optical melodies the way someone who reproduces a song finds his way from one tone to the next."[60]

We have not brought in all these observations and theories from animal psychology for their own sake; rather, they should provide us only with a contrasting image, in order to help determine the specific value of the individual "symbolic forms" for the structure of intellectual consciousness. This consciousness is a consciousness of objects insofar as it is self-consciousness— and it is self-consciousness only in and by virtue of the fact that it is a consciousness of objects. Whether this turn, to which the content is not so much subjected as the mode of experiencing is in human beings, is a *product* of symbolic forms or, whether, on the other hand, the latter is only an expression, a characteristic "symptom" of this turn, this question is basically as pointless as it is unanswerable. For both of these determinations can be grasped only as existing "in addition" to each other; we have here neither a "prior" nor "subsequent" independent element, but always only a correlation of aspects. From the purely analytic point of view, which cannot be confused with questions of genesis, only one thing is essential here: that

59. Hans Volkelt, *Über die Vorstellungen der Tiere.* Leipzig and Berlin: 1914, pp. 79ff.—Cassirer.

60. Volkelt, above [*Über die Vorstellungen der Tiere*], pp. 125f.—Cassirer.

the basic relationship we have before us is capable of closer determination insofar as it is graduated within itself in the different symbolic forms. Myth, language, art, knowledge—they are all basic intellectual potencies participating in the transfiguration and reorientation which organic life experiences as soon as it enters into the specifically human sphere, but they do not participate in this process equally. This inequality provides us with new methodological means for working out the particular phases of the unified process of "anthropogeny."[61] The change in viewpoints which takes place in the transition from one form to another provides us with various different perspectival aspects, and what results for us from the combination of these is the complete image of this anthropogeny.

If we begin here by considering the mythic world, then this appears at first glance to reveal the same relatively diffuse configuration that we found to be characteristic of the representational world of animals. For it is a basic feature of mythic "objects" that they are not at all sharply delimited according to classes and species, but rather that they are capable of almost unlimited transfigurations. Mythic being is subject to the fundamental law of metamorphosis; it cannot manifest itself in any way but through cloaking itself in ever new forms. All "natural" limits, all the opposites between the kingdom of the "organic" and the "inorganic," or between plant, animal, and human experience, as they appear to be immediately offered to empirical observation, are skipped over here, and it is this jump that appears to provide the principle of myth and the "beginning of its motion."[62] No matter how far myth may seem to go beyond this beginning, the general direction in which it progresses always remains the same. Nowhere in myth do we find the kind of objective determinateness and objective constancy that is required and posited by experiential thought. The *principium individuationis* which governs this latter, the separation of objects according to their "here" and "now," according to a fixed and definite place that they acquire in space and time, fails us here. In fact, it appears to turn into its opposite, for the singularity of a space-time determi-

---

61. This term also appears in the introduction to *PSF*, vol. 2: Cassirer compares the methodological dispositions of mythic thematization in Schelling's metaphysics with those of folk psychology. The former proceeds from a previously existing identity of the Absolute; the latter proceeds from the identity of human nature. See p. 12: "And with this question the subject of myth takes a new turn. Metaphysics and psychology have answered it in opposite senses, metaphysics from the standpoint of theogony, psychology from the standpoint of 'anthropogeny.' "—Eds.

62. On all this cf. esp. [*PSF*] vol. 2, pp. 179ff.—Cassirer.

nation and fixed space and time limits are not found in mythic thought. *Its* space and *its* time are not given as some clear and sharp "separateness" of elements; rather, we find in them a continual going-over-into-another, a complete melting together of individual places as well as of moments. Things are governed by what Lévy-Bruhl called *multiprésence*,[63] by means of which a mythic reality can be found simultaneously at any number of different places without this thereby in the least meaning that it is no longer "the same" thing. In this changeability, in this fluidity and fleetingness of its contents, the mythic world seems still to be very close to the forms of the animals' experience and the animals' "representations" as they can be reconstructed on the basis of the animals' behavioral patterns. In fact, modern developmental psychology has tried to explain both worlds by means of the same principle: the concept of the "complex quality" had been used as a key for the representation of animal "consciousness" just as one has pointed to the form of "complex thought" in order to designate the peculiar "logic" of mythic forms.[64] But this is not actually a true parallelism, for the common element that provides the basis of the comparison, the *tertium comparationis*, is essentially a negative and not a positive one. It expresses well the contrast between it and the "objective" configuration of the empirical-theoretical image of the world, but it threatens, on the other hand, to blur the specific difference by virtue of which the "complexion" of mythic consciousness is distinguished from that of animal consciousness.

Vignoli reports in his original and remarkable book *Mito e scienza*[65] about a long series of animal observations that he made during a period of years, which were supposed to serve as a proof that the true roots of mythic awareness and mythic thought generally reach down into the animal realm, for even animals possess the gift of "personification"[66] from which the mythic world grows. If we consider these observations and experiments more closely, then we can see that on the contrary they serve clearly to display the sharp distinction between the animal and the human world. They serve to show that the animal world, instead of possessing an objec-

63. On *multiprésence*, see Lucien Lévy-Bruhl, *How Natives Think*, trans. Lilian A. Clare (New York: Washington Square Press, 1966), p. 96.—Eds.

64. More in Heinz Werner, *Einführung in die Entwicklungspsychologie* [4th ed. (Leipzig: J. A. Barth, 1926)], esp. §§13, 22, 34ff.—Cassirer.

65. Vignoli, *Mito e scienza* (Milan: Fratelli Dumolard, 1879); English trans., *Myth and Science: An Essay* (New York: D. Appleton, 1882).—Eds.

66. See Vignoli, *Myth and Science*, pp. 48–67, esp. p. 65: "Every object of animal perception is therefore felt, or implicitly assumed, to be a living, conscious, acting subject."—Eds.

tive, factual character, is primarily if not exclusively "physiognomic" in character, that it is a collection not of "thing qualities," but of expressive values. The extraordinary sensitivity to such expressive values which the higher animals especially possess is thereby attested to. Köhler reports, for example, how his anthropoids immediately responded "sympathetically" to a certain human facial expression—for instance, how they immediately responded to an expression of fear with fright and horror even when there was not the least "objective" reason for it.[67] In fact, everything seems to suggest that animal "knowledge" always takes this direction, that the different "functional circles" the animal lives in are differentiated according to "physiognomic" criteria rather than according to any specific, objective "characteristics."[68] The circles of prey, of sex, of the enemy, of the same species—these all appear to be differentiated not so much by factual distinguishing "features" as through such affective qualities that differentiate between the attractive and the repulsive, the luring and the frightful, and so forth. But it would be a false conclusion if we were to infer from this unobjective and nonfactual character of the animal world that it has to be organized along personal lines. We can never, by simple conversion, acquire or infer a positive definition from this negative one alone. Rather, this also presupposes a positive intellectual principle of interpretation and formation. Vignoli's theory must attribute to the animal a capacity of not only personification but also of "entification." It should be capable of grasping a variety of levels and shadings of expression in its immediate experience, and it should be able to reshape these experienced differences into differences regarding its "essence."[69]

It is this last feature that reveals the real problem with this theory. For "entification," the "elevation to being," always remains an act *sui generis*, an independent, intellectual action which, as such, lies far beyond the limits of animal "consciousness." We found again and again in the course of analyzing the mythic form of thought how much it too is rooted in and remains bound to primordial expressive experience. But the variety of mythic forms does not spring immediately from these experiences themselves; rather, it

67. Cf. above, p. -.—Cassirer. The manuscript gives no page number here. Perhaps this is a reference to *PSF*, vol. 3, p. 66 n., citing Köhler's "Zur Psychologie des Schimpansen," in *Psychologische Forschung* 1 (1921): 27f., 39; see also *PSF*, vol. 1, p. 189 n., which gives essentially the same reference to Köhler.—Eds.

68. Examples are again found in Werner, *Entwicklungspsychologie*, §13, and in other places.—Cassirer.

69. On Vignoli's theory, cf. [*PSF*] vol. 2, p. 20 n.—Cassirer.

comes from the particular "concentration" that they undergo. The world of expression as such is nowhere transcended, but a concentration takes place in it, a gathering together of particular "points of judgment." Only in this gathering together and combination does it become the *demonic* world. The demon may be conceived as ever so vague and fleeting, but it always has some kind of personal "character" by means of which it can be distinguished and recognized. It is helpful or hostile, cruel or good, ready to give protection or malicious and treacherous. It may be quite unpredictable in its behavior, moody and changeable in its particular expressions, yet it possesses certain limits to its essence and particular character from which it does not depart. All the arbitrariness and chance in its activities and actions do not serve to eliminate this specific nature of its being. So here too in these first, primitive structures of myth the decisive step has already been made. The chaos of affects has begun to clear, and particular configurations emerge from it that acquire an enduring nature. The mythic process of demonization provides the preparations and preconditions for the individualization of reality. Now the world of life surrounding mankind is not grasped through indefinite shared feelings but seems to be divided up and to begin to take on form around fixed centers. Where man attains to this mythic configuration of reality the various noises of reality no longer just impinge on him from outside. Rather, he begins to hold onto them as something constant and recurring.

In his writings on the cults of the forest and fields,[70] Mannhardt shows how a host of the figures with which mythic thinking populates the fields and meadows, the groves and bushes, originates thanks to such an emphasis, as they are formed from the rustling of the trees and of the foliage on the ground, from the groaning of the wind, and the whispering of the brook. Here too Herder sees one of the deepest roots of all mythical feeling and thought. "Just as all nature makes sounds, so there is nothing more natural for sensuous peoples than to think that it is alive, speaks, and acts. Those wild peoples saw a tall tree with its astonishing crown and marveled: the crown resounds! That is an acting divinity! The primitive falls to the ground and worships it!"[71] In such acts of adoration, of elevation to the divine, mankind does not remain "passive" toward such existence. Individual voices are now singled out of this muffled confusion of voices, and the

70. See Johann Wilhelm Emmanuel Mannhardt, *Wald- und Feldkulte*, 2 vols. (Berlin: Gebrüder Borntraeger, 1875–1877).—Eds.

71. [Johann Gottfried Herder], "Über den Ursprung der Sprache," [*Herders Sämmtliche Werke*, ed. Bernhard Suphan (Berlin: Weidmann, 1891), vol.] 5, p. 53.—Cassirer.

more that mythic interpretation progresses, the more that these voices, by remaining specific, come together to form a unity and a whole, the sound of a choir of spirits. The examination of the mythical world has of course showed us how slowly this process moves forward. In its early forms, there appear to be such developments that have no definite limits or individualization. Such developments as we find them in the Melanesian's *mana*, the *orenda* of the Iroquois, the *wakanda* of the Sioux[72] designate an indefinite composition rather than a clearly defined essence. They are not themselves demons, but a kind of designation for the demonic in general—for what is to be worshiped, for the fearsome, the terrible, the overpowering, the dangerous and threatening, the foreign and uncanny.

If anywhere, we are standing within the sphere of expression, in a mythic feeling that is not yet differentiated, has not yet been concentrated to form particular configurations. But the further that the mythic process progresses, the more this indefiniteness dissipates. We now move from the world of impersonal, magic forces to that of individual mythic forms and, finally, to that of personal gods. We have seen how this advance also stands for an inner transformation in human self-consciousness. Mankind does not form the gods after man's own image as if this were itself something already fixed at the beginning, as if this were an original datum; rather, it is found only in the process of mythic and religious formation. It attains its essence by bringing it forth in this formative process.[73]

But we have already overstepped the circle to which myth and religion belong and without noticing it have attained a new level of thought. As we have shown earlier, it is language that plays a decisive part in the process of this "theogony." The god's definite nature is achieved only through the name that he receives; the proper *name* is what secures for him his own *being*. In the name, his essence, his individual character is unified in such a way that, according to the general, mythic conception, knowledge of the god's name enables the one who possesses it also to possess all the god's powers.[74] As such the name encompasses a fundamentally broader area and exercises a still more general influence. It is not primarily a "proper name";

72. On *mana*, *orenda*, and *wakanda*, see *PSF*, vol. 2, pp. 75ff.—Eds.

73. For a more detailed explanation the reader is referred to the explication in *Sprache und Mythos, Studien der Bibliothek Warburg*, VI (1925), pp. 51ff.; see also [*PSF*] vol. 2, pp. 199ff.—Cassirer. *Language and Myth*, trans. Susanne K. Langer (New York: Dover, 1953), pp. 62ff.—Eds.

74. Documentation esp. in *Sprache und Mythos*, pp. 37ff.—Cassirer. *Language and Myth*, pp. 44ff.—Eds.

rather, its true power emerges when it is used as a "thing name." As we said above, the god's name is what first constitutes its "character" as a personal god, and now the same development occurs in the opposite direction. The function of "naming" becomes the starting point and vehicle for the function of defining objects—or, to put it a better way, for the function of establishing objects. In naming a content, it then becomes ripe for perceiving and observing as an object. With the name, it acquires a constancy, a persistence, and a permanence that is denied to the fleeting contents of experience that are given no names. Whatever is not taken out of the uniform flow of contents by the name, whatever is not determined through some indicator or signpost of language, cannot emerge as something solid and enduring. It does not in this way achieve independent "existence," insofar as this is understood to mean *ex-sistere*, the stepping out or stepping forward from the flowing constant series of appearances.[75]

It is only through the purely demonstrative functions of "pointing out" and "showing," as found in language in the use of articles,[76] that such a sphere of existence is delimited. Now arises the notion of the "thing" as something identical and persisting to which various, changing characteristics or states accrue, a "center" of objectivity, in which all changing existence is drawn together and to which it is related. Empiricism and Skepticism tend in their criticism of language primarily to regard it as a deficiency that it has a relatively small number of names at its disposal; language is far from being in a position to address, let alone to have the right word for, all reality. In place of the individual fullness and individual differences in our perceptual contents language can only provide a meager general term in which all the particular nuances are lost and eradicated. What is here attributed to language as a deficiency, what is objected to as its fundamental limitation, holds instead the basis of its richness and greatest strength. Only by this limitation is language able to prove its mastery. Not by shining its light evenly on all parts of the perceptual world, but by collecting it in certain focal points, language creates a "centering," an organization of this world. Whatever falls in this way under the beam of language emerges as a gestalt from a relatively undetermined background. This distribution of accents and the partitioning off of a "foreground" and a "background" provide the intellectual articulation of the world as we represent it, and of

75. See Goethe, *Faust*, lines 146–147.—Eds.

76. On the function of the article and its relation to demonstrative pronouns, cf. [*PSF*] vol. 1, pp. 202ff.—Cassirer.

which the spoken articulation is only an outer expression. From the standpoint of immediate experience every such distinction, every stronger emphasis of particular elements must always appear to be a kind of violation, but it is through this very application of force to immediacy that a separation from immediacy and the delimitation and definition of an objective reality become possible. Naming singles out a particular aspect of the passing contents, which never recur with any strict uniformity, providing it with a stable *sign*, and on the basis of this, if you will, an "artificial" unity, regarding and treating it as "the same."[77] This provides the foundation[78] for the interpretation that does not simply accept the given as a sum of elements that are similar in nature and in value, but which divides them up into the relatively important and relatively unimportant, into "typical" and "coincidental" qualities.

As long as the function of language has not yet completely developed or achieved its full strength, there are as yet no really sharp distinctions of such areas of "importance," and the presupposition is missing for structuring the given in terms of things, so a persistent, substantial "kernel" could be singled out and distinguished from changing, accidental qualities. Not only in the world of the animal, but also in the world of the child, there does not yet seem to be such a difference, such a separation of the enduring from the changing or of the central from the peripheral, *before* the child's feelings and thought come under the all-powerful influence of language. Among the best-known findings in child psychology is that the child no longer "recognizes" an otherwise well known object from his environment as soon as it appears to be in the least bit modified, that, for example, a minor change in the mother's clothing is sufficient to make her appear unrecognizable, so that she does not seem "the same." If we were to try to explain this fact by declaring that the child has not yet learned to distinguish the "essential" from the "unessential" characteristics, then such a claim would obviously contain a *petitio principii*; it would use the fact that is to be explained as the principle of explanation. For the difference between the "essential" and the "unessential" does not precede the development of language and logical concept formation as some self-evident, pure given, but holds only from the standpoint of this latter development. Only after

---

77. Cassirer discusses this notion of artificial signs in *PSF*, vol. 1, pp. 105f.—Eds.

78. *Marginal note:* recogn. / path. / sine Met. / Tel? / στατ.—Cassirer. "recogn." probably refers to the synthesis of recognition in the concept in Kant, *Kritik der reinen Vernunft, Werke*, vol. 3, pp. 614–618 (A 103–110). *Critique of Pure Reason*, pp. 133–138.—Eds.

fixed linguistic concepts have been coined and aspects of perceptual experience have been especially designated in some way can we turn around and find in them a difference between the sphere of the "necessary" and of "chance," the "essential" and the "unessential."

That is the kernel of truth in nominalism's thesis that the "concept" and the "word" cannot be separated. The word taken as a *flatus vocis* does not create the concept, but without the support that it gives to it, without the assistance that it gets from the word, the concept would, as soon as it arose, come apart and melt into nothing. The same holds for the perception of objects in general, which can be acquired only through the medium of concepts and can be secured and fixed only by the strength of these. Hence "object" and "name" belong together, not in the sense that the name in any way "imitates" or reproduces the object as some previously given nature of the thing, but in the sense that by virtue of it, by virtue of the general function of naming, is consciousness able to raise itself to the sphere of objective thinking at all. Language becomes the precondition of "recognition in concepts," and this itself again provides a definite stage, a necessary transitional phase for the "unity of the manifold," for the form of "synthesis," on which rests the possibility of relating a representation to an "object."[79] By virtue of this particular, linguistic-logical relationship consciousness has now stepped beyond that delicate balance which still governed things in the mythic world of form. Its particular contents now no longer appear to be subject to a restless transformation; rather, they have an independent content, a peculiar "stability" of their own. How much this process of "consolidation" owes to language and how much it remains bound to it can best be confirmed by the pathological *disorders* of language.

As we have seen they never concern just name-giving alone; rather, with its loss or disturbance the whole of consciousness seems to be thrown back to an entirely different level. Instead of being organized by reference to fixed and sharp thing unities, it appears now to move again among those "sensory melodies" that we found to be characteristic of the way animals perceive. It fades into a series of external determinations without separating out of them anything enduring, without binding them to an objective "substratum." The particular qualities, of warm and cold, of hard and soft, of smooth and rough, are distinguished from one another, but an object is

---

79. For a closer argument on this cf. the earlier discussion, Part -, Chap. -, pp. -ff.—Cassirer. The manuscript gives no page number here. Perhaps this is a reference to *PSF*, vol. 1, pp. 283f.; vol. 3, pp. 108, 114.—Eds.

not "recognized" on the basis of all these distinctions and a definite name attributed to it as a thing.[80] The world is in a way once again fluid and fleeting—the I is carried away by the course of its individual sensory experiences, but the will does not build up in it, as in Goethe's "Legend," to form a ball of crystal.[81]

The analysis of language has shown us that it never attains or performs its unique achievements immediately; rather, a variety of preparations are necessary for them and their completion in language and in its world of thought. The "primacy of action," which is characteristic of the way animals perceive and notice, appears still to govern completely the original concepts of language. They clearly reveal a "teleological" structure; they relate not so much to the circle of "things" and their "characteristics," as rather to the circle of means and ends as they are defined by wishing and wanting in human action and effort. A content is "named" not according to what it "is" in a purely objective sense but according to what it is good for. Its "meaning" accrues to it only in its use, and it is with reference to this that the primary linguistic as well as the primary mythical concepts acquire their order. The formation of class and serial concepts in myth is understandable only in terms of this principle. They do not collect what belongs together according to "objective" categories of some kind, but fit them together in the mythic functional circle, for example, in the circle of activities and practices relating to magic. The elements that can take one another's place within this circle are brought together as one, without paying any attention to the differences in their objective structure and specific nature. From the mythic point of view they no longer form a plurality, but rather a single "object." By reference to this principle we are in a position to understand those remarkable unities that not only join together things that—for a purely objective orientation—are completely disparate, but declare them to be strictly *identical*.[82] Language appears at

---

80. For more on this see Part -, Chap. -, esp. pp. -ff.—Cassirer. The manuscript gives no page numbers here. Perhaps this is a reference to *PSF*, vol. 3, pt. 2, chap. 2, pp. 120–142. See Cassirer's discussion of sensory melodies in Volkelt, *Über die Vorstellungen der Tiere*, above in this chapter.—Eds.

81. See Goethe's poem "Legend" (Part II of "The Pariah"), trans. E. A. Bowring, *The Poems of Goethe: Translated in the Original Metres*, various translators, Household Edition (New York: John W. Lovell, 1882), pp. 138ff., lines 8–11 (after the Brahmin's wife goes to fetch water without a pail or pitcher): "She of neither stands in need / For with pure heart, hands unsullied, / She the water lifts, and rolls it / To a wondrous ball of crystal." Goethe, "Legende," *WA*, Abt. 1, vol. 3, p. 10.—Eds.

82. I refer here, for instance, to the identity that exists in the mythic thought of the

first to continue along the same lines, and the language of children is especially rich in formulations that show this basic tendency, in which there is a desire to bring together in one basic concept not what is objectively the same in *kind*, but what is the same in its *meaning* or affect, what excites or appeals to the will in the same way.[83]

But in its highest logical achievements language moves far beyond this circle. It makes the transition from the sphere of emotion to the "theoretical" sphere. Order according to means and ends gives way to an order according to objective characteristics and objective contexts. Now it attains to a form of observation that is no longer confined exclusively to the task of accomplishing practical ends; it not only takes in and circumscribes the circle of human activity, it gains a clear overview of the whole of reality. It attains to an intellectual horizon, a circle of vision in which it comprehends this whole. This advance from the "circle of action" to the "circle of vision" marks one of the most characteristic differences between the human world of consciousness and the animal's world of experience. The animal too would not be able to assert itself in the face of its surrounding world if its actions were not adapted to it, if it was not able, in a specific way, to answer the questions put to it by its environment through a more or less purposive movement. But these answers as a whole reveal a thoroughly rigid structure. Certain situations call forth certain series of actions which always occur in the same way. The animal *performs* these actions, but it does not stand apart from them and is not able to regard them objectively, either individually or as a whole.

In order to elucidate this, we recall the example mentioned earlier given by Fabre in his *Souvenirs entomologiques*.[84] The sand wasp does not usually

---

Huichol Indians between grain, deer, and peyote, a kind of cactus. Cf. Carl Lumholtz, *Symbolism of the Huichol Indians, Memoirs of the American Museum of Natural History* (New York, 1900), vol. 3, pp. 17ff. For details see [*PSF*] vol. 2, pp. 180ff. Cf. also Lévy-Bruhl, *How Natives Think*, pp. 116–136.—Cassirer.

83. Illustrations for this are given in *Sprache und Mythos*, pp. 33ff.—Cassirer. *Language and Myth*, pp. 39ff.—Eds.

84. Volkelt, *Über die Vorstellung der Tiere*, p. 29; cf. above p. -.—Cassirer. Fabre's works are collected in *Souvenirs entomologiques: Études sur l'instinct et les moeurs des insectes*, 10 vols. (Paris: Ch. Delagrave, 1879–1915). The manuscript gives no page numbers here. This is probably a reference to *PSF*, vol. 3, pp. 275ff. There Cassirer also refers to Volkelt's discussion of Fabre's investigations of the sand wasp. Volkelt refers to Fabre's conclusions without naming the publication. The discussion in question first appeared in Fabre's "Étude sur l'instinct et les métamorphoses des sphégiens," *Annales des sciences naturelles*, série 4: Zoologie 6 (1856): 137–182, on p. 148. See Fabre's *The Hunting Wasps*, trans. Alexander Teixiera de

take the prey it brings home directly into its lair; rather, it places it in front of the entrance, goes into the lair, and only after it has found it to be ready, does it drag the prey inside. If the prey is then removed while the animal is inside the den, the wasp is then able to find it again but it cannot now just simply carry it into the lair; rather, it must first again undertake the examination of the lair that it had just completed—and this cycle of activities can be repeated indefinitely, if the observer continues to interrupt it. We can hardly come any closer to an explanation of this situation if we were to assume that the animal, immediately after getting the image of the lair, forgets it again, that it is unable to hold and retain it even for such a short period. Here too it is necessary to go back a step.

The lack of memory, of "retaining inside," according to all that can be inferred otherwise about animal "mental life," is an original lack of any turn inward. Genuine "memory" is correlative with what opposes it; it is connected with its seeming opposite. We only remember what we, in a way, have brought forth from ourselves, a view that we have conceived to be about something independent and objective. But it is just this setting in opposition that we do not find with any real sharpness among animals. Its precondition is "representation," and this is itself closely connected with the representational function of language. When the latter is not yet sufficiently developed, consciousness consists in the simple present of its contents, but it is lacking the most important means for their objectivization, their "presentation" and representation. In the case we just examined the investigation of the lair constitutes a part of the animal's circle of *action*, but this part cannot be freed from its linkage and bondage to the action as a whole; it cannot enter as an independent element into the animal's circle of *vision*.

It is again the pathological disturbances of language that, in an advanced

---

Mattos (New York: Dodd, Mead, 1915), pp. 76–77: "It has been proved that these ruses are singularly invariable. In this connection, I will mention an experiment which interested me greatly. Here are the particulars: at the moment when the Sphex is making her domiciliary visit, I take the Cricket left at the entrance to the dwelling and place her a few inches farther away. The Sphex comes up, utters her usual cry, looks here and there in astonishment and, seeing the game too far off, comes out of her hole to seize it and bring it back to its right place. Having done this, she goes down again, but alone. I play the same trick upon her; and the Sphex has the same disappointment on her arrival at the entrance. The victim is once more dragged back to the edge of the hole, but the Wasp always goes down alone; and this goes on as long as my patience is not exhausted. Time after time, forty times over, did I repeat the same experiment on the same Wasp; her persistency vanquished mine and her tactics never varied."—Eds.

stage of human language, can make the differences between both spheres evident to us. One of the most frequently observed symptoms of persons suffering from aphasia is that the names of things, the use of which the patient has lost, are replaced by other locutions in which the object itself is not named but its use is described. The patient cannot find the name of the knife, but he can indicate that it is there "for cutting"; he does not use the word "meat," but he indicates that it is "for eating." In such cases language seems to have taken a step backward, it appears to turn to the mere reproduction of actions instead of the representation of objects. In this regression we can indirectly recognize its true achievement all the more clearly and forcefully—what we can designate as the intellectual conquest of the objective attitude.

In this, its basic function, language does not stand alone; it is closely connected from the outset with another potency of the mind. The attainment of objectivity takes place not only by means of the power to give names, but through the formation of images as well. This is the second, highly productive root of every type of objective view. We always gain access to the depiction of the world through the gateway of "representation"; however, this has two different basic forms, neither of which can be reduced to the other. The same process of objectification, of "making present" that we met with before in language, is found in a kind of new dimension in the different fine arts. As was true of the intellectual achievement of language, it is completely insufficient to describe art as a mere "reproduction" of an already present world of form. Here, as there, this reproduction is based upon a primordial "production." Mankind attains a view of the form of things not by simply reading it off from them as though it were some determination adhering to them but by making an internal image of them and then bringing this image forth. In this act of embodying and fashioning, the world attains a shape and bodily nature, attains borders and definition. The basic act of this determination is therefore bound as much to the function of language as to that of art. It has the same task to manage as does language. It cannot simply sketch the image of reality after some copy that it has at hand, according to a given "model"; rather, it must produce it itself. It does not merely trace the contour of things, which it passively receives. Its power consists in the creation of this contour, in ideally drawing it out. Together with language, aesthetic composition creates a clear and distinct outline of the world of objects. It makes use here of the same means as does the former: the basic means of "concentration." Just as language in the act of naming divided up the immediate flow of sensory experiences by means of making selections and creating fixed centers of "meaning" with them, as it gave a different depth, a foreground and a background, to what, so to speak, previously existed side by side on a plane—so too this occurs in the creation of every artistic image and composition. Here is the kernel of that more than *merely* "aesthetic," that truly "theoretical" achievement which every genuine work of art realizes. It contains a representation of the world which is also a true world-discovery.

Goethe said of artistic style that it rests upon the foundations of *knowledge*: "upon the essence of things, insofar as we are permitted to know it through visible and tangible forms."[85] So for him "The Beautiful is a manifestation of secret laws of nature, which, without its presence, would never have been revealed."[86] But these laws are not like those that the understanding "introduces" into nature; they are, rather, like those that the productive, artistic imagination grasps in pure sensory vision. The compositions of this imagination are neither arbitrary nor occur by chance, nor are they essentially "subjective"; a genuine and necessary lawfulness of form is expressed in them. These are not shadows created by madness, but *essences* that we possess in them—and yet these essential forms *stand* before us in reality only because the eye of the artist has *released* them there.

Here too, as with language, the act of determination moves in a direction from inside to outside, not from outside to inside. To put it more precisely, there is never, of course, any such opposition in itself; rather, we introduce it by bringing in a false way of looking at things when we consider the unitary process of "determining objects." This determining is always and necessarily two-sided; it is a revelation enacted from the inside on the outside and from the outside on the inside.

This revelation is by equal necessity an unfolding as well as a limitation. Max Liebermann once said that the art of drawing consists in the "art of leaving out."[87] In this "leaving out," or "disregarding" of coincidental

85. Goethe, "Einfache Nachahmung der Natur, Manier, und Stil," *WA*, Abt. 1, vol. 47, p. 80: "Wie die einfache Nachahmung auf dem ruhigen Dasein und einer liebevollen Gegenwart beruht, die Manier eine Erscheinung mit einem leichten fähigen Gemüth ergreift, so ruht der *Stil* auf den tiefsten Grundfesten der Erkenntniss, auf dem Wesen der Dinge, in so fern uns erlaubt ist es in sichtbaren und greiflichen Gestalten zu erkennen."—Eds.

86. Goethe, *The Maxims and Reflections of Goethe*, trans. Bailey Saunders (New York: Macmillan, 1893), no. 481, p. 171.—Eds. *Marginal note:* space- / Renaissance- / Leonardo- good [*illegible word*] / saper vedere!—Cassirer. On Leonardo's saying "saper vedere!" or knowledge as "vision," see Cassirer, *The Individual and the Cosmos in Renaissance Philosophy*, p. 158.—Eds.

87. Probably a personal communication. According to Günter Busch, Liebermann often quoted this saying by Berlin sculptor Johann Gottfried Schadow (1764–1850). See Busch's

determinations in order to bring out a perceptual form, the same gift of negativity and "abstraction" is manifested as we constantly found it in language and as we have recognized it to be the precondition of its highest positive achievements. For each genuine intellectual *production* must at the same time appear, in contrast to the immediately given and the immediately experienced, to be a *reduction*.

The way in which this reduction takes place, the law to which it is subject, the "viewpoint" from which it is undertaken, determines the nature of the individual arts. Each of them proceeds differently; each sets a different accent of meaning, and according to its own "meaning" it extracts a different essential world of form. Painting, sculpture, architecture—they all go their own way, and the specific way of rendering space that prevails in each of them corresponds to a specific way of rendering objects. It is the task of systematic aesthetics to follow out all these particular ways of rendering and to show the characteristic "principle" that they obey.

This task cannot be taken up here; we must be content with showing the general course and direction of such types of configuration in general. In the context of the present problem this topic interests us not so much for its own sake as for the interrelationships and differences that exist between it and the other "symbolic forms." Art is closely connected to all of them, in regard to both its basic meaning and its development, yet on the other hand it must also become separate from them in order to find what is unique to its essence and task. In its earliest beginnings it appears to belong completely to the mythic sphere; the images it creates do not exist for their own sake but are interwoven with certain magical purposes. As with the *word*, so too the *image* is conceived from the outset not as something purely "ideal," but as having its own efficacy which goes beyond the surrounding circle of the "natural," of the physically real, and yet is considered to be quite real. Word magic and picture magic stand in the center of the magical worldview; they appear to be the true means by which man makes the powers of nature serve him. Emancipation from this circle takes place only gradually and step by step.[88] But even after this liberation has taken place, after image making has recognized its own complete independence and

---

"Einleitung" to Liebermann, *Die Phantasie in der Malerei* (Frankfurt am Main: S. Fischer, 1978), p. 12: "He [Liebermann] loved Schadow's saying: 'Drawing is leaving out' and used it often to describe his own notion of drawing."—Eds.

88. Cf. on this, e.g., *Sprache und Mythos*, pp. 37ff., 79f.—Cassirer. *Language and Myth*, pp. 44ff., 98f.—Eds.

autarchy, it remains interwoven with the world of language as if by secret, delicate threads. For no matter how much they differ in the *medium* of form giving, art is connected with language with respect to a comprehensive intellectual goal. In language as well as in art, mankind is elevated from sensory "perception" to actual "seeing." They are two organs that belong together and work together in order to achieve an image of the world—what Leonardo da Vinci called "saper vedere,"[89] and what Goethe called "Sehen mit Geistes Augen."[90]

The inner systematic relationship between the basic problem of aesthetics and the problems of the philosophy of language that result from this has hardly ever been clearly understood. Only Benedetto Croce has recognied the fact that aesthetics and the philosophy of language correlatively condition each other, and he has tried to derive both from a common root. But he looks for their unity in another place; he does not try to base them so much upon the function of representation [*Darstellung*] and on what they achieve for the construction of the world of objects as upon the function of "expression." Aesthetics becomes the general "science of expression,"[91] to which the philosophy of language belongs as a partial aspect.

The modern aesthetician whose starting point and philosophical method are closest to our own defines this relationship differently, as well as the opposition between the phenomenon of language and the primary phenomenon which is the basis of image formation. Konrad Fiedler, of all nineteenth-century aestheticians, is the one who most clearly saw the necessity of constructing aesthetics on a basis secured by the criticism of knowledge. Fiedler was perhaps the first who took the "Copernican revolution,"[92] which Kant had discovered for the world of knowledge, and carried it over into the world of artistic activity. As Kant had shown that the theoretical world does not reproduce an existing outside object, but rather that the object of knowledge is actually constituted through it, so Fiedler sought to provide an analogous proof for the artistic world of form. In the course of this he was confronted by language, which is something

89. Cassirer, *The Individual and the Cosmos in Renaissance Philosophy*, p. 158.—Eds.

90. "Seeing with the eyes of the mind." Goethe, "Zur Morphologie," *WA*, Abt. 2, vol. 8, p. 37: "We learn to see with the eyes of the mind, without which we would search about blindly everywhere, but especially in the study of nature."—Eds.

91. Benedetto Croce, *Estetica come scienza dell'espressione e linguistica generale*, 2 vols. (Milan: R. Sandron, 1902).—Eds.

92. See Kant, *Kritik der reinen Vernunft, Werke*, vol. 3, pp. 17f., 21 (B xxii n.). *Critique of Pure Reason*, p. 25 n.—Eds.

intermediate between theoretical and aesthetic form. Fiedler showed that we cannot adhere to "naive realism" here either. We fail to understand language and devaluate it if we attribute to it only the task of merely reproducing a reality possessing the right of "being present at hand" independent of language and making this an object for thought and knowledge.[93]

Language does not merely contain signs or designations for a being; rather, language is a form of being itself. The meaning which the miracle of language has is not that it refers to a being, but that it *is* a being. We may not, however, here interpret this being as a kind of thing; rather, we must take it as determinative of things.[94] This means that vague and flowing sensory consciousness is enriched by a new element, a new material through the word, in which it becomes possible to attain a coherent and definite organization of reality at all. We find this kind of organization in figurative art too, yet it moves in a very different direction from language and uses quite different means. "Just as from time immemorial two great principles, that of imitation and that of the transformation of reality, have laid claim to being the true essential principle of artistic activity, so too it seems that the only way to decide this dispute is to find a third principle to take the place of these two: the principle of the production of reality. For art is none other than the means by which man first came to achieve reality."[95]

In order to understand this thesis in all its significance and depth we must break radically with the presupposition that what we call the visible reality of things is given and present at hand as a finished substratum, prior to all formative activities of mind. "The problem of the work of art"—as Fiedler puts this, in perhaps the briefest and most pregnant way in an aphorism from his *Nachlass*—"can only be understood by someone who recognizes that nature as we see it is not something fixed, something that is

---

93. See Konrad Fiedler, "Über den Ursprung der künstlerischen Tätigkeit," *Fiedlers Schriften über Kunst*, ed. Hermann Konnerth, 2 vols. (Munich: R. Piper, 1913–1914), vol. 1, pp. 188–195, esp. pp. 195f.: "If we keep in mind that a linguistic expression is able to refer to something real and bring it to mind, something which has a claim to existence independent of the linguistic form, then we can do this only by retaining the standpoint of naive realism. That is, we assume that reality is given without considering that we first have to perceive it, so that it can be given." See also pp. 196f.: "It is not reality per se that we grasp when we conceive and grasp things in language, as we would like to believe, but always only reality insofar as it has achieved existence in the developed form of language."—Eds.

94. This is an untranslatable pun on the words *dinglich* and *bedingend*.—Eds.

95. Konrad Fiedler, "Moderner Naturalismus und künstlerische Wahrheit," in *Schriften über Kunst*, ed. H. Konnerth, 2 vols. (Munich, 1913), vol. 1, p. 180.—Cassirer.

not real in the normal sense of the word, just as the problem of knowledge can be grasped only by someone who has recognized that it is not the reality of things which endures but only the form which reality assumes through us."[96] Hence, the theory of art must repeat the transcendental question of the "possibility of the relationship of our representations to an object," but it directs this question toward the object not as an object of knowledge, conceived in terms of the conceptual apparatus of science, but as an object that is simply looked at. It does not approach it as something to conceive or determine in thought, but simply as something that can be *seen*.

This "seeability," we must recognize, is neither a predicate attributed to things as such, as absolute things, nor does it consist in the simple passive possession of certain sense-data, certain optical sensations or perceptions. It requires an act of mind, an act of spontaneity. "Things" attain a "look" because the mind lends it to them through a particular kind or direction of activity. This activity is none other than that of artistic production. It does not imitate what has been seen; rather, its basic significance and true achievement consist in transforming the merely sensed or dully felt into something seen. With this, we have the second and decisive step toward objectifying and grasping the world as configured whole. "If a man in the end finally is unable to deal with all the glory that confronts the eye all at once, and can only stare dumbly, and can only make all this which is available to him accessible to the development of consciousness by putting it into another medium, that of language, then the capacity that he finds within himself, to make that which he sees an object for pictorial representation, shows him the way in which it will be possible for consciousness of the visible world to enter onto its own path of development."[97]

Here is a clear and sharp designation of the intellectual bond that ties language to the figurative arts and creates a kind of "union" between them. This union is only imperfectly recognized if we begin with the expressive function alone, if we grasp only the lyrical, expressive aspect of language and art. The true foundation, the legitimation, of this union is found only if we understand both language and art as basic ways of objectification, of raising consciousness to the level of seeing objects. This raising is in the end possible only when "discursive" thinking in language and the "intuitive"

---

96. [Fiedler], Aphorismen aus dem Nachlass (Ausgabe Konnerth, No. 88), [in *Schriften über Kunst*,] vol. 2, p. 65[–66].—Cassirer.

97. Fiedler, "Über den Ursprung der künstlerischen Tätigkeit," in *Schriften über Kunst*, vol. 1, p. 276.—Cassirer.

activity of artistic seeing and creating interact so as together to weave the cloak of "reality."[98]

In Fiedler's own aesthetic system a barrier to the completion of this project was set from the outset—a barrier that is closely related to that aspect of his thought on which the true power of the system rests. The "objectivistic" founding of aesthetics finally undergoes a methodological overstatement and exaggeration insofar as it tends to push aside completely the subjective factors in aesthetic experience. Although they in fact cannot be eliminated, nothing follows for Fiedler from this fact, that they are always there, for their significance and validity. The psychological context may not be confused with the constitutive; the feelings that are elicited while taking in a work of art may not be regarded as belonging to its essential aspects. They are purely coincidental features that do not concern the work of art as such, and which may not therefore be used in the definition of the artistic "primary phenomenon." The "visibility of nature" is the actual, even the only goal of artistic activity.

From the recognition that the human mind cannot attain to the pure, clear realm of the visible form of things as long as it tries to grasp them only through immediate or reproduced *perceptions* we are led to the additional insight that artistic activity is necessary to bring out this form and make it visible. "Only by virtue of the fact that man is not merely a perceiving and thinking creature, but also is active—externally active—and so participates in the visible appearance of things, is this thereby something fully present to him, and the more he is filled with its living presence, the more everything else is pushed aside which otherwise forces itself into his consciousness and darkens visibility when he looks at things."[99] Fiedler in the end regards everything that belongs to the "subjective" side, to the "emotional" world instead of the world of the visible, as merely *obscuring* pure visibility. Art's relationship to this sphere seems in the last analysis to be merely sentimental confusion. Only those will be able to understand art in its own language who have learned to grasp works of art purely as they are "in themselves" and to abstain from the enjoyment provided by the exploitation of an impression through feeling. The attainment of complete and pure objectivity can hence come only at the price of an asceticism that must

98. On the difference between the "discursive" form of language and the "intuitive" form of art, cf. especially Fiedler's discussions in "Wirklichkeit und Kunst," zweites Bruchstück, in *Schriften über Kunst*, vol. 2, pp. 238ff. [238–250].—Cassirer.

99. Fiedler, "Ursprung der künstlerischen Tätigkeit," in *Schriften*, vol. 1, p. 319.—Cassirer.

be imposed by the artistic creator as well as the beholder of art upon their own selves and their emotional stirrings.

This interpretation not only threatens us with the loss of the unity of artistic experience, but on closer examination it also contains a violation of the basic presuppositions of Fiedler's own doctrine of knowledge. For there can be no doubt in this theory that "subjective" reality is any more immediately "given" than "objective" reality is. Again and again it is emphasized that for a view of knowledge to assume the existence of an already available world of ideas is no less dogmatic than to assume the existence of a finished world of things. All being, whether we regard it as "objective" or "subjective" being, depends on an act of determination and on certain forms in which this act takes place. If this is so, then the philosophical analysis and the philosophical foundation of these forms cannot stop with simply showing what these forms achieve in the rise of the consciousness of objects. It must also look for them where they seem to be active in the opposite way, in helping with the formation of the "I," of "self-consciousness." We have already examined in detail what language and myth in particular contribute to the constitution of self-consciousness.[100] We saw everywhere that in both of them we have not a finished, closed world of the ego emerging from itself but rather the formation of this world in and through these forms.

This conclusion is enlarged and deepened if we reflect upon the form and the origin of historical consciousness. The necessity of mediation to which we were directed at every point here emerges again into the brightest light. When we are concerned with the objectivity of "nature," we need first to engage in a reflective criticism of knowledge in order to have this mediation sharply and clearly emerge for us. This is where "naive realism" appears to have its proper place; reality as it is found in the forms of experience, in the forms of space and time, of substantiality and causality, are regarded as "absolute" reality. By contrast, as far as the reality of history is concerned, it is impossible to take it as some rigid thing-like object. We must arrive at the conviction that a historical world is always to be defined only as relative to a historical consciousness and that this form of consciousness defines what we conceive under the name of "history." On the other hand, we see that the circle of specifically human existence closes here. The new dimension into which we enter when we move from the different

---

100. Cf. [PSF] vol. 1, pp. 249ff.; vol. 2, pp. 155ff.; 175ff.—Cassirer.

forms of organic life into the human world is perhaps most obviously different at this point.

No matter how richly developed we conceive the animal's world of perceptions and feelings to be or how much we are willing to attribute to the "feats of intelligence" in the higher animals, none of this even comes close to the most primitive achievements of historical consciousness. Of course, one can *define* the organism in such a way that it is designated as a being not limited to a mere present point here and now, but in whose presence the traces of the past are preserved. But this *real* keeping, this mere aftereffect that the past exercises, does not make up an existence or a life in history. This presupposes, rather, the decisive turn or transition from the mere "circle of action" to the "circle of vision." Even in the world of the higher animals the circle of action is no longer completely rigid and closed; it not only encompasses actions that must always occur in the same way according to interlocking rules of "instinct," but is also open to influence and reorientation through earlier experience. But this type of animal "learning" does not involve that specific form of "turning inward" that we designate by the name of "recollection." Here is memory, not recollection; "habit-memory," not "knowledge-memory."[101] The latter function requires something quite different from the simple continuation of the past in a modified form of existence; it demands a unique reorientation in our outlook by means of which the past "appears" in the present and by means of which it is at the same time known as past.

This change in outlook, this grasping in the present without really "remaining" in it in the true sense, without being bound to the here and now, is the beginning of all historical consciousness. In order to go back and enter into its beginning, however, it is not sufficient for us to consider the form of consciousness it attains to in the phase of theoretical knowledge and the shape it takes on by making use of the resources of thought that influence and govern thinking at that level. Rather, the same demand holds for history as for nature that Hegel sets forth in the *Phenomenology of Spirit*. If the *concept* of history and of nature is completed only in the "science" of both, then we must demand on the other hand that science itself not be satisfied with discovering and showing the world of nature and

---

101. On this difference cf. Bertrand Russell, *The Analysis of Mind* (London: George Allen & Unwin, 1921), Lecture 9, "Memory." (Cf. above p. -.)—Cassirer. The manuscript gives no page number here. Perhaps this is an incompletely expressed reference to Cassirer's discussion in *PSF*, vol. 3, pp. 174–176.—Eds.

of history in the forms and categories valid for science. It should, rather, "provide us with the ladder"[102] to consciousness that will then lead consciousness to this standpoint of theoretical knowledge. The configurations wrought by myth, language, and art turn out to be the most important rungs on this ladder.[103]

The historical self-consciousness of mankind, the turning inward of its own awareness, is never immediately given in the form of a historical narrative; it is in the form of myth. As in the realm of nature, where demonization appeared as the beginning and precondition of all individualization in the interpretation of the world of objects, so too heroization appears in the realm of history as the only primordial means to isolate individual figures in the flow of events and the indefinite prehistorical dawn. Mankind first gains knowledge of itself and the phases of life that it has traversed in its development when these phases become concentrated into mythic individuals. Mankind emerges from and confronts itself for the first time in the mythic-heroic view of existence. All the achievements of culture are seen in this way, not as things, as mere results and products, but understood in the mythic hypostasis, as the acts of heroes and saviors.

The cult of the hero, the cult of the heroic ancestors, now provides the firmest and most secure bond to connect mankind with the prehistorical past. Through it, this prehistorical past is not only recalled but also seen; past events are not merely renewed subjectively in the imagination but stand objectively before the people with an immediate presence in the form of the cult. The long-forgotten and submerged now finds its resurrection, because the life of the hero, his acts and sufferings, are not only what the rituals of the cult represent but something constantly brought back by them. The cult does not simply serve the memory of the ancestors; they are reborn in it and newly brought together with the present generation.

---

102. See G. W. F. Hegel, *Phänomenologie des Geistes, Sämtliche Werke*, Jubiläumsausgabe, 20 vols., ed. Hermann Glockner (Stuttgart: F. Frommann, 1927), vol. 2, pp. 28f. *The Phenomenology of Spirit*, trans. A. V. Miller (Oxford: Oxford Univ. Press, 1977), sec. 26, pp. 14–15: "Science on its part requires that self-consciousness should have raised itself into this Aether in order to be able to live—and [actually] to live—with Science and in Science. Conversely, the individual has the right to demand that science should at least provide him with the ladder to this standpoint, should show him this standpoint within himself."—Eds.

103. See Cassirer's remarks on his extended interpretation of Hegel's phenomenology, in which the connection to myth is already made; *PSF*, vol. 2, pp. xv–xvi: "If then, in accordance with Hegel's demand, science is to provide the natural consciousness with a ladder leading to itself, it must first set this ladder a step lower [into mythical consciousness]."—Eds.

When the circle of generations is closed, mankind attains certainty of the unity of becoming and a feeling of indestructible endurance. In this feeling the chain of events now takes on the form of history; in this feeling becoming has itself been elevated to the form of being. Only myth is originally capable of such an elevation, for it alone succeeds in seeing the past as past and nonetheless putting it into the pure form of presence. In the *image* of the past, as it is found in the figure of the heroic ancestor, mankind has outgrown the passing away of things as a fact of nature. The organic phenomenon of death, of having to die, is now met and overcome by an intellectual phenomenon, by an act of freedom. In the immortality which it lends to its mythic hero, mankind has attained for itself, for its own species, an ideal immortality.

In this context it finally becomes fully clear to us why the oldest form of language in which human historical consciousness can be expressed can be none other than the language of myth. If the science of history must draw a sharp line between itself and myth, the philosophy of history may not draw this dividing line in the same way. For it, myth, insofar as it is seen and understood in a truly comprehensive manner, provides the magic key that unlocks the world of history. Herder was fully aware of this. He was the first to promulgate the doctrine that mythic-religious narratives are not to be taken as merely poetic stories, but that they are to be conceived and used as the "oldest *documents* of the human race."[104] A sharp intellectual foundation for this method and its ingenious application had to wait, however, for the philosophy of history as developed in the works of Bachofen. The center of Bachofen's comprehensive view consists of his interpretation of myth as an original intellectual form of historical knowledge.[105] In it we must see the principle of knowledge which animates and guides all his particular investigations.[106] "Aside from language and the works of human hands," as he stresses, "there is still another class of monument available for our comparative research, namely myth. Indeed, it is myth that provides our

104. See Johann Gottfried Herder, *Älteste Urkunde des Menschengeschlechts* (2 vols., 1774, 1776), *Herders Sämmtliche Werke*, vols. 6 and 7.—Eds.

105. See Bäumler, "Bachofen der Mythologe der Romantik," in Bachofen, *Der Mythos von Orient und Occident: Eine Metaphysik der alten Welt*, in *Werken von Johann Jakob Bachofen*, ed. Manfred Schroeter, intro. Alfred Bäumler (Munich: C. H. Beck, 1926), pp. xxiii–ccxciv. See esp. p. cxc: "We need only to go back to myth, in order to find the origins of the historical world and to attain to a comprehensive knowledge of the fate of the human race."—Eds.

106. Cf. now on this esp. Alfred Bäumler, "Bachofen der Mythologe der Romantik." Introduction to the Bachofen edition by Bäumler and Schroeter. (Munich 1926), esp. pp. clxxxixff.—Cassirer.

richest and most reliable insights regarding the cultural relations among the various peoples. For although migrant peoples not infrequently change their language along with their abode or, through their contacts with other peoples, quickly distort it to the point of unrecognizability, although the products of the arts and crafts are very much affected by climate and other local conditions, no nation, in changing its abode, changes its god, its basic religious view, and its traditional ritual observances. Myth is nothing other than a picture of the national experience in light of religious faith."[107]

Here we find an objectivity in myth which, correctly understood and made use of, is not only not inferior to mere historical facticity, but in a certain regard is far superior to it. The mythic narrative is not really deprived of all meaning through the denial of its historicity. "What cannot have happened was nonetheless thought. External truth is replaced by inner truth. Instead of facts we find actions of the spirit."[108] Bachofen could develop this interpretation because from the outset he was pursuing a "tautegorical"[109] understanding of myth, in Schelling's sense, instead of a merely "allegorical" interpretation.[110] He began by assuming that while myth takes on many forms and its outer appearances change, it nonetheless follows certain laws and generally is the result of a single universal law of the mind. "Everywhere there is system, everywhere cohesion; in every detail the expression of a great fundamental law whose abundant manifestations demonstrate its inner truth and natural necessity."[111] Such "natu-

---

107. *Marginal note:* 540f.—Cassirer. This is a reference to Bachofen, *Der Mythos von Orient und Occident*, pp. 540–541. The passage as quoted here was translated into English as "The Myth of Tanaquil," in *Myth, Religion, and Mother Right*, trans. Ralph Manheim (New York: Bollingen Foundation, 1967), pp. 212–213.—Eds.

108. Bachofen, "Die Sage von Tanaquil" (1869), Einleitung, edition by Bäumler and Schroeter, pp. 539ff. [p. 542.]—Cassirer. Bachofen, "The Myth of Tanaquil," p. 214.—Eds.

109. See *PSF*, vol. 2, p. 4: "He [Schelling] replaces the allegorical interpretation of the world of myths by a tautegorical interpretation, i.e., he looks upon mythical figures as autonomous configurations of the human spirit, which one must understand from within by knowing the way in which they take on meaning and form." Cassirer refers here to Friedrich Wilhelm Joseph von Schelling, *Einleitung in die Philosophie der Mythologie, Sämmtliche Werke* (Stuttgart and Augsburg: J. G. Cotta, 1856), vol. 1, pt. 2, pp. 195f.: "Mythology is not allegorical, it is tautegorical. The gods are its actually existing essence, which are nothing else than and have no meaning other than only what they are." Schelling says in a note on p. 196 that he has taken over this concept from Coleridge.—Eds.

110. Cf. on this [*PSF*] vol. 2, pp. 3ff.—Cassirer.

111. Bachofen, Vorrede zum Mutterrecht, edition by Bäumler and Schroeter, p. 11.—Cassirer. Bachofen, Introduction to "Mother Right," in *Myth, Religion, and Mother Right*, p. 76.—Eds.

ral necessity" is inaccessible to history as long as it is concerned simply with facts and is satisfied with stringing together individual happenings on the thread of time. History can find a necessary, internally meaningful structure only when it delves into acts of the mind rather than into particular facts gathered at random and when it conceives these acts as its true object. For these acts, even when they are conceived as free acts, have an unchanging specificity and a fixed rhythm of their own. They do not follow one another by chance, but develop from one another according to an immanent lawfulness.

This sequence, not of events, but of the intellectual aging of the world, is what the philosophy of history wants to discover. It must struggle against the basic positivistic error "as if research into past ages was concerned with finding out facts rather than with the spiritual truth, with the empirical nature of events rather than with the spirit of the times contained in traditions."[112] The spirit of the times can be grasped only in the form of myth, which does not provide mere wrapping for them, but is the only possible way to conceive them. Thus for Bachofen myth becomes the indispensable basis of knowledge, the *ratio cognoscendi* of history. But this is only possible because it is in a sense the ground of its being, its *ratio essendi*. By means of myth specific primordial experiences and states that mankind has passed through are first perceived in an objective form and so made accessible to recollection, to historical thought and memory.

Here, however, we again meet the same basic relationship that we found in the formation of "external" reality. In the work that myth accomplishes in history we again find that it never stands alone. It is one member of the great triad of mind consisting of myth, language, and art. When Hamann calls poetry the "mother tongue of the human race,"[113] this claim applies especially to the language of historical consciousness. By expressing his different situations and fate in mythic-poetic form, man is able not only to live and exist in them but to become aware of himself as the subject undergoing these different states and fates. But poetry as a form is superior to myth in a particular respect. With poetry a new view of time emerges. Schelling said that myth is governed by a completely prehistoric temporality—a temporality in which the end is like the beginning, the beginning

112. Quotation from Bachofen, "Die Sage von Tanaquil" (1869), p. 578.—Eds.

113. Cf. Johann Georg Hamann, "Aesthetica in nuce." in *A Study in Christian Existence with Selections from His Writings*, ed. and trans. Ronald Gregor Smith (London: Collins, 1960), p. 196.—Eds.

like the end.[114] Myth pushes the contents perceived in it off into an indefinite temporal distance, but this distance has not yet, so to speak, achieved any temporal depth. All aspects of its temporality are still as if of one piece. They lie in the same layer of the past as such without any further differentiation among them. This relationship begins to give way to another as soon as the heroic song or epic narrative strives to call up the past or hold it in memory. Just as the narrative itself attains its objective clarity and specificity only by forming a structured whole—as it starts with a particular beginning and must move through a series of intermediate portions to a particular end—so too does it provide this structure to the content to which it refers.

By entering into the form of the epic, narrative undergoes an increasingly clear temporal organization. The events are divided into particular phases which follow a specific order of sequence, or epic succession. As long as man is primarily bound to a primordial time by means of the cult, as long as his knowledge of the ancestors and the feeling of inner community with them is based on the fact that they appear to be immediately present in the actions of the cult, everything which is understood in this way remains essentially in the pure present. But the epic report brings an end to this kind of presence. The mythic "it is" is transformed into the "there was" of the fable and the legend. But while fable and legend move in the same circle of contents as does the cult, they also contain a new form which ultimately springs from the basic form of "saying," of representation found in language itself. In the cult and in the rite the mythic is itself still something lived; it is put into living action. In the legend it then becomes something enunciated and through this enunciation it attains a new objective distance. With this, for the first time the foundation is laid on which a view of specifically historical time, a time of human history, can grow.

The ring surrounding human and divine things now closes from a new side. In myth the link connecting mankind and god is the figure of the hero who becomes a god, who experiences an apotheosis. The epic takes largely the opposite course. In it we can see into an intellectual process that can be called the humanization of the gods. The measure of the human is no longer extended so as completely to transcend mankind; rather, it is the god himself who subjects himself to these standards, who descends into the narrow human world with its passions and struggles, its victories and defeats. Here a new point of view is created; we enter the new era of

---

114. Cf. on this [*PSF*] vol. 2, pp. 106ff.—Cassirer.

human, specifically historical time. One may still dispute whether Achilles is not, according to his "actual" original mythological meaning, really a sun hero; for the epic Achilles, the Achilles of Homer, however, this dispute makes no sense. Even the very question that is raised here violates the epic's laws of style. The Achilles of the *Iliad* is no longer a mythologem; he is completely defined as an individual human being with limits, who rejoices and mourns, who loves and rages before us. The epic stands here at the side of the fine arts as their ally in this process of individualization and humanization. Sculpture in particular is effective in contributing to this movement.

The oldest form of sculpture, that of the Egyptians, seems still to stand entirely under the spell of a particular mythico-religious view of things. The human image stands in service to the religious idea of immortality; its appearance, the bodily form must be preserved if its eternity, its unlimited continuation is to be ensured. In their further development the fine arts emerge more and more from this circle; the representation of figures becomes a goal in itself, an aesthetic value itself. In this autonomy of the aesthetic a new autonomy of the human is achieved. In the animation that the human body receives through artistic activity, it attains a new meaning and a new dignity. It alone now appears to be the pure medium through which divinity becomes visible. Divinity is no longer portrayed with half-animal and half-human features; the god, insofar as it can be embodied at all, can no longer be revealed in any other than human form. Here again we see that the configuration of the "external" and the "inner" cannot be separated from each other. The arts, by helping man to attain to a complete view of his own body, by chiseling out this body in a clear and definite outline, separates the specifically human feeling of the ego from the sphere of the general, mythic feeling of life.[115] In the same sense as the spatial delimitation, so too the temporal delimitation takes shape. Only when mankind divides its past from its present, when both are regarded as separated from each other and nonetheless conceived as interwoven in the closest way, does there arise in such connections and separations an image of historical being and an image of mankind itself as the "subject" of history.

Here too, where the circle of formation appears finally to close, where "inner" and "outer" reality enter into each other and join to form a cosmos, we are not yet at the end of the course of intellectual development. It is

---

115. On all this cf. [*PSF*] vol. 2, pp. 127ff., 194ff.—Cassirer.

typical of this development that, just as it sets the "limits of human nature"[116] in the first place, at the same time it also pushes beyond these limits. All objective and subjective truth, all certainty about the outer world as well as all certainty about itself that mankind is able to attain, appears to depend on the function of representation. Man knows the world and himself only through the image that he makes of both. But it also turns out that he is not able to remain within this sphere of perceptual truth and knowledge, that the striving after knowledge cannot be met or satisfied in this way. The process of cognition dares to leave behind this basis after just barely taking possession of it; it goes its way "into the unknown, not to be trespassed."[117] Its intellectual horizon is not the same as the horizon of concrete perception; the ideal meaning of the world does not appear limited to the dimension of representation. A new dimension is constructed now over the dimension of representation: the dimension of pure "signification." We have sought to follow in detail the path that leads from the one to the other.[118]

We saw in the development of the knowledge of nature how the more sharply it reflects on the true task of objectification the more it has to give up the attempt to meet this task by means of purely perceptual thought. Again and again, the images and models in which thought seeks to grasp reality, and in which it strives to organize it, are pushed back, and their place is taken by pure symbols of thought. In them there is no longer present either a real or a possible perception of things, no description of either a concrete "datum" or a perceptual *dabile*. Rather, a purely relational order is grasped, a law for connecting a series is set out, and a constructive principle—the "unity of a manifold"—is created in pure thought from it. This confronted us most clearly in the transformation that the basic and original form of "pure intuition," that of space itself, gradually undergoes.

If we review once again in a brief retrospective summary the various intervening phases that lead from the first primitive "feeling of space" to the scientific "concept of space" in exact, theoretical knowledge, then we see that this whole development stands under the sign of a particular dialectic. Here no simple, straight "progress" takes place; rather, at a par-

---

116. A reference to Goethe's poem "Limits of Human Nature," in *Goethe's Collected Works*, vol. 1, pp. 82–85. "Gränzen der Menschheit," *WA*, Abt. 1, vol. 2, pp. 81f.—Eds.

117. Goethe, *Faust* II, lines 6222f.: "ins Unbetretene, nicht zu Betretende."—Eds.

118. See *PSF*, vol. 3, pt. 2, "The Problem of Representation and the Building of the Intuitive World," and pt. 3, "The Function of Signification and the Building Up of Scientific Knowledge."—Eds.

ticular point this development appears to bend backward and to undergo a kind of intellectual peripeteia. It is as if, by virtue of this turning back, the end had returned to the beginning, as though a particular result of the formative process, once achieved, was then given up and abandoned. At the intellectual center of this development we are confronted by space in its pure objectivity, in, so to speak, its substantial solidity. This is the place of admission, the πρῶτον δεκτικόν,[119] to the world of objects in general; it gives every being its fixed place and thus a firm footing. In the early stages this kind of "solidification" of space—or, to put it a better way, this kind of solidification into an objective perceptual space—is not yet attained, while in the final phases it has already been left behind and overcome. In these phases a purely functional interpretation of space has again taken the place of the purely substantial one. Space is no longer the space of things but a pure system-space. In this way the starting point and the result appear to meet in a common feature, that to an extent both manifest a particular opposition to the structure of the "world of things," to the world of empirical objects. But this opposition does not, of course, have the same meaning and direction for both.

We can say that the "primitive" interpretation of space is still prior to the world of things and that the conceptual, exact interpretation lies beyond it, that the one is sub-thing-space, the other supra-thing-space. The space of animal "perception" and "representation" and, in a certain sense, mythic space too, is *not yet* the fixed space of objects characteristic and determinative of the empirical view; the mathematical-physical space of order is not this space any longer. The former is not so much a complete totality of things as a totality of actions, directions of actions; the latter is not so much a complex of objective elements as it is a system of relations. The question about which way and on the basis of which sensory data the spatial orientation of animals takes place appears to have received little detailed clarification, despite all the efforts that have been expended upon it in the fields of biology and animal psychology. A truly satisfactory and exhaustive theory that does justice to all the phenomena observed does not seem so far to have been achieved.[120]

But one thing appears certain, that the space of the animal is not actually

---

119. "one's initial understanding."

120. Cf. on this question e.g. the rich material in Rudolf Brun, *Die Raumorientierung der Ameisen und das Orientierungsproblem im allgemeinen* [*Eine kritisch-experimentelle Studie; zugleich ein Beitrag zur Theorie der Mneme*] (Jena: [Gustav Fischer,] 1914).—Cassirer.

"space seen," in which particular elements are distinguished and separated according to objective "features"; rather, it must be conceived purely as an "action space." In a series of careful observations, Bethe established that bees returning home always find again with great certainty the place in space from which they flew away, but that on the other hand they were not able immediately to find their hive when its position was altered slightly during their absence.[121] On the basis of this and similar experiments, Rádl concludes that what we might call the "space" of the animals is nothing other than a system of directed energies, each of which puts the organism into a kind of equilibrium with itself. "This equilibrium is the animal's orientation. Spatiality is not the same for different animals. While for one a space of light is more developed, for another it is a space of gravity and with yet another it is a horizontal space or a space of touch that is best developed. It is probable that many such spaces occur for the same organism, but that here the one prevails and there the other has the upper hand."[122]

Such a purely dynamic character appears also to be a feature of space in the mythic image of the world. Again, the differences in spatial orientation are not acquired here by separating out from the whole surrounding world certain objective unities differentiated by objective features and used as fixed coordinate middle points. Rather, we find the opposite process: the order of objective reality is structured on the basis of the difference between particular primitive feelings of direction. "Above" and "below," "right" and "left," they all have a primary, mythic "meaning." A peculiar, mythic feeling of value clings to them, in which all contents of reality share in some way and in accordance with which they now begin to organize and grade themselves. Here too demonization proves to be the beginning and the end of all individualization. North, south, east, and west—they are all originally conceived as demonic forces, each of which possesses a particular direction of action and attention. The totality of these lines of force is the basis on which space as a mythic force field is constructed.[123]

We meet with a fundamentally different turn, a new mode of configur-

---

121. [Albrecht] Bethe, "Dürfen wir den Ameisen und Bienen psychische Qualitäten zuschreiben?," *Pflugers Archiv* [*Archiv für die gesamte Physiologie des Menschen und der Thiere*], vol. 70, 1898 [pp. 15–100]; see H. Volkelt, above [*Über die Vorstellung der Tiere*], pp. 23ff.—Cassirer.

122. [Emanuel] Rádl, *Untersuchungen über den Phototropoismus der Tiere* (Leipzig: [Wilhelm Engelmann,] 1903). (Quoted by Uexküll, *Umwelt und Innenwelt der Tiere*, p. 208.)—Cassirer. The quotation is from Rádl, p. 174.—Eds.

123. For further information see [*PSF*] vol. 2, pp. 83ff., 96ff.—Cassirer.

ing, in the sphere of language. The world of language is distinguished here by the fact that in it the unstable balance begins to be stabilized. By designating through language, not only particular spatial features are fixed; it also creates a new relationship between them. Now they prove to be distinguishable and to be steadfast in relationship to each other; they come together in an objective all-encompassing space. Language provides the means of expression for referring to a "here" or "there," to "closeness" or "distance," so that from a particular point in space it is possible to have an objective overview of the whole.[124] But this kind of overview, based on linguistic concepts and the empirical concepts of objects conditioned and brought about through language, in no way constitutes the final or highest result of pure theory. It never stops with a mere synopsis of reality, but demands and creates a new form of synthesis.

This pure intellectual synthesis has the peculiar character that in it space can no longer be exhibited as an isolated or isolatable "object." It can no longer be imagined or conceived as any kind of object at all. Rather, it is only a kind of basic means of objectification, namely, one whose task can be fulfilled only in conjunction with other categories of the knowledge of nature, especially in "union" with the concept of time. With this dispersal of the rigid spatial schematism, this elevation of space to a purely conceptual level, to a symbol of order,[125] reality seems to have regained some of the flexibility and fluidity that it possessed in its earlier phases when it was "closer to life." It now appears again to be not so much a totality of things as a totality of events. The liquidity that it gains has none of the instability and volubility in common with the fleeting character that it had at the beginning. For thought now has found the means by which it can hold fast the phenomena in the midst of endless variability and by virtue of which it can assert itself. No longer does it conquer and control the sea of becoming by means of the concept of the thing; rather it does so by the concept of law. In place of the presupposition of constant things, it is now served by the assumption of invariants as its foothold and basis. There appears to be movement in a circle here; we seem to be led in our observations from their end back to the beginning. Between the beginning and the end lies a world,

124. On this whole matter cf. [*PSF*] vol. 1, pp. 198ff., vol. 3, pp. -ff., and other places.—Cassirer. The second reference was left incomplete; Cassirer probably is referring to the discussion of the "deictic" function of language and spatial words in *PSF*, vol. 3, pp. 151ff.—Eds.

125. *Marginal note:* No longer ἀπρὶξ τοῖν χεροῖν the space of modern physics [is] so difficult to grasp because it is no longer something to be "grasped" with the hands.—Cassirer. See Plato *Theaetetus* 155E5.—Eds.

the world that is constituted through the pure concepts of order themselves, through the presuppositions and principles of scientific knowledge.

On the other hand we have of course seen the difficulties that stand in the way of the ascent into this last sphere. Pure theory must take possession of this new ground step by step. It is as if thought did not dare to tear itself away from the true basic means of objectification that it owes to the structure of the empirical world of perception. With all its organs grasping it,[126] thought adheres to this basic category of the thing. Even when it no longer appears to the world of perception—from the standpoint of content—to be the final, "true" reality, where thought grasps the necessity of going on to another reality, it does not dispense with the form in which it grasps them. It now requires a firmer foundation; in place of sensory qualities it has other determinations in which it believes that it only now possesses the true "essence" of things. But this new ontological determination changes nothing in the purely methodological approach. For the "second reality" is, like the first, grasped according to the manner of things. When thought strips the contents of perception of their absolute, substantial character, it does not thereby eliminate this character as such but relocates it somewhere else. Behind the first world of things, which is now surrendered to "subjectivity," another arises, and it seems to possess the true character of the thing—true solidity and endurance. When theoretical knowledge proceeds with showing the structure of this world and with defining its details, it is aware of being in a new domain; its attempt remains nonetheless directed to assimilating this domain to the previous one as far as possible, to grasping it by means of its "similarity" to the earlier one. It is repeatedly subject to the force of this kind of analogical thinking. Again and again, an image taken from the concrete, particular gestalt of sensory things creeps into the formulation of basic laws. In place of thinking in terms of principles we have thinking in schemata and models. Constant efforts are required in order to ward off this effacement, not just to make use of the basic theoretical means of objectification but also to understand its true function and to concede its proper meaning to it. The entire modern history of our knowledge of nature is filled with this struggle. Finally, the goal that it strove for from the beginning with a more or less definite methodological consciousness seems to have been achieved; its form of the concept is clearly and sharply separated from the notion of the thing.[127]

126. See Goethe, *Faust*, lines 1112–1117.—Eds.
127. On the whole cf. the earlier presentation; esp. Book -, Chap. -, pp. -ff.—Cassirer. The

We have here recalled this transition from the dimension of "representation" to the new dimension of "significance," as it takes place in theoretical knowledge of nature, only in order to attend to another, more general question. Can an analogous "change in meaning" also be exposed when we consider the "inner" world instead of the "outer" one? That both worlds conform methodologically to each other in regard to their organizational principles, that they show the same sort of architectonic rhythm, was confirmed anew throughout the course of our investigation. This is reason enough for us to suppose that this last great change, through which the concept of the thing grows beyond itself, corresponds to a no less significant transformation in the area of "inner experience." While the organization of the outer world is governed by the category of the thing, the structure of the inner world depends on the category of personality. While in the former we remain in the sphere of spatial perception, in the latter we move in the medium of time. We may therefore state our problem as follows: is there a way to transcend the personal sphere in the same sense in which a transcendence of the sphere of things proves to be possible and necessary? Can and must our investigation rise above the form of time and, in a sense, tear itself away from it in the way that it had to go beyond the schematism of spatial perception? From the standpoint of a pure "philosophy of life" this very question must appear paradoxical and objectionable. For the philosophy of life distinguishes the "inner" from the "outer" and time from space by conceiving us to have in the one a mediated and derivative being, in the other a completely primordial, immediately certain being. Once we are on the level of this primordial being, we have left behind the picture-world of space in order to go back and enter fully into the world of time so that there can no longer be any "beyond" for us, no more "transcendence."

We stand here at the pillars of Hercules: it is the absolute itself that opens up to us in the intuition of pure duration, of *durée réelle*. So, as necessary as it was to break out of the forms of space and the thing, every attempt to break free of the form of time and the ego is senseless. But here too we are forced to take a different view if we carefully examine the structure of that "experiential time" which the philosophy of life takes to be the fundamental given and certain. It proves to be no such simple fact; rather, it contains in itself a peculiar tension, a relationship between two opposing poles. It was the process of symbolic formation that revealed this polarity to us and

---

manuscript gives no reference. Cassirer probably is referring to the discussion entitled "Language and Science: Thing Signs and Ordinal Signs," *PSF*, vol. 3, pt. 3, chap. 3, pp. 328ff.—Eds.

demonstrated it over and over again. It is only the series of experiences itself, not what is grasped and experienced in it, that remains bound to the form of time; only the acts of intending and opining, but not the facts they refer to, belong to it.[128]

With this insight we again stand before a methodological limit to the temporal view, as we did before in regard to the spatial view. The ideal world of form provided by the medium, without whose stability individual worlds of experience could not enter into relationships with one another, could not be made understandable to one another, cannot be reduced either to a particular, temporally bound and temporally limited circle of experience or to the totality of these circles. In contrast to them, it possesses its own content, which can no longer be designated in the language of the temporal viewpoint and no longer measured by its standards. Here we are concerned not so much with something *trans*-temporal as with a being that is in principle *non*-temporal, a pure "enduring in itself" that belongs to a dimension completely different from all becoming, all existence, and all persistence in time. Every kind of symbolic formation works in its own way and with its own aim toward such a pure sense of the I, which is specifically distinguished from a mere ego-meaning. This sense of the I appears in language most characteristically where it is able to achieve the kind of expression most adequate to it, where it sharply and clearly distinguishes the "is" of the copula—which expresses the validity and stability of a pure relation—from asssertions of mere existence, assertions about spatial and temporal *dasein*.[129]

Even myth, which more than all other forms appears to be rooted in the personal world and seems to merge completely with it, has introduced us to certain themes that already distinctly point in another direction. In the middle of the mythic, personal world of demons and personal gods we meet now and then with figures that seem to us to be like "strangers." They possess nothing of that individual fullness of life, of that concrete immediateness that we otherwise find in the mythic pantheon. They seem in comparison to be strangely abstract, shapes without body or blood. Yet they have a very particular significance and function in the whole of mythic "meaning." They appear as the administrators and executors of a power of

128. The following footnote was deleted in the manuscript: "That all psychological 'Understanding' is bound to the recognition of such an ideal 'World of Form' has been shown in detail by Spranger; cf. his essay 'Zur Theorie des Verstehens und zur geisteswissenschaftlichen Psychologie,' *Festschrift für Joh. Volkelt*, Munich, 1918."—Eds.

129. For more see [*PSF*] vol. 1, pp. 313ff.—Cassirer.

fate standing above all the chance aspects of personal will and personal activity and conceived as free from all individual arbitrariness. They no longer act but rather measure, and the standards that they apply do no change with time but are ordered and prescribed from the earliest of times. In this way the power of *moira* stands in Greek thought above the being and all the actions of the gods.

But the Greeks did not create the shape of *moira*; they only gave it expression. In it we have a truly typical feature common in the history of religions to almost all peoples. Again and again we meet with this notion that the entire course of events in time stands under the control of a single force, which itself does not belong to events and is not defined by them. The order, according to which time moves on and according to which everything that happens is granted a particular length of time, a limited life span, is not itself something which has come about. It is a being, something nontemporal and eternal. In Chinese religious thought this view is found in the notion of the *Tao*, in Indian thought it is the notion of *Rita*, in the Avesta it appears as that of the *Asha*.[130] All of them express the belief that a law holds which is above time and governs the rise and fall of everything but that this law itself is not of the temporal order, so that it is a power above time and so also above the personal. Even here, where we are still moving in a basic sphere of mythic thought and awareness, consciousness has an early inkling that the law of coming to be and passing away to which all life is subject can no longer be conceived to belong completely to the circle of life and particular things. In the organization of mythic consciousness a basic tension remains, a latent contradiction: the image of the mythic universe, an all-encompassing and all-controlling order of time and fate, is attained only through a gradual dissolution and release from the mythic category of individuality.

This antithetical situation continues and becomes more acute as soon as the mythic conception of the world rises to the level of a religious one. For in the latter both of these opposing themes have gained new power and depth. The conception of individuals now appears with true definition and clarity. The step has been taken from mythic awareness to the feeling of the self and to self-consciousness. But we have seen again and again that religious thought cannot in the end find complete and adequate expression

---

130. For specific references see [*PSF*] vol. 2, section 2, Chap. 2, esp. pp. 193ff.—Cassirer. References to *Tao, Rita,* and *Asha* are found in *PSF*, vol. 2, p. 115.—Eds.

in this sphere, which it itself has created and constituted. For individuality appears at the same time also to mean limitation: *omnis determinatio est negatio*.[131] We see the entire history of philosophical theism caught up in this conflict; we see how it struggles again and again with the task of retaining the personality of God without thereby binding the divinity to the circle of finite, limited existence. It is philosophical idealism that here drew the final, decisive conclusion from this dialectic. It renounces the attempt to force the intelligent order, which it conceives the divinity to be, into the form of an individual being or an individual personality. It is able to hold fast to this renunciation and to carry it through because for it the value relationship between "being" and "meaning" has been reversed, because it does not base meaning on being, but rather being on meaning.

This turnabout and its consequences for thought emerge most sharply and clearly in Fichte's philosophy of religion. It strives to establish the "reality," that is, in its sense the pure significance of the divine, by distinguishing it from all kinds and forms of existence and empirical reality. In this philosophy God is not the creator of the intelligent order; he is this order itself, insofar as it is not conceived as a finished order but rather one in the process of completion, an *ordo ordinans*, not an *ordo ordinatus*.[132] The meaning of the completion of this order does not stem from an absolute being, is not posited or brought forth by it, but is genuinely original and the foundation of being. With this radical inference, however, with this primacy of the category of meaning before the category of existence, as established by Fichte's guiding transcendental principle and the foundation of his philosophy of religion, we now stand again before the same great shift that we were led to before in another field and in connection with a completely different problem. The same step is again demanded of us. In order to grasp a particular intellectual "meaning" we are now required to give ourselves over completely to it instead of clothing it in images that we derive from the given world of perceptual reality, so as to picture it to ourselves. Here too we have to leave behind the habit of thinking in mere "analogies" and of "schematizing" in order to enter into the sphere of

[131]. "All determination is negation." See Spinoza, Epistola 50, *Opera quotquot reperta sunt*, ed. J. van Vloten and J. P. N. Land, 3d ed., 4 vols. (The Hague: Martinus Nijhoff, 1914), vol. 3, p. 173; *Spinoza Selections*, ed. John Wild (New York: Scribner's, 1930), p. 454.—Eds.

[132]. These terms—an active ordering, in contrast to an existing order—are explained in Fichte, "Aus einem Privatschreiben," in *Sämmtliche Werke*, ed. J. H. Fichte, 8 vols. (Berlin: Verlag von Veit & Comp., 1845), vol. 5, pp. 381f.—Eds.

thought in terms of pure significance. For this a further sacrifice is necessary. As before we had to give up the substantial thing, we now have to give up the substantial "person." Fichte's philosophy of religion sharply and forcefully puts forward this decisive postulate of method against its opponents.[133] But it is of course understandable that antagonism to the acceptance of this postulate led again and again to ever greater opposition. At first glance it seems that nothing less is demanded here of thought than that it renounce every firm grasp on the "reality" of things, as well as on individual subjects. But if thought attempts this, does any other kind of being remain for it to think about, besides its own being, that of its own "abstractions"? Does it not now seem to be contained in a kind of void, in a space of "pure validity," of "truth in itself," from which no way leads back to the richness and immediacy of life?

There seems in the end to be only one solution to this dilemma. Thought cannot arrest the ascent from the particular to the universal, the progression from perception and sensory awareness to the sphere of pure "signification," but thought seems to be as little able to give up seeing the universal in the image of the particular. So it must attempt here to find a middle way from which it may hope to be able at least to retain a relationship to both poles, although it cannot fully amalgamate them into a unity. We have seen earlier the way this occurs in regard to the standpoint of the *thing*. Instead of breaking away from its principle, from the very category of the thing, thought only alters the quality, the makeup of things. It provides them with new characteristics that are not contained or presented in immediate perception, but it does not disturb the core of the world of things itself. The way out seems even more obvious, seems even more clearly to be the only possible and practicable course if we are dealing with the makeup of the inner world, the world of the "geist," instead of with the organization of the world of things. Here too every attempt to explain the structures of the "objective geist" by reference to the mere data and means of individual consciousness must fail. Compared to such consciousness they always re-

133. Cf. e.g. Fichte's "Appellation an das Publikum gegen die Anklage des Atheismus": "I say that the concept of God, as a particular *substance*, is an impossible and contradictory concept.... I say, that the proof of the existence of God from the existence of a sensory world is impossible and contradictory. I thereby deny of course the existence of God as *a substance, and as inferred from the world of sense*. Because of this I am considered to deny God ... in every sense. What I affirm is therefore, for my accusers, nothing, absolutely nothing: for them nothing at all is real for them except insofar as it is a substance and sensory, hence there can only be a substantial God, inferred from the world of sense." (*Sämtliche Werke*, vol. 5, pp. 216f.)—Cassirer.

tain an independent, irreducible "essence"; they prove to be, as Plato said of the idea of the Good, superior to it in age and dignity.[134]

Here too it seems possible to grant these structures their proper significance and dignity without completely removing and alienating them from the sphere of subjective thought. Just as thought at a particular level of the process of theoretical objectification had to posit things of a new kind and composition, so now it has to discover another kind of intellectual subject than the sort that we take as the basis for the phenomena of individual consciousness. That seems to solve the problem all at once, seems to allay the conflict between the demands of the individual and the universal. Pure forms of meaning appear to be infinitely superior to the mere ego-worlds of particular individual subjects, but this superiority consists in nothing other than that a kind of transindividual intellect is expressed and becomes effective in them. In order to do justice to the objective, universally valid contents of these forms, we do not have to elevate them above the bounds of life and temporal reality. In fact, we can conceive of them as belonging to life itself and springing forth from its own depths, insofar as we are able to elevate ourselves to a view of truly comprehensive and universal centers of life. The opposition between the universal and the particular is then resolved within the level of the living occurrences themselves, for in the end it is one and the same process from which the organic forms and cultural forms proceed, from which purely vital configurations and those of language and of religion, of science and art all arise.

This solution seems so tempting and enticing that it has been put forth many times as long as there has been such a thing as an independent "philosophy of culture." Again and again, it thus seems indispensable to assume the existence of transindividual unities of life, which seemed to offer the only firm point of rest or support. The basic ideas of an organological philosophy of history,[135] as they were developed since Vico[136] and

---

134. See Plato *Republic* 509B. *Collected Dialogues*, p. 744: "In like manner, then, you are to say that the objects of knowledge not only receive from the presence of the good their being known, but their very existence and essence is derived to them from it, though the good itself is not essence but still transcends essence in dignity and surpassing power."—Eds.

135. Cassirer uses the term "Organologie" to designate those doctrines that interpret processes of meaning in culture by reference to the image of the growth and death of a living organism. Here he follows Theodor Litt, who speaks about the subsumption of a "transpersonal effective relationship [*überpersönlichen Wirkungszusammenhang*] under the idea of an 'organism.'" See Litt, *Individuum und Gemeinschaft*, 3d exp. and rev. ed. (Leipzig: B. G. Teubner, 1926), p. 281; see pp. 327–332. See also Cassirer, "Naturalistic and Humanistic

given definite shape in the Romantic period, have provided all along the actual moving forces of the philosophy of culture. It is hardly saying too much, if we were to claim that the modern "philosophy of spirit" first came into its own with these ideas and that it delineated its problems through them. But no matter how highly we may value the historical achievement of this basic organological view, this cannot distract us from its fundamental, systematic limit. This limit lies in the fact that it too attempts to solve problems concerning pure "meaning" by relegating them to the level of occurrences and so transforms them into problems concerning actual events. "Meaning," which in itself is transtemporal, is taken to emerge from the temporal development itself, to be born from it. But here there is only one alternative. Either we must, with Hegel, *posit* that the realm of meaning, the realm of the "Idea," exists beforehand as something for itself, as the true substance of the mind which then emerges into history, but is in no way constituted by it, by the shifts and changes in the course of time as such, or we may transfer all intellectual contents to the process of history itself. Then we look for the idea only in the order and rhythm of historical configurations. In the end, then, this content is defined by nothing but the temporal position it occupies. It appears to be so bound in this way that even the mere *attempt* to conceive it independently of its temporal context and of the conditions surrounding its temporal emergence turn out to be a nonsensical undertaking.

The individual determinations to which all events as such are subject must now also be applied without limitation to the pure contents of meaning. Whatever they "are," they do not owe their character to some universal sense that surpasses time; rather, they are as they are only for an instant and just for that instant. This, their present, this existence in a single unmistakable "now," does not pose a limit to which they are subject; it provides the only possible form of their activity, their being real. That this interpretation is already contained in the general premises of the organological metaphysics of history cannot be denied. It was reserved for the last historical stage of this metaphysics to draw the truly decisive, methodological conclu-

---

Philosophies of Culture," in Cassirer, *The Logic of the Humanities*, trans. Clarence Smith Howe (New Haven: Yale Univ. Press, 1961), p. 8.—Eds.

136. Cassirer's reference is to the conception of history in Giambattista Vico's major work, *Principi di scienza nuova di Giambattista Vico d'intorno alla comune natura delle nazioni*, 3d ed. (Naples: Stamperia Muziana, 1744). *The New Science of Giambattista Vico*, trans. Thomas Goddard Bergin and Max Harold Fisch (Ithaca, N.Y.: Cornell Univ. Press, 1984 [1948]).—Eds.

sions from it. The form of organology that prevailed in the Romantic systems was still all too filled with ideas and ideals deriving from other regions of thought for it to follow out this line of thought to the end.

Not until Spengler's philosophy of history was the keystone added to the edifice of organology. Spengler was not the first to introduce a strain of skepticism into the organological philosophy of history, but he was perhaps the first to possess the courage to accept this skepticism. If the pure structures of meaning found in poetry and language, in religions or in scientific knowledge are nothing but the creations and products of the spirit of a particular people or culture, then it is completely consistent to conceive them as also perishing with it, just as they had arisen from it. Their rise and perseverance, their wilting and decay now also mean the aging and death of these structures, for they no longer have any independent stability of their own outside the *process* in which they unfold. They "exist" in the strict sense, they have meaning and value, only as long as they stand in the gleam of the immediate, historical present and as long as they are able to maintain this, their place in the sun of historical reality. Any endurance that continues beyond this is denied them—and must remain denied them, since all organic *existence* is bound to fixed organic dimensions, to being here and now. Spengler's philosophy of the decline of culture is therefore only a supplement, only the methodological continuation and methodological conversion of philosophy's interest in the "birth of culture" as it had been asserted by nearly the entire metaphysics of organology before him. "These cultures, sublimated life-essences, grow with the same superb aimlessness as the flowers of the field. They belong, like the plants and animals, to the living nature of Goethe, and not to the dead nature of Newton. I see world-history as a picture of endless formations and transformations, of the marvelous waxing and waning of organic forms."[137]

Here we will not go into the details of how Spengler developed this image; we limit ourselves merely to drawing attention to those features that are significant for our own systematic problem of symbolic formation. Spengler seems to have grasped this problem in its depth and breadth and in its true universality, because for him the entire language of culture and the language of history are written in symbols. Only by penetrating these symbols and grasping the essence that appears in them are we able to

137. Oswald Spengler, *Untergang des Abendlandes*, Einleitung [vol. 1 (1923), p. 29].—Cassirer. See *The Decline of the West*, auth. trans. Charles Francis Atkinson, 2 vols. (New York: Knopf, 1929), vol. 1, pp. 21–22.—Eds.

unlock the meaning-structure of processes. Although the concept of the symbol seems to be the actual methodological focal point of Spengler's philosophy, in practice it recognizes only a single specific facet, one basic intellectual aspect. This is because for Spengler the entire achievement of the symbolic function is limited to the function of expression. His characteristic procedure, which he applies everywhere, is, to state it in our own terminology, to transform all representation and significance into purely expressive meaning. Here again we see with great sharpness and clarity the attitude toward the problem of the symbol that we found in Klages' doctrine of expression.[138] Pure "physiognomics" alone, rather than an abstract logic of factual matters, a logic of ideal facts, is able to open up and interpret for us the secrets of historical existence. Not only religion and art, but even theoretical knowledge—not just music but also mathematics—appear limited to purely proclamatory functions. In them we find represented no structural relationships possessing their own objective meaning and with their own objective "truth"; rather, we find only inner states, which of course belong not just to individual souls but to the soul of all, to the "cultural souls."

Changing the morphology of world history this way into a "universal symbolism" means that all claims by thought to possess universal and timeless truths turn out to be empty, for "truths" exist only in the context of a particular group of people. The singularity and uniqueness characteristic of all genuine expressive phenomena make the belief in the universality of truth untenable. If the expressive function is not just the only *organ* for knowing the world, not just the only means through which mankind grasps reality, but if everything *known*—all the "objects" of knowledge—is also included in it, then the notion of a truth transcending it and its temporally conditioned individuality turns out to be an empty and dangerous illusion. It is dangerous because it threatens to dull and weaken our awareness and sensitivity to the unique and irrecoverable nature of the particular moment that can never be repeated.

The conclusions that Spengler draws from this are well known. There no longer is any sculpture, painting, mathematics, or physics, if by that we mean some universal way of representing and giving form based upon specific general principles of organization. Instead, we have only a plurality of kinds of sculptures, paintings, mathematics, and physics, each com-

---

138. Cf. above p. -.—Cassirer. The manuscript gives no reference. Cassirer probably is referring to his discussion of Klages in Chapter One above.—Eds.

pletely separate and different from the other. Each of them has "reality" only as long and to the extent that it remains alive, to the extent that it fills its necessarily limited life span. The specificity that we think we can find in them does not derive from the enduring nature of any "timeless" truths or timeless forms, but is only the expression of a purely physiognomic character of a culture and temporal epoch. The object-pole disappears from all these worlds of form, and in their place only the ego-pole remains, the pole of the soul. Even different types of mathematics claiming to be a scientific system can be nothing but such a proclamation of a soul. "If it is true that the intentional accomplishments of a mathematics only belong to the surface of history, it is equally true that its unconscious element, its number-as-such, and the style in which it builds up its self-contained cosmos of forms are an expression of its existence, its blood."[139]

We here will pass over all the fundamental objections that could be made from the standpoint of the critique of knowledge to this dissolution of mathematics into psychology and of "Being" into "Existence." We remain exclusively on the basis of historical narrative and take this problem solely in the same sense as Spengler himself does. If we assume Spengler's own point of view, a methodological surprise and a methodological paradox result. For the theoretical objectivity and factual character of knowledge that just now appeared to have been overcome, that seemed to be a mirage created by abstract, unhistorical thinking, now reemerge at the very same point when we deal with the foundation of the *philosophy* of history and its specific "truth." Such a "truth" can never be obtained by means of physiognomic vision as such, for *its* power and strength consist precisely in leaving alone what it observes, in not attempting to take it out of its historical context or to "transpose" it into another point in time. Without this act of transposition we then lose every possibility of "comparing" two temporally separated contents with each other or even of simply identifying them with each other according to their "meaning." Every content is what it is only in relationship to itself, not in relation to something different from itself, belonging to a different time and situation. If we conceive existence and knowledge in terms of the Heraclitean river, then Heraclitus' claim holds that nobody can step into the same river twice,[140] since there are

---

139. Spengler, *The Decline of the West*, p. 101. This quotation reflects the wording in the 1923 edition (Munich: C. H. Beck), which Spengler revised considerably from the 1918 edition (Vienna and Leipzig: Wilhelm Braumüller); cf. p. 148 of the 1918 edition and p. 137 of the 1923 edition.—Eds.

140. See Heraclitus frag. B 91 (Diels, vol. 1, p. 96; Freeman, p. 31).—Eds.

ever new currents. But even if we assume that all historical life consists in nothing other than this flowing movement, this can never hold for historical knowledge, let alone for the philosophy of history. For this can be developed only to the extent that it is possible for it to establish certain fixed points of reference for itself, that it is able to grasp a unity and similarity of form among the various configurations that rush past.

Spengler's own philosophy of history is completely in line with this methodological demand, for it strives to be a doctrine of form, a "morphology" of world history. But even in the pursuit of this task it has gone beyond the dimension of merely physiognomic expression. The unique power and independence of the "logos" are once again presupposed and recognized in the basic topic of a morpho-*logy*. What is more, it is not just implicitly assumed here, but rather comes before us with a peculiar intensity, in a kind of increased and exaggerated form. For Spengler's doctrine to succeed where all other philosophies of history have failed, it proposes to go so far in its grasp of the pure laws of form governing what happens that it thereby is able not only to attain a comprehensive view of the past, a synopsis, but also to predict the future. This prediction of the future stands as its true goal. The image of world history takes shape only for those who have learned to grasp its immanent "logic," who recognize what is typical in the changing histories of individual cultures, what is necessary in the boundless, chance elements. Here we come to the end of Spengler's skepticism, for the very closed and unbroken necessity that he denied to the "logic of mathematics" he now imparts in increased measure to the "logic of history." Nothing particular, no singular existence and no individual event can escape from it and its universality. The fate of our future culture thereby becomes, in regard to its form and duration, a strictly limited and unavoidable event. From the examples we possess we can obtain an overview and *calculate* its essential features.[141]

Here we see that two completely different ways of looking at things stand out in Spengler's doctrine. The ideal of a "morphology," which he himself regards as perfecting the ideal of a "physiognomy," in fact is unmistakably in total and irreconcilable opposition to it. For how can we conceive a physiognomy that wants not to observe and interpret but rather to *calculate*? We could try to weaken this objection by pointing out that the concept of "calculation," which Spengler attributes to and reserves for the

141. Cf. esp. *Untergang des Abendlandes*, Einleitung, nos. 13 and 14 [pp. 51–58].—Cassirer. See *The Decline of the West*, vol. 1, intro., pp. 36–41.—Eds.

philosophy of history, is specifically distinguished from all forms of mathematical calculation and definition. The "chronological number" is totally different from the mathematical number. Mathematical laws are the means for knowing dead forms; the means for understanding living forms is analogy. Analogy unveils history's language of forms. It shows that the number of forms that appear in world history is strictly limited, that ages, epochs, locations, and persons re-occur according to types. Here again the question arises whether this repetition, assuming that it in fact takes place, could also be grasped as such and *known* if every sphere of life remained strictly within its own limits, if it only moved at the level of its own experiences without ever reaching beyond them into a purely ideal medium of objective "meaning." A consciousness that consisted simply of expressive values and that was able only to understand purely expressive phenomena would in fact be as little able to think in terms of analogies as it would be able to think in terms of mathematical laws. For in the end knowledge by analogy also presupposes insight into specific, objective facts, and without them it would have no footing and no definiteness.

One may distinguish between a Faustian and an Apollonian form of mathematics and a Faustian and an Apollonian natural science and see in both nothing but ways of giving expression to the Apollonian and Faustian soul. But even this distinction can never be obtained from the dimension of the soul alone; rather, it results only when we bring in standards that no longer stem from the soul itself. An act of knowing that was no longer capable of retaining in thought the meaning and essence of a mathematical principle as such, as a kind of propositional meaning, would also have no way of holding fast to and retaining the various shapes of this meaning in different "cultural souls." We must have already grasped the idea of mathematics as a definite area of objectively possible propositions. We must, so to speak, have recognized this logical type of being before we can show how it changes and becomes differentiated in the field of history. Every historical epoch would then be able to emphasize a particular field in this area, but it would thereby neither create nor exhaust it; it only gives it a limited historical realization and currency. In this way the *genus proximum* of mathematics remains finally the only means for making visible the specific differences between the various particular "mathematics."

What Plato said about phenomena in general, that they can be known only through their participation in ideas, then stands out with particular sharpness and clarity in all areas of thought, in all the phenomena of "culture." We must have already recognized them according to their ideal type and sorted them out before we can begin to interpret them as phenomena of life and in this sense to understand them as organic types. Once we have grasped the essence, the eidos of the mathematical, then we can begin to follow it out in various temporal forms in which it is represented and realized in the totality of its historical manifestations. But the heaping up of all these manifestations does not help us to find and grasp this essence itself if we were not already able to experience it paradigmatically in a single case of its realization. This holds not only for mathematics but also for sculpture or music—for here too a productive principle of formation, as well as a characteristic form of the image itself, can be found in the richness of the particular works that have come forth in time. We cannot "explain" these principles or come to a deeper understanding of them by conceiving them as emerging from the transindividual unities of life as postulated by organological metaphysics. At best we can only obtain back from these unities of life the contents that we have previously introduced into them. One has to have included the entire range of the "objective spirit" and the different basic directions of objective meaning in the *concept* of these subjects, in order to let them seem to arise and emerge from them as a result of their work.[142]

And now we also can see here quite clearly the extent to which the makeup of the specifically "intellectual" world can be completed—that is insofar as thought at a specific level of its development overcomes not only the category of the thing and thingness but also categories of "personal" being. It is this last form of "transcendence" that truly opens up the sphere of the mind. It is, of course, understandable that thought can decide only with great difficulty to overstep limits this way and that it can maintain its newly found standpoint only with effort. By going beyond the sphere of things and beyond the personal sphere, it has left the firm ground of specifically human existence. In Goethe's *Prometheus* fragment, Prome-

---

142. In this criticism of the "organological" view, I agree especially with Theodor Litt. "Since its entry into the experiential structure of social reality is the occasion for the self to objectify its inner life in the symbolic forms"—writes Litt in the same sense as the basic methodological view that we uphold throughout this work—"it also finds itself on the plane of another, wider, differently structured, kind of 'World': a world of 'meaning' distinguished from all references to 'time' and 'reality.' Just as every world, it leads the ego irresistibly beyond itself, by drawing it away from its limited particular contents of meaning so that it acquires new meaning in the surrounding area.... A temporal-ideal relationship must ... encompass all the meaning claims among different individual subjects wherever psychological life enters into a symbolic formation" (Litt, *Individuum und Gemeinschaft*, 2d ed., Leipzig: [B. G. Teubner,] 1924, pp. 180, 183).—Cassirer.

theus, as the symbol of mankind, replies to the question, "How much then is yours?" by answering: "Whatever space my energies can fill, Nothing more nor less!"[143] The circle of human activity appears to be defined in fact by the two opposing poles of "I" and "World" and exhausted by the space between them. Mankind cannot be productive except by dividing the whole of being into partial unities, by separating it into thing-configurations and I-configurations. As with man's productive efforts, so too his entire concrete, perceptual grasp of the world is bound to these two basic forms and constantly harnessed to them. Yet man is not limited by this immanent boundary to his perception and action, but ventures to fly beyond them. So man comes to share in a new heaven and earth, in an "intelligible cosmos." It would be self-contradictory, a falling back into old habits of thinking and seeing, if man were again to try to grasp and describe this cosmos in images. It can be conceived only in *symbols*, the symbols of language, art, religion, and theoretical cognition.

Throughout the course of our investigation, at the end of which we now stand, we have sought to show how the course of human knowledge leads from "representation" to "signification," from the schematism of perception to the symbolic grasp of pure relationships and orders of meaning. All these orders, no matter how absolute we may take them to be, existing in and of themselves, are there "for" man only to the extent that he participates in their development. Man's life in them cannot consist of passive awareness; his life is bound up with their production so that he raises these orders up into his consciousness by means of this course of knowledge. In this act of becoming conscious and of making himself conscious we do not find the power of fate which governs organic processes. Here we attain the realm of freedom. The true and highest achievement of every "symbolic form" consists in its contribution toward this goal; by means of its resources and its own unique way, every symbolic form works toward the transition from the realm of "nature" to that of "freedom."[144]

---

143. Goethe, "Prometheus, A Dramatic Fragment," trans. Frank Ryder, *Early Verse Drama and Prose Plays*, ed. Cyrus Hamlin and Frank Ryder, *Goethe's Collected Works*, vol. 7 (New York: Suhrkamp, 1988), p. 242. See *WA*, Abt. 1, vol. 39, p. 198.—Eds.

144. Note at bottom right of page: "completed 16/IV 28."—Cassirer.

PART II

On Basis Phenomena
c. 1940

Chapter One

Presentation of the Problem

Objective Character (truth value)
    α) of perception (taking something as true)
        the organization of "external" perception
            Physics, etc.—"nature"
    β) of the "expressive" function
        the organization of "inner" experience
            the world of the "mind"—culture

How is this objectivity to be secured?[1]
Possible ways of securing it:

[1. The Objective Character of Perception]

(A.) Securing it by (Formal)-logical means: through "inference," "proof," *syllogism*.

Defects of these procedures:
In regard to "external" experience—perception.

If it had no particular truth *content* "in itself," then it could not gain it through proof (syllogistically). For the syllogism (inference, proof) cannot "generate" any truth *content* at all. It can only "pass it on," transfer it. It says that *if* A is true, then also B and C, but it never says *that* A is true. It consists of purely *hypothetical* statements, not of assertions (statements about truth or statements about reality). "Assertion" must always enter in from *another* source. "Being" can therefore only be "asserted," not "proven."

---

[1]. *Marginal note: cf.* sheet a.—Cassirer. This is a reference to the section entitled "The Objective Character of the Expressive Function."—Eds.

All the syllogistic *proofs* that have been attempted for the "reality" of things, become entangled again and again in a circle (Descartes—*veracitas Dei*).[2]

What follows from this *rejection* of syllogistic attempts to secure the truth (securing it through proof), objectivity, and the "truthfulness" of "perception"?

Several theoretical possibilities present themselves.

FUNDAMENTAL SKEPTICISM[3]

The tropes of Aenesidemus[4]—Denial of the truth value of sensory perception; Veil of Maya—World as Illusion; "what even the poets sing of"[5]—sensory illusions.

[The] character of illusion [is] transferred to the whole—

Greek Skepticism—"problematic" Skepticism of Descartes

(No function is to be trusted, if it can fool us even *once*.)

Since therefore the "absolute" *truth* of what is supposedly true ("taken for true" in perception) can never be secured, we are now left with *absolute*

2. See Arnauld's formulation of the circle in Descartes' proofs of reality in "Objectiones," *Oeuvres de Descartes*, ed. Charles Adam and Paul Tannery, 12 vols. (Paris: L. Cerf, 1896–1913), vol. 7, p. 214, lines 7–14. *The Philosophical Writings of Descartes*, trans. J. Cottingham et al., 2 vols. (Cambridge: Cambridge Univ. Press, 1984), vol. 2, p. 150: "I have one further worry, namely how the author avoids reasoning in a circle when he says that we are sure that what we clearly and distinctly perceive is true only because God exists.—But we can be sure that God exists only because we clearly and distinctly perceive this. Hence, before we can be sure that God exists, we ought to be able to be sure that whatever we perceive clearly and evidently is true."—Eds.

3. *Marginal note:* Litt: R. Richter, Skept / Hönigswald.—Cassirer. Litt discusses Skepticism in his *Einleitung in die Philosophie* (Leipzig and Berlin: B. G. Teubner, 1933), pp. 26–34. "R. Richter, Skept" refers to Raoul Richter, *Der Skeptizismus in der Philosophie*, 2 vols. (Leipzig: Dürr, 1904–1908). "Hönigswald" is probably a reference to Richard Hönigswald, *Die Skepsis in Philosophie und Wissenschaft* (Göttingen: Vandenhoeck & Ruprecht, 1914).—Eds.

4. Aenesidemus of Knossos (fl. 1st century B.C.), who taught in Alexandria, put forth ten tropes or ways of argumentation directed against the reliability of perception. These τρόποι take their starting point from the differences between people, the various senses, social customs, and so forth. See Sext. Emp. I, 36–163.—Eds.

5. See Plato *Phaedo* 65A9–B3: οἷον τὸ τοιόνδε λέγω· ἆρα ἔχει ἀλήθειάν τινα ὄψις τε καὶ ἀκοὴ τοῖς ἀνθρώποις, ἢ τά γε τοιαῦτα καὶ οἱ ποιηταὶ ἡμῖν ἀεὶ θρυλοῦσιν, ὅτι οὔτ' ἀκούομεν ἀκριβὲς οὐδὲν οὔτε ὁρῶμεν. *Collected Dialogues*, p. 48: "What I mean is this. Is there any certainty in human sight and hearing, or is it true, as the poets are always dinning in our ears, that we neither hear nor see anything accurately?"—Eds.

PRESENTATION OF THE PROBLEM 117

illusion; nothing is worth our trust. *"Life is a dream."*[6] This view seems, in principle, incapable of [being] refuted.

There remains only *one* form of refutation. We do not need "absolute" truth; rather, in fact, we need relative truth.

We don't need "being-true" (= a *mirror image* of an absolute true being); we need "being truer," an expression of the *whole* of experience. This question—whether something is true or untrue—loses its meaning if it is applied to the *whole*. The *predicate* true or untrue is not applicable in this case because this *predicate* always applies only *in relation to this whole*. I can no more raise the question of truth in regard to the *whole* of experience than I can raise the question of *"where?"* for the whole of the universe—

This [is] the theoretical way to repel *absolute* skepticism (cf. also Hönigswald).[7]

Other [solutions] (at bottom, are not critical but metaphysical solutions).

(B.) The Theory of "Immediate Knowledge"

It is *justified* insofar as it can serve as a *defense*, in the defense against syllogistic *proof* as a means to secure the "objectivity" of perception.

The questionable thing is what it would put *in place of* this proof.

The philosophy of *"common sense"* in the form given to it by Reid.[8]

Every *generally held* opinion is *eo ipso* secure against all theoretical doubt. *Philosophy* cannot overturn the judgment of "healthy human understanding." It can establish no "higher" reason in place of commonplace human reason. It can only *register* the latter's opinions, only *take note of* what is generally believed or not believed, but there is no possibility for it to

---

6. Reference to Pedro Calderón de la Barca, *Life Is a Dream* (*La vida es sueño*, 1636). This work was well known in Germany; Lessing began a German translation of the drama, and Goethe had the play performed in 1811 in Weimar.—Eds.

7. See Hönigswald, *Die Skepsis in Philosophie und Wissenschaft*, p. 85: "Doubt can be raised, in other words, only against *relative* claims to validity—more precisely, against those that can be defined only from the standpoint of reference to absolute claims to validity."—Eds.

8. See Thomas Reid, *An Inquiry into the Human Mind*, 2d ed. (Edinburgh, 1765), chap. 2, sect. 6, p. 41: "If there are certain principles, as I think there are, which the constitution of our nature leads us to believe, and which we are under a necessity to take for granted in the common concerns of life, without being able to give a reason for them—these are what we call the principles of common sense; and what is manifestly contrary to them, is what we call absurd."—Eds.

criticize these judgments. For *with what* would it want to carry out this criticism? What *organ* does it possess for this purpose—besides this "commonplace" human reason?

There is, of course, no *particular* organ of philosophical thought and of philosophical "truth"—outside of thought in general. There is therefore no "critique" of reason. For what would we want to criticize reason with besides *through* reason?

The thing is therefore to establish reason's most universal claims and the ways it asserts itself, in order thereby to be sure of the validity of its claims. As far as actual basic truths are concerned, the *"quid facti"* and the *"quid juris"* collapse into each other.

Other (more modern) forms of the *same* standpoint:

(α) Fries' Theory of the "Self-Confidence of Reason"[9] in Nelson's version: the impossibility of theory of knowledge.[10]

([This is] *correct*, if we understand it to mean the rejection of syllogistic proofs, [but it is] *incorrect*, if it refers to the *relative* criticism of knowledge—this cannot be dismissed.)

(β) Hume's Theory of "Belief"—Pragmatic Theory—

In contrast to the philosophy of common sense, Hume does not dismiss the question of *"quid juris"*; rather, he poses it in the sharpest terms. But it is

---

9. See Jacob Friedrich Fries, *Neue Kritik der Vernunft*, 1st ed. (Heidelberg: Muhr & Zimmer, 1807), vol. 2, pp. 37f.: "The highest subjective principle of all human judgments is the *principle of human reason's self-trust*: every human being trusts the power of human mind to be able to attain the truth."—Eds.

10. See the summary of Nelson's argument in "Die Unmöglichkeit der Erkenntnistheorie," *Abhandlungen der Fries'schen Schule* 3 (1912): 594f.: "It is the task of epistemology to examine the truth or objective validity of our knowledge. I maintain that it is *impossible* to solve this problem, and I prove this in the following manner. In order to solve the problem as stated we must be in possession of a criterion through whose application we are able to decide if a cognition is true or not. I will call it the 'epistemological criterion' for short. This criterion will itself either be a cognition or not. If it was a cognition, then it would belong to the same problematic area that we are concerned with and whose validity we intend to decide about with the aid of the epistemological criterion. Hence, it cannot itself be a cognition. But if the epistemological criterion is not a cognition, it must nonetheless be known in order to be applicable, that is, we must be able to recognize that it is a criterion of the truth. But in order to attain knowledge of this criterion we must apply it first. In both cases, therefore, we meet with a contradiction.—Consequently, an epistemological criterion is impossible and so epistemology is an impossible undertaking."—Eds.

declared to be theoretically *unanswerable*. It can be "solved" only practically, by chopping through the knot—biologically, not logically—[by] putting all theoretical scruples aside. "Carelessness" (Hume cf. *Treatise* . . .) alone can afford us any remedy.[11] Our (psychological) belief is incapable of justification by proof, yet such belief is unavoidable. Its "*quid juris*" is quite problematic, but nothing can oppose the overwhelming power of its "*quid facti*." This [is] the role of "imagination"—a completely atheoretical function—in Hume's system.[12]

(γ) Jacobi's Doctrine of "Belief"[13] as a religious-metaphysical variety of Hume's theory of belief—

The "grounds" for our "belief in the reality of the external world" cannot be theoretical, logical grounds. For this we must look elsewhere.[14]

But Hume's *psychological* solution is only an apparent solution. It gives skepticism free rein by posing the question of "*quid juris*" while at the same time declaring this question to be unanswerable. We can and must answer this question. But this is only possible by recourse to another source of *certainty*—the source of religious *intuition* ("belief" in the religious-intuitive sense as the final grounds of *certainty*, something that cannot be attained by any kind of "knowledge"). "Knowledge" never attains to "Being"—Being can only be grasped through "belief," and that holds not only for pure "transcendent" Being, but for *immanent* being as well.

---

11. See Hume, *Treatise of Human Nature*, ed. L. A. Selby-Bigge (Oxford: Clarendon Press, 1896), p. 218: "As the sceptical doubt arises naturally from a profound and intense reflection on those subjects, it always encreases, the farther we carry our reflections, whether in opposition or conformity to it. Carelessness and in-attention alone can afford us any remedy."—Eds.

12. See Hume, *Treatise of Human Nature*, bk. 1, pt. 3, sec. 10, pp. 118–123: "Of the influence of belief."—Eds.

13. See Jacobi's description of his view of "belief," in *The Spinoza Conversations Between Lessing and Jacobi*, trans. G. Vallée et al. (New York: Univ. Press of America, 1988), p. 120: "Conviction through proofs is a second-hand certainty and rests on comparison; it can never be altogether certain and total. Now, if every *taking-to-be-true* [Fürwahrhalten] which does not have its origins in rational grounds, is faith, then conviction based on rational grounds, is faith, then conviction based on rational grounds must itself come from faith and from faith alone must draw its strength.—It is through faith that we know we have a body and that other bodies and other thinking beings exist apart from us." See Cassirer, *Das Erkenntnisproblem in der Philosophie und Wissenschaft der neueren Zeit* (Berlin: Bruno Cassirer, 1920), vol. 3, p. 32, where he stresses the importance of this passage.—Eds.

14. *Marginal note:* s. Jacobi . . / u. Erkprbl, III.—Cassirer. On Jacobi see Cassirer, *Das Erkenntnisproblem*, vol. 3, pp. 17–33.—Eds.

(δ) Analogous solutions in Dilthey, *On the Grounds*—[15]

[He offers an] atheoretical solution—as in Jacobi—but on a different foundation: voluntaristic—based on the "will's experiences," instead of upon religious "belief." [This is] an expansion of "lived experience" as a basis.

But opposed to all these "absolute" solutions stands the *critical* solution, as the "relative" solution.

It does not ask about the "truth" of perception as a *whole*.

It asks about the *place* of each particular perception (*"Wahrnehmung"*) within the whole, in the "context of experience." This *context*, the "system," does not need to have its truth demonstrated or "tested"—it is the measure, not what is measured.

But every *individual* perception must be measured within this whole and tested if it is "true" or "false."

None can lay claim to "immediate" certainty.

The final "invariants" are not given, they must be *searched* out, and "established." Yet this "establishing" is never something "absolute," but rather depends upon the continuing course of science.

The "invariants" shift "from place to place," such as in the general theory of relativity.[16] *This* [is] the significance of "subjectification"—but this subjectification can never apply to "experience as a whole." Hence, an "invariant" "framework" always remains. But this framework itself is not fixed, but can change. Analogous considerations [apply] to the *expressive function*.

---

15. See Dilthey, "Beiträge zur Lösung der Frage vom Ursprung unseres Glaubens an die Realität der Aussenwelt und seinem Recht," *Sitzungsberichte der Königlich Preussischen Akademie der Wissenschaften zu Berlin* (1890): 977–1022, esp. "Das Prinzip der Erklärung," pp. 982f., "Die herrschende naturwissenschaftliche Hypothese über den Ursprung des Glaubens an die Realität von Objekten": "I do not explain our belief in the outer world by reference to a structure of thought, but by reference to a structure of life given through drives, will, and feeling, which is mediated by processes that are the equivalent of modes of thought. . . . It is from our own life, from the drives, feelings, and willing that create this life and whose outside is our body, that the distinction between self and object, it seems to me now, arises within our perceptions."—Eds.

16. On the theory of relativity as an illustration of the dependent character of all invariants, see Cassirer, *Substance and Function* and *Einstein's Theory of Relativity* (two books bound as one), auth. trans. W. C. Swabey and M. C. Swabey (New York: Dover Books, 1953), chap. 2, pp. 367–386.—Eds.

PRESENTATION OF THE PROBLEM   121

The "Positivism" of the Vienna Circle[17] sees correctly that "reality" in the strict sense is never to be apprehended through any merely formal procedure (through pure "logic," through "proofs" and argumentation). It calls for an independent basis,[18] on which all (mediate) inference builds. Positivism looks for this basis in "perception."[19] Perception is the only thing that discloses reality. We do not make inferences (logically, formally) from perception to reality; rather, perception is what opens up reality. Perception gives us the only (immediate) insight concerning reality, something which can never be obtained from conceptual, logical means. To this extent, the particular status of the "basis" [is] recognized. But in "physicalism" this basis is taken too narrowly.[20]

17. Included among the members of the Vienna Circle, which met from approximately 1907 until the end of the 1930s in Vienna, were the mathematicians Hans Hahn and Kurt Gödel, the physicist Philipp Frank, the philosopher and economist Otto Neurath, and the philosophers Rudolf Carnap, Herbert Feigl, Moritz Schlick, and Friedrich Waismann. Their main publication was the journal *Erkenntnis*.—Eds.

18. Here and in the following discussion Cassirer uses the German word *Basis* with reference to but not in the same sense as in Rudolf Carnap's *The Logical Structure of the World*, trans. (2d ed.) Rolf A. George (Berkeley: Univ. of California Press, 1967). See pt. 3, C (entitled "The Basis"), secs. 61–83 (pp. 98–136). In Carnap's book (first published in 1928) *Basis* means the "basic objects" of a "constructional system" (*Konstitutionssystem*), i.e., "a step-by-step ordering of objects in such a way that the objects of each level are constructed from those of the lower levels" (sec. 2, p. 6). Carnap proceeds on what he calls an "autopsychological basis" (*eigenpsychischen Basis*), and so he calls his method "methodological solipsism" (sec. 64, pp. 101–103).—Eds.

19. Here Cassirer probably has in mind Carnap's doctrine of "elementary experiences" (*Elementarerlebnisse*). See Carnap, *The Logical Structure of the World*, pt. 3, C ("The Basis"), sec. 67, "The Choice of Basic Elements: The 'Elementary Experiences.'" Carnap criticizes Ernst Mach's view, according to which simple sensations provide a theoretical starting point. In opposition to this, Carnap explicitly turns to the gestalt theory of Wertheimer and Köhler: "One could perhaps think of choosing the final constituents of experience at which one arrives through psychological or phenomenological analysis (such as the most simple sensations, as in Mach [Anal.]) or, more generally, psychological elements of different types from which experiences can be formed. However, upon closer inspection, we realize that in this case we do not take the given as it is, but abstractions from it (i.e., something that is epistemologically secondary) as basic elements. It must be understood that constructional systems which proceed from such basic elements are as much justified and practicable as, for example, systems with a physical basis. However, since we wish to require of our constructional system that it should agree with the epistemic order of the objects (section 54), we have to proceed from that which is epistemically primary, that is to say, from the 'given,' i.e., from experiences themselves in their totality and undivided unity (pp. 107f.).—Eds.

20. For Carnap, following Neurath, "physicalism" is the view that physicalistic language is the "universal language." Hence, all observation reports are private descriptions until they are

"Expression" must also be taken into account as a second dimension, as the key to the world of "life," the "psyche," the "mind." If there were no such thing as perception of expression, these three worlds would remain closed to us forever; no path leads to them from the bare perception of things. Physicalism's "reality" is balanced upon the tip of perception in the sense of taking something to be true. It has no sense for what we mean by "psyche," "life," or "mind." In fact, physicalism is only a confession that perception, in the sense of mere objectification, finds no meaning in any such realms of experience. But it is wrong to conclude from this that they are in fact objectively senseless or meaningless. We can only conclude that it is not possible to make this meaning visible from the standpoint of physics and through its methods. Hence, "The spirit world is not sealed off—*your* mind is closed, *your* heart is dead."[21]

[2.] *The Objective Character of the Expressive Function*

Here too the same problems recur that we were able to follow in the perception of truth (the organization of "outer" experience).

Preliminary phase: uncritical, undifferentiated acceptance of the expressive function. It is taken to be the very expression of "reality," that is, "mythic" reality. [This is a] magic-demonic image of the world (momentary gods, etc.). This corresponds to that theoretical image of the world in which no "criticism of the senses" has been undertaken, in which everything perceived (as something taken as true) is also *eo ipso* "true." Doubts about this "reality" emerge with the development of science (Greek philosophy, etc.) and this doubt finally leads to its complete destruction. In modern thought [there are] two forms of this destruction (total denial): behaviorism and physicalism.

This denial leads in its most extreme form to the denial of the question

---

brought into the form of physical description. This leads to the thesis of the "unity of science." See Carnap, "Die physikalische Sprache als Universalsprache der Wissenschaft," *Erkenntnis* 2 (1932): 462. *The Unity of Science*, trans. Max Black (London: Kegan Paul, Trench, Teubner, 1934), pp. 95–96: "For the sake of precision we might supplement or replace 'physical language' by the term '*physicalistic language*'; denoting by the latter the universal language which contains not only physical terms (in the narrow sense) but also all the various special terminologies (of Biology, of Psychology, Sociology, etc.) understood as reduced by definitions to their basis in physical determinations."—Eds.

21. A reference to Goethe, *Faust*, lines 443f.—Eds.

of meaning (Carnap). We cannot meaningfully inquire into any kind of being except physical being. Physics is the "universal language of science."[22] There are no other scientific claims except those that can be formulated in physical terms.

(Here we [can raise] the objection that philosophy is concerned not just with science alone, but with all forms of "world understanding." That there is a difference here is something that Carnap himself must admit.)[23] Here too it most probably will be like absolute "skepticism" regarding perception of truth. We can of course critically limit the "truth" of perception (and of the expressive function), but we cannot eliminate it or skeptically deny it completely.

It is negatively correct that there can be no formal, syllogistic proof of the "birthright" (*quid juris*) of the expressive function. Logically, "Solipsism" is a "possible" attitude and yet in practice it is nonetheless "absurd" (Schopenhauer—fortress—madhouse, and so on).[24] What does "in practice" mean in contrast to "logically"? Here [we have], the same alternatives as in the case of the theoretical problem (of perception).[25]

---

22. A reference to Carnap's essay "Die physikalische Sprache als Universalsprache der Wissenschaft." Eng. trans. *The Unity of Science.*—Eds.

23. Worm-objection. Cf. the expressive function. That is a *demonstrable* difference in any case. The question is not meaningless.—Cassirer. Cassirer is referring to the phenomenon of expression as described by Carnap: "The statement 'this animal has consciousness' must contain more than the mere report that this animal shows certain observable reactions to given stimuli; for this statement influences my actions; for if I know that the worm feels pain, I do not step on it, while the mere observation that it writhes does not necessarily prevent me from doing so." See *Pseudoproblems in Philosophy*, trans. Rolf A. George (Berkeley: Univ. of California Press, 1967), p. 137.—Eds.

24. See Arthur Schopenhauer, *The World as Will and Representation*, trans. E. F. J. Payne (New York: Dover Books, 1969), vol. 1, bk. 2, sec. 19, p. 104: "Theoretical egoism, of course, can never be refuted by proofs, yet in philosophy it has never been positively used otherwise than as a sceptical sophism, i.e., for the sake of appearance. As a serious conviction, on the other hand, it could be found only in a madhouse; as such it would then need not so much a refutation as a cure. Therefore we . . . shall regard this sceptical argument of theoretical egoism, which here confronts us, as a small frontier fortress. Admittedly, the fortress is impregnable, but the garrison can never sally forth from it, and therefore we can pass it by and leave it in our rear without danger." Schopenhauer, *Die Welt als Wille und Vorstellung*, 3d ed. (Leipzig: F. A. Brockhaus, 1859), vol. 1, bk. 2, §19, pp. 124f.—Eds.

25. (Cf. A 1).—Cassirer. This probably refers to a discussion at the beginning of envelope 184c marked "(A 1)" in which Cassirer considers the alternatives to syllogistic proof, which he terms the "theory of immediate knowledge" and the "critical solution."—Eds.

Theory of Immediate Knowledge

We do not need to infer "other minds"; we experience the other directly, "immediately," with more certainty and more immediately than the being of things.

Rejection of inferential theories. The theory of the "analogical inference" and so on is rightly repudiated, for example, by Scheler.[26]

Instead [we have a] leap into the metaphysics of "immediate knowledge," either in terms of "common sense" (cf. Reid) or of metaphysical "intuitionism" (this agrees with Jacobi's standpoint—in regard to the problem of expression as represented by Scheler and Bergson). Bergson: all reality is the reality of "life." The so-called world of things (physics, physicalism) is an illusion of "science"; scientific knowledge is necessarily the reification, stabilization, deadening of life. Life [is] absolutely real, but incognizable, only graspable by intuition.

[This is the] inversion of physicalism. Now physics is an illusion; life (which is manifested in the expressive function) alone is real, given, true. The expressive function [is] a *donnée immediate de la conscience*.[27] The same [holds for] Klages.

Our standpoint [is] "critical"; we uphold neither the falsity (skepticism) nor the truth (metaphysics) of the expressive function. Rather, we seek to limit critically and justify critically its achievements in the construction of the "cultural world."

The fact always remains as a certain starting point that cannot be challenged by any scientific skepticism that a person's "own I" is given as a phenomenon which is not "physicalistically" describable. Physics as the "universal language of science" lets us down when it is confronted with this phenomenon. It is not possible to describe, to "define," what the "I" means in a mathematical-physicalistic way. (Leibniz already saw this. "Perception" is not a phenomenon that can be expressed in physicalistic terms.—if we could go around, like in a mill[28]—His entire philosophy is based on this: *ce a moy qui dit beaucoup.*)[29]

---

26. See Max Scheler, *Wesen und Formen der Sympathie*, 2d ed. (Bonn: F. Cohen, 1923), pp. 274–277. *The Nature of Sympathy*, trans. Peter Heath (London: Routledge & Kegan Paul, 1958), pp. 238–241.—Eds.

27. Reference to Bergson.—Eds.

28. See Leibniz, *Monadologie*, §17, *Die philosophischen Schriften von Leibniz*, ed. C. J. Ger-

PRESENTATION OF THE PROBLEM 125

The sentence "I will" [or] "I think" is "meaningful" without being "physical." (Cf. on this "irreducibility" of the "I" (not reducible to "something seen" etc.) the comments Jonas Cohn directs against Carnap, pp. 65f.)[30] But another and more difficult question is whether this foundation, this δός

---

hardt, 7 vols. (Berlin: Weidmann, 1875–1890), vol. 6, p. 609: "Et feignant, qu'il y ait une Machine, dont la structure fasse penser, sentir, avoir perception, on pourra la concevoir aggrandie en conservant les mêmes proportions, en sorte qu'en y puisse entrer comme dans un moulin. Et cela posé, on ne trouvera en la visitant au dedans que des pieces qui poussent les unes les autres, et jemais de quoy expliquer une perception." See "Monadology" in Leibniz, *Discourse on Metaphysics, Correspondence with Arnauld and Monadology*, trans. George K. Montgomery (LaSalle, Ill.: Open Court, 1902), p. 254: "Supposing that there were a machine whose structure produced thought, sensation, and perception, we could conceive of it as increased in size with the same proportions until one was able to enter into its interior, as he would into a mill. Now, on going into it he would find only pieces working upon one another, but never would he find anything to explain Perception." Leibniz's undated letter to Bayle, no. 10, *Philosophische Schriften*, vol. 3, p. 68: "Et quand on auroit les yeux aussi penetrans qu'on voudroit, pour voir les moindres parties de la structure du corps, je ne voy pas qu'on seroit plus avancé, et l'on y trouveroit l'origine de la perception aussi peu qu'on la trouve maintenant ou dans une montre où les parties constitutives de la machine sont toutes visibles, ou dans un moulin, où même on peut se promener entre les roues: puisque la difference du moulin et d'une machine plus subtile n'est que de plus et de moins. On peut concevoir que la machine produise les plus belles choses du monde, mais jamais qu'elle s'en aperçoive" (And even if one had the sharpest eyes, in order to see the smallest parts in the structure of the body, I do not see how one would be better able to discover the origin of perception or to find this in a clock, in the components of a machine, in which everything was visible, or in a mill, even if we could walk between its wheels: for the difference between a mill and a much finer machine is only a distinction of more or less. One can understand how a machine can produce the most beautiful things in the world, but never that it can perceive them).—Eds.

29. See Leibniz, *Discours de métaphysique, Philosophische Schriften*, vol. 4, pp. 459f.: "Mais l'ame intelligente connoissant ce qu'elle est, et pouvant dire ce MOY, qui dit beaucoup, ne demeure pas seulement et subsiste Metaphysiquement, bien plus que les autres, mais elle demeure encor la même moralement et fait le même personnage. Car c'est le souvenir, ou la connoissance de ce *moy*, qui la rend capable de chastiment et de recompense." Leibniz, *Discourse on Metaphysics, Correspondence with Arnauld and Monadology*, p. 58: "But the intelligent soul, knowing that it is and having the ability to say that word 'I' so full of meaning, not only continues and exists, metaphysically far more certainly than do the others, but it remains the same from the moral standpoint, and constitutes the same personality, for it is its memory or knowledge of this ego which renders it open to punishment and reward."—Eds.

30. See Jonas Cohn, "Kritische Bemerkungen zur neupositivistischen Erkenntnislehre, namentlich zu der Carnaps (Methodenmonismus und Problemabweisung)," *Philosophische Hefte* 5: 1/2 (1936): 51–74, esp. 66 n.: "Carnap's objectivism, his misunderstanding of the subject, is seen in the fact that he derives 'my own body' from the experience of a 'thing seen' (Aufbau §94, p. 132; §129, p. 171)." This reference corresponds to pp. 149 and 199f. in the translation, *The Logical Structure of the World*.—Eds.

μοὶ ποῦ στῶ,[31] can be extended beyond a person's "own" I—whether knowledge of the I or of the "other" is physically possible. Here we receive a surprising answer from Schrödinger, the "Hypothesis π":[32] such knowledge is not only possible, it is necessary. Physics as a science must also incorporate Hypothesis π into its complete system. It cannot get along without the presupposition that the "perceived" is "given" not only to me, but also to others. "Given" means always given to a subject, given to "me" or to "others." Even the "data" of physics also include this physically irreducible phenomenon (cf. Schrödinger . . .) in [the] expressive function. Schrödinger's hypothesis gives us at least this, that the I as a starting point, although it is physically irreducible—inexpressible in the language of physics—in no way contradicts the language of physics; rather, it "tacitly" enters into it (i.e., without explicitly being expressed, in fact incapable of being expressed). There are, namely, such implicit, inexpressible "premises."

That the data of physics are given to "somebody" is something generally characteristic of these data and applies to them generally; hence it is something physically insignificant (something understood that goes without saying) that can be left aside in all physical statements ("bracketed out"). But this characteristic is present despite this "bracketing out"; it is not philosophically insignificant but belongs to the complete description of reality.

So even the positivistic, physicalistic theory of knowledge speaks about sensory "experiences." But such "experiences" always include the I-factor, which is indescribable in physical terms and can only be defined as a general "point of reference."[33]

31. Archimedes is reputed to have said: δός μοὶ ποῦ στῶ καὶ κινῶ τὴν γῆν ("Give me a place to stand on and I can move the earth"). See *Pappi Alexandrini collectionis quae supersunt, e libris manu scriptis edidit, latina interpretatione et commentariis instruxit Fridericus Hultsch* (Berlin: Weidmann, 1878), vol. 3, p. 1060, lines 3f.—Eds.

32. π = "personality." See Erwin Schrödinger, "Quelques remarques au sujet des bases de la connaissance scientifique," in *Scientia: Rivista internazionale di sintesi scientifica* 57 (1935): 181–191, esp. 186: "Pour être bref, je désignerai l'hypothèse qui *s'oppose* au solipsisme par la lettre P ('personalité') des créatures qui m'entourent" (To be brief, I designate the hypothesis that is opposed to solipsism with the letter P ["personality"] for those creatures that surround me).—Eds.

33. Cf. also Natorp, Psychologie, 1.ed.—Cassirer. See Paul Natorp, *Einleitung in die Psychologie nach kritischer Methode* (Freiburg i. B.: J. C. B. Mohr [Paul Siebeck], 1888), §4, esp. p. 13: "The I, as the subjective point of reference of all contents conscious to me, stands opposite all these contents as something different from them."—Eds.

[Chapter Two]

[Basis Phenomena]

[1.] Basis Phenomena (Primary phenomenon)

Goethe's Maxims 391–93.

[391.] The highest gift we have received from God and nature[1] [is life, the rotating movement of the monad about itself, knowing neither pause nor rest. The impulse to nurture this life is ineradicably implanted in each individual, although its specific nature remains a mystery to ourselves and to others.[2]

392. The second benefit from active higher beings is the experienced, our becoming truly aware, the living-moving monad's intervention into the surroundings of the outer world. Through this it becomes truly aware of itself as internal lack of limits, and as externally limited. Although it requires a predisposition, attention, and luck, we can become clear ourselves about what we experience; but to others it remains a mystery.

393. As the third there now arises what we direct toward the outer world as actions and deed, as speech and writing; these belong to it more than to us ourselves; this is why the outer world can more readily attain an understanding about it than we ourselves are able to. However, in the

---

1. These three Goethe maxims are referred to throughout this chapter. In the manuscript Cassirer wrote out only the first lines of maxim 391, followed by ellipses. The numbering indicates that Cassirer used Hecker's edition: *Maximen und Reflexionen*, Schriften der Goethe-Gesellschaft, 21, ed. Max Hecker (Weimar: Verlag der Goethe-Gesellschaft, 1907), pp. 76–77.—Eds.

2. Goethe, *Wisdom and Experience*, ed. Ludwig Curtis and Hermann Weigand, trans. H. Weigand (New York: Pantheon, 1949), p. 135. Maxims 392–393 are not translated in *Wisdom and Experience*.—Eds.

outer world one senses that in order to really be clear about this, it is necessary to learn as much as possible about what we have experienced. This is why people are so greatly interested in youthful beginnings, stages of education, biographical details, anecdotes, and the like.]

Here [we have the] attempt to reconstruct life according to the character of its being and the way in which we ourselves and others can come to know it according to the kind of knowledge that we can have of it. Both questions belong together inherently, for human life is conscious of itself. It does not simply exist; rather, it "knows of itself" and this "knowing of itself" is constitutive for it, defines its specific difference. Goethe attempts to distinguish three levels here.

[First Level:] Life is given to us in the form of "monadic" being—a "being" that is not to be understood, however, as at rest in itself, but as a process, as movement—the "stream of consciousness"[3] which constantly flows and knows neither rest nor quiet.

We must take it as a primary phenomenon [*Urphaenomen*] without attempting to give an "explanation" of it. Must I not also simply accept (admit) myself insofar as the *monas* remains unknown, but not a "mysterium"? It is, rather, unknown and revealed to all, the primary revelation itself.[4]

[Second Level:] The second thing that Goethe distinguishes here is "becoming aware" in the sense of doing—both action and reaction. The "life" of the *monas* does not remain a kind of closed existence. It comes forth "to the outside" and testifies to its own existence by being effective and reactive. It is only through this form of activity that we find the *monas* in a new sense: as something internally unbounded, as externally bounded.[5]

---

3. See William James, *The Principles of Psychology*, 2 vols. (London: Macmillan, 1901), vol. 1, chap. 9, "The Stream of Thought," p. 239: "*In talking of it* [consciousness] *hereafter, let us call it the stream of thought, of consciousness, or of subjective life.*"—Eds.

4. *Marginal note:* Urworte, Orphisch: Δαιμχν.—Cassirer. See Goethe's verse "Δαιμων, Daemon" from "Primal Words—Orphic," in Goethe, *Selected Poems*, ed. Christopher Middleton, trans. Michael Hamburger et al. (Boston: Suhrkamp/Insel, 1983), p. 231: "As stood the sun to the salute of planets / Upon the day that gave you to the earth / You grew forthwith, and prospered, in your growing / Heeded the law presiding at your birth. / Sibyls and prophets told it: You must be / None but yourself, from self you cannot flee. / No time there is, no power, can decompose / The minted form that lives and living grows." Goethe, "Urworte, Orphisch: Δαιμων, Dämon," *WA*, Abt. 1, vol. 3, p. 95.—Eds.

5. Cf. Fichte: the I limits, defines itself through a not-I.—Cassirer. Reference to Fichte, "System der Sittenlehre nach den Principien der Wissenschaftslehre," in *Sämmtliche Werke*, ed. J. H. Fichte, 8 vols. (Berlin: Verlag von Veit & Comp., 1845), vol. 4, p. 93.—Eds.

> Und dem *un*bedingten Triebe
> Folget Freude, folget Rath;
> Und dein Streben, sei's in Liebe,
> Und das Leben sei die That.[6]

"Moral" striving does not remain isolated within itself. It gives up its centripetal (ego-centric) movement, the "rotating movement of the *monas* around itself." It turns to the outside, to others; it gives itself over to the "world" and thereby to "externalities," to τύχη (the second level of the "Primal Words").[7] Now the "I," the *monas*, is no longer "unconditioned," no longer absolute and self-satisfied. It "conditions" itself by turning to other living things. The primary phenomenon of the "I" comes together with the primary phenomenon of love. And from love follows the act. (Insufficiently expressed: the *monas*, the "I," as an "individual" turns toward the "social" world. The ethical primary phenomenon: the "I" recognizes others "next" to it, "outside" itself, not *extra* but rather *praeter nos* and enters into an active relationship toward them.)[8] In its regard for others, mankind observes the first clarification about itself. It can never, according to Goethe's basic conviction, attain a view of itself by means of mere self-study: by introspection never, but through action. Try to do your duty, and you know your mettle straightway.[9] Mankind can only recognize itself in others. By introspection no man can discover his inmost heart (Tasso).[10]

---

6. Goethe, "Wanderlied," *WA*, Abt. 1, vol. 3, p. 58. "And the *un*conditioned drives / follow rapture, follow wisdom; / And your striving, should be Love, / And your life should be Action."—Eds.

7. See Goethe's verse "TYXH, Chance" from "Primal Words—Orphic," in *Selected Poems*, p. 231: "Strict the limit, yet a drifting, pleasant, / Moves around it, with us, circling us: / You are not long alone, you learn decorum, / And likely act as any manjack does: / It comes and goes, in life, you lose or win, / It is a trinket, toyed with, wearing thin. / Full circle come the years, the end is sighted, / The lamp awaits the flame, to be ignited." "Urworte. Orphisch. TYXH, das Zufällige," *WA*, Abt. 1, vol. 3, p. 95.—Eds.

8. Cf., again Fichte, *Sittenlehre*.—Cassirer. Probably a reference to the discussion of the "Freedom of the other" in Fichte's "System der Sittenlehre nach den Principien der Wissenschaftslehre," in *Sämmtliche Werke*, vol. 4, pp. 221f.—Eds.

9. Goethe, *Maximen und Reflexionen*, no. 442, p. 93: "Wie kann man sich selbst kennen lernen? Durch Betrachten niemals, wohl aber durch Handeln. Versuche, deine Pflicht zu thun, und du weisst gleich, was an dir ist." *Wisdom and Experience*, p. 208: "How can one learn to know oneself? Introspection is a hopeless method, whereas action may lead to success. Try to do your duty, and you know your mettle straightway."—Eds.

10. See *Torquato Tasso*, *WA*, Abt. 1, vol. 10, p. 154. Goethe, "Torquato Tasso," in *Goethe's Plays*, trans. Charles E. Passage (New York: Ungar, 1980), pp. 526f.: "By introspection no man

Third Level: How do others come to know us? Not through ourselves, not by means of how we live or the way we are, but only through objectification, through the "works" that we create. Others can know us only in our work, as what we do and make, as what we say and write, as πρᾶξις and ποίησις[11] (Aristotle).[12] But here a strange turnabout [takes place]. These works no longer belong to us; they mark the first level of "alienation." They stand in an order of their own, which follows objective standards. The "I" can no longer really find itself again in it.[13] It feels hemmed in.

Faust: Alas, the things we do, no less than those we suffer, impose restraints upon our drive to live.[14]

These works belong now more to the outer world than to us. They are also no longer recognizable in full measure. For the being of the works outlives that of their creator. These works are in a certain sense more than their creator and so possess a peculiar kind of "transcendence."[15] The work

---

can discover / His inmost heart; by his own measure he / Will judge himself too small, or else, alas, / Too great. Man knows himself through man alone / And only life can teach him what he is."—Eds.

11. Praxis ("acting") and Poiesis ("making"). On this distinction see Aristotle *Metaphysics* 1025b25 and *Nicomachean Ethics* 1140a1–22.—Eds.

12. Cf. Bühler on language as Poiesis.—Cassirer. Bühler, *Sprachtheorie* (Jena: G. Fischer, 1934), pp. 52–53.—Eds.

13. Spricht die Seele. Cf. Simmel, the "Tragedy of culture," that it forces the I into alien forms.—Cassirer. See Schiller's adage "Sprache": "Warum kann der lebendige Geist dem Geist nicht erscheinen? / *Spricht* die Seele, so spricht, ach! schon die *Seele* nicht mehr." From "Votivtafeln," no. 41, *Sämtliche Werke*, Säkular-Ausgabe, 16 vols., ed. Eduard von der Hellen (Stuttgart and Berlin: J. G. Cotta, 1904), vol. 1, p. 149. "Why can the living spirit never to the spirit appear? / Speaks the soul, then what speaks, alas, is the soul no more." The other reference is to Georg Simmel, "Der Begriff und die Tragödie der Kultur," *Philosophische Kultur: Gesammelte Essais*, 3d ed. (Potsdam: Gustav Kiepenhauer Verlag, 1923), pp. 236–267.—Eds.

14. Cassirer writes: "ach unsre Taten selbst, so gut als unsre Leiden / Sie *hemmen* unseres Lebens Drang." See *Faust*, lines 632f.: "Ach! unsre Thaten selbst, so gut als unsre Leiden, / Sie hemmen unseres Lebens Gang" (Alas, the things we do, no less than those we suffer, impose restraints upon our lives). Cassirer changes "Lebens Gang" (course of our life) to "Lebens Drang" (our drive to live).—Eds.

15. Cf. Goethes Prometheus. I know it, . . . they are eternal—for they are.—Cassirer. See *Prometheus. Dramatisches Fragment*, WA, Abt. 1, vol. 39, p. 201: "So bin ich ewig, denn ich bin!" Goethe, "Prometheus, A Dramatic Fragment," trans. Frank Ryder, *Early Verse Drama and Prose Plays*, ed. Cyrus Hamlin and Frank Ryder, *Goethe's Collected Works*, vol. 7 (New York: Suhrkamp, 1988), p. 244: "So I'm eternal, since I am!" Cassirer changes "I am" to "they are."—Eds.

has a unique οὐσία—a *form* or εἶδος which persists as something enduring. This is its eternity which enables it to have continuing effects that the creative individual, the *monas*, could never foresee. In this sense the saying is true that "What it weaves no weaver knows."[16] Here the "outer world" (which in this case is the historical world) can "come to a better understanding than we are able to ourselves."[17] What Plato's work "is" does not lie enclosed in Plato's monadic "consciousness," because it extends over the centuries. It only becomes clear in the total course of its consequences and interpretations.

The Turn Against the "Primary Phenomena":
The Onset of "Reflection"[18]

With the three claims that Goethe puts forth (maxims 391–393) he wants to retain the "natural" attitude of mind that he feels so close to as an artist. Art requires no "metaphysical" depth—it must protect itself from this supposed deepness. It must be on its guard against it insofar as it does not want to lose itself. For it is concerned with the "surface"[19] of the phenomena, the "many-hued reflection"[20] of life.[21] Goethe wants to pre-

16. See Heine, "Jehuda ben Halevy," from the cycle of poems *Romanzero* (1851), in *The Complete Poems of Heinrich Heine*, trans. Hal Draper (Boston: Suhrkamp/Insel, 1982), p. 660: "Years come round and years pass onward—/ in the loom the spool is whirring, / Busy flying hither-thither—/ What it weaves no weaver knows." See Heine, "Jehuda ben Halevy," *Heines sämtliche Werke* (Stuttgart and Berlin: J. G. Cotta, 1887), vol. 3, p. 126.—Eds.

17. Probably a reference to Kant's comment (Kant, *Critique of Pure Reason*, p. 310), that "it is by no means unusual, upon comparing the thoughts which an author has expressed in regard to his subject, whether in ordinary conversation or in writing, to find that we understand him better than he understood himself." *Kritik der reinen Vernunft*, *Werke*, vol. 3, pp. 256f. (A 314/B 370).—Eds.

18. Litt, *Einleitung*, pp. 4ff.—Cassirer. See Theodor Litt, *Einleitung in die Philosophie* (Leipzig and Berlin: B. G. Teubner, 1933), pp. 5–10, "Die Reflexion," and pp. 10–14, "Die Reflexion zweiten Grades."—Eds.

19. Diderot, "Vers. über die Malerei."—Cassirer. Reference to Goethe's translation of Diderot's "Essai sur la peinture." "Diderot's Versuch über die Malerei," *WA*, Abt. 1, vol. 45, pp. 245–322, esp. p. 254: "A perfect imitation of nature is in no sense possible, the artist is only called upon to provide a representation of its surface." *Diderot's Selected Writings*, ed. L. G. Crocker, trans. D. Coltman (New York: Macmillan, 1966), pp. 161–167.—Eds.

20. See Goethe, *Faust* II, line 4727: "What we have as life is many-hued reflection" (Am farbigen Abglanz haben wir das Leben).—Eds.

21. Cf. Goethe und Platon.—Cassirer. See Cassirer, "Goethe und Platon" (1922), in *Goethe und die geschichtliche Welt: Drei Aufsätze* (Berlin: Bruno Cassirer, 1932), pp. 105–148.—Eds.

serve this standpoint even as a thinker.[22] So he protests against every attempt to go behind the primary phenomena—against every attempt to "explain" them. We should let them stand as they are in all their prominence and incomprehensibility.

Goethe is no systematic philosopher; he does not want to unveil and reveal the nature of the absolute. But he has an incomparable feeling for the primary phenomena which only appear and are, but which cannot be given any further explanation.[23] So we can use him as the true divining rod[24] that can lead us to the hidden treasure of the primary phenomena. He rages against the "Procuress[25] Understanding,"[26] which thwarts this again and again and tries to reduce the immediately certain to something else which is quite questionable (physics, color!). The understanding is always at work to mediate this immediacy, but thereby depriving it of its true and original meaning by this alleged mediation.

This coming to rest and stopping with the primary phenomena—this is

---

22. "Vom Absoluten," Max 261.—Cassirer. See Goethe, *Maximen und Reflexionen*, no. 261, p. 47: "Vom Absoluten in theoretischen Sinne wag' ich nicht zu reden; behaupten aber darf ich, dass, wer es in der Erscheinung anerkannt und immer im Auge behalten hat, sehr grossen Gewinn davon erfahren wird." *Maxims and Reflections of Goethe*, 2d ed., trans. Bailey Saunders (New York: Macmillan, 1908), p. 110: "Of the Absolute in the theoretical sense, I do not venture to speak; but this I maintain: that if a man recognizes it in its manifestations, and always keeps his gaze fixed upon it, he will experience very great reward."—Eds.

23. See, e.g., Goethe's comments to Eckermann, February 18, 1829, in *Goethes Gespräche*, vol. 4, p. 72, no. 2661, which Cassirer cites in *The Logic of the Humanities*, trans. Clarence Smith Howe (New Haven: Yale Univ. Press, 1961), p. 176: "The height of human attainment is amazement; and if the object of a man's amazement is an *Urphänomen*, he will have attained tranquillity; he can have no higher awareness and he ought not to seek anything beyond it; for here is the absolute limit. But to average human beings contemplation of an *Urphänomen* is not enough; they think there must be something beyond; they are like children who, upon peeping into a mirror, instantly turn it over to see that which lies on the other side."—Eds.

24. See Goethe, *Maximen und Reflexionen*, no. 713, p. 158: "Lichtenbergs Schriften können wir uns als der wunderbarsten Wünschelruthe bedienen: wo er einen Spass macht, liegt ein Problem verborgen" (We can use Lichtenberg's writings as a wonderful divining rod; where he makes jokes, that's where a problem lies hidden).—Eds.

25. *Marginal note:* Goethe Urphän[omen]: / cf. Formbegr[iff] und / Kausalbegriff, / Bl. I.—Cassirer. See Cassirer's discussion of *Urphänomen* in "Formproblem und Kausalproblem," *Zur Logik der Kulturwissenschaften: Fünf Studien*, in *Göteborgs Högskolas Årsskrift*, 48, Heft 1 (1942), pp. 109f. This marginal note probably refers to the manuscript of that text.—Eds.

26. See Goethe, *Maximen und Reflexionen*, no. 412, p. 82: "Vor den Urphänomenen, wenn sie unseren Sinnen enthüllt erscheinen, fühlen wir eine Art von Scheu, bis zur Angst. Die sinnlichen Menschen retten sich in's Erstaunen; geschwind aber kommt der thätige Kuppler Verstand und will auf seine Weise das Edelste mit dem Gemeinsten vermitteln."—Eds.

the attitude which Goethe demands of us, especially with regard to the primary phenomena of life, the act, and conduct. Life and activity (in the sense of πρᾶξις and ποίησις) are finalities. There is nothing further to be "known" about them or to explain. We are in them, but we cannot conceive them as objects, cannot observe them from outside or "from above."

But is such an attitude, as Goethe demands it of the artist and practices it himself, possible for the whole of our intellectual life? Do we here have such an "immediate," unbroken unity? No, this brokenness appears itself to be immanent ("dialectical") necessity. For even the understanding's function of questioning belongs to the original and essential functions of the mind, to those through which it truly becomes itself, what it "is." This function stands at the beginning of all philosophy (not only at the beginning of so-called metaphysics)—θαυμάζειν[27] as the beginning of philosophy. It begins with the question of τί ἐστι.[28] That is the onset of the Socratic concept, the onset of reflection. Socrates directs the question toward moral self-consciousness, toward the "I," the monad and its πρᾶξις and ποίησις. He does not ask (metaphysically) whence this allness, but he asks (ethically) about the "What for," about the εἶδος as τέλος.

The transfiguration of "life" through the form of the "question": that is the specifically Socratic achievement. This is what gives life its value: ὁ δὲ ἀνεξέταστος βίος οὐ βιωτὸς ἀνθρώπῳ.[29] But where do we find limits here—where is our protection against the "busy Procuress Understanding"?

What distinguishes Socrates' method from the Sophists', which Aristophanes completely confuses with each other?[30] One important and central thing is common to them both: that they regard life itself and all its forms as something worth asking about, that they do not simply accept it and take it as it is, that they do not accept it as a primary phenomenon. They

27. "wonder." See Aristotle *Metaphysics* 982b11–21; Plato *Theaetetus* 155D and *Philebus* 14C–D.—Eds.

28. "what is." See Cassirer, *Die Philosophie der Griechen von den Anfängen bis Platon* (Berlin: Ullstein, 1925), p. 80, on Socrates' use of the question: τί ἐστι.—Eds.

29. Plato *Apology* 38A5–6. *Collected Dialogues*, p. 23: "Life without ... examination is not worth living."—Eds.

30. A reference to Aristophanes, *The Clouds* (112ff.), in which Socrates is a character who takes money for teaching. See *The Clouds*, trans. and ed. Moses Hadas, *The Complete Plays of Aristophanes* (New York: Bantam, 1962), p. 105: "Strepsiades: That is the Think-shop of sage souls. There dwell men / Who maintain the heaven's a snuffer and we men coals. / They teach (if you pay them) how to win any case, / Right or wrong. / Pheidippides: Who are they? / Strepsiades: I don't rightly know the name, but they are deep thinkers / And fine gentlemen. / Pheidippides: They're scoundrels, I know them. You mean those imposters, / Pale and barefoot. That miserable Socrates is one, / Chaerephon another."—Eds.

cannot do so (assume it is something that is to be "taken for granted"); they want to understand it by means of something else. They ask about its "basis," its "logos." Life is given to us, but we are the ones who have to give an account of it. This "accountability" is the beginning of all philosophical "integrity." But "integrity" without accountability is nothing, is mere ἐμπειρία καὶ τριβή.[31] Socrates and the Sophists understand it in completely different ways. The Sophists' manner of accountability—which in its kind is completely justified and necessary and may not be regarded from the outset as defective—is essentially a kind of intellectual accountability. It conceives an entity or concept to be understood when it is possible to break it down into its elements and to determine their "origins." That is the Sophists' question of the ἀρχή.[32] This question can be answered essentially in historical terms. Sophistic "knowledge," σοφία, is essentially "news" (ἱστορίη).

The Sophists ask whence language, whence justice, whence the state, morality, and so forth. The general answer is: all this exists differently than things in nature do, independently of mankind, and strictly objectively. Rather, it is all the work of people. It did not "grow" (φύσει), as things in nature do, but was "made"; it was fabricated by human beings' νόμῳ; θέσει.[33] For this reason they do not possess the unchanging being of natural things, which exist and remain as they are. They do not merely "exist," they also have "validity" for us, but only as long as the act of positing (of νόμος or of θέσις) this validity continues to be in effect and is not superseded or canceled.

In the field of customary morality there is no thing-like objectivity. Such an "objective" morality would be a logical monstrosity in the eyes of the Sophists, a *contradictio in adjecto*, for it would make morality into a φύσει ὄν (into a physical thing) that existed and endured by virtue of its own "nature," while morality is always the very opposite. Morality exists only by undergoing change, for it is rooted in νόμος, and this νόμος changes into another and then another as the people who set it out and follow it themselves change: πάντων χρημάτων.[34]

31. Socrates, Phaedo; life of the bees and ants, etc.—Cassirer. In *Phaedo* 82 B 1, Socrates compares a life of self-control and honesty without philosophy and reason with the life of the bees, wasps, and ants. The translation of the Greek is "experience and practice."—Eds.

32. "beginning."—Eds.

33. "convention, command."—Eds.

34. Reference to Protagoras frag. 74 B 1 (Diels, vol. 2, p. 228; Freeman, p. 125): πάντων χρημάτων μέτρον ἐστὶν ἄνθρωπον εἶναι ("Of all things the measure is Man").—Eds.

The "basis" of morality is therefore its development. The question about its "why" can only be answered historically. Here and here alone lies its ἀρχή—not in any unchanging "elements" as in the case of the things in φύσις, such as fire, water, air, and earth. Socratic "reflection" is not satisfied with this kind of foundation and explanation. It looks for "another kind of cause" (ἄλλο αἰτίας τὸ εἶδος).[35] The αἰτία, the true αἰτία, cannot be found in a thing's historical origin, at the beginning of its ἀρχή. The true αἰτία lies, rather, in its "end," in its telos.

Despite this radical difference in the sophistic and Socratic way of asking questions, both of them remain united in one thing, which, in a sense, is what is essential to both of them: that they "ask" at all, that they regard not only the being of nature, but that they also—and primarily—regard human reality as something which we need to raise questions about and which it is worth raising questions about. From now on nothing escapes from the sphere of questioning. Nothing is so certain, so taken for granted, so old and venerable that we cannot—for indeed we must—ask: Who are you? From whence do you come? What is the source of your demands? Your authority? Your dignity?

The onset of "reflection" has thereby begun—and it stops now at nothing, at no "last things." It subjects everything to its corrosive "criticism." Philosophy, at least, was henceforth addicted to this criticism and it cannot protect itself from it without forfeiting its own nature. In scholasticism (Greek) ratio sought to become reconciled with (Christian) "belief," but from this union there arose only λογισμός νόθος,[36] a kind of bastard birth (the scholastic "systems" of Nominalism and Realism).

The spirit of criticism in Descartes and in Kant dissolves this "marriage," and it leads to sharper forms of questioning and of doubting. Criticism extends to the limits of skepticism: *de omnibus dubitandum*. But no limits can be set to "reflection," λόγον διδόναι.[37] In the Middle Ages—we read in Wolfram: "Ist zwîvel [herzen nâchgebûr, daz muoz der sêle werden sûr]"[38] but here the opposite [holds]. Doubt is the positive instrument of knowledge and expresses the function of philosophical knowledge.

---

35. Plato, *Phaedo*.—Cassirer. See Plato *Phaedo* 97D5–E5. *Collected Dialogues*, p. 79: "These reflections made me suppose, to my delight, that in Anaxagoras I had found an authority on causation who was after my own heart. . . . I was prepared to give up hankering after any other kind of cause."—Eds.

36. "illegitimate reasoning."—Eds.

37. "give a justification."—Eds.

38. "If there is too much doubt in the heart, the soul turns sour." From the "Vorspruch" to

Here our question arises: How can both be brought together and reconciled? How can we do justice to the Goethean demand for the recognition of "primary phenomena" and to the Cartesian-Kantian demand for "reflection" in knowledge and philosophy? How can we uphold that form of certainty and "immediateness," which Goethe attributes to primary phenomena and at the same time grant the no less unassailable right of "thought," which wants to bring everything before its bench for investigation and accreditation? Is there still some sort of synthesis possible here? Or must this remain an irreconcilable conflict?

This conflict, this antinomy, has been set forth again and again, and has left an indelible mark in particular on the present-day philosophical combatants. All the well-known oppositions can be traced to it. The "intellect" [is] hated, denigrated, and rejected in the name of another deeper, more original substance—that might be called soul, life, or whatever. The striving for "immediacy," instead of the mere "mediations" of thought; intention is called upon in opposition to mere reflection—primacy is attributed to the will and the life of desire, in contrast to the "intellect." These are the main themes of "metaphysics" since its renewal through romanticism. Here romanticism, there positivism; here "reason and science," there their opposite—even their complete rejection—here "irrationalism," here rationalism, here mysticism, here "physicalism"—that is the comprehensive theme of philosophy during the last 150 years (1781–1831).[39] Must we necessarily declare ourselves for one of these alternatives? Or is there a way to reconcile them, which is more than—and principally different from—an eclectic mixture? Can we preserve respect for the primary phenomena, without acting in opposition to the critical spirit, without becoming guilty of sinning against the mind, which occurs when we deny its original right—its autonomy—so that we treat it as something foreign, as an intruder (*l'intrus*)? This is the question that we want to raise in what follows.

[2. Overview of Basis Phenomena]

We return here again to Goethe's Maxims 391–393 in order to attain an overview of the basis phenomena, from which we must take our starting

---

Parzival 1, lines 1–2. In *Wolfram von Eschenbach*, 6th ed., ed. Karl Lachmann (Berlin and Leipzig: Walter de Gruyter, 1926), p. 13. Cassirer quotes only the first two words.—Eds.

39. Probably this should read: "1781–1931." Kant's *Critique of Pure Reason* appeared in 1781.—Eds.

point in order to attain any access to "reality," and in which all that we call "reality" originally is disclosed and opened up. It is not "we," in the sense of logical conscious subjects, who "infer" the existence of reality in the form of *cogitatio* and *argumentatio*. As we will later have to show more fully, this form of inference is not applicable to the basis phenomena. They are "prior" to all thought and inference and are the basis of both. Rather [it] is they themselves that first "open up," that is, reveal, make manifest. They are the "originär-gebenden"[40] intentions in Husserl's sense. They are for us the actual sources of knowledge of reality. If we conceive these sources as obstructed, then the stream of our knowledge of reality will also run dry. The concept "reality" then attains its meaning only to the extent that it is fed by these sources, is filled concretely by them. The basis phenomena and that which reality in all its various forms, directions, and dimensions makes accessible to us; these are not a "result" which we have to infer in a mediated way; rather, they are "the light and the way."[41] We cannot correctly describe them as "something" that "is," as present-at-hand in the sense of an absolute being, nor can their "being," understood in this way, be something "inferred," its absolute being something that can be logically derived (as Descartes, for example, infers the existence of matter, the world of bodies from the *veracitas Dei*).[42] Such derived "being" has nothing to do with real basis phenomena; they are not something which is mediated for us; rather, they are the ways, the modes of mediation itself. To speak in terms of images: they are not something present-at-hand, which in some way comes to us through the windows[43] of our consciousness (whether through the windows of our "sense organs" or through other "mental,"

---

40. "primordially giving." See Husserl, *Ideen zu einer reinen Phänomenologie und phänomenologischen Philosophie*, vol. 1, pt. 1, *Jahrbuch für Philosophie und phänomenologische Forschung* 1 (1913): §§1, 19, 24, esp. p. 36. Husserl, *Ideas: General Introduction to Pure Phenomenology*, trans. W. R. Boyce Gibson (New York: Collier Books, 1962), pp. 45f., 74–76, esp. p. 45: "Every science has its own object-domain as field of research, and to all it knows . . . there correspond as original sources of the reasoned justification that support them certain intuitions in which objects of the region appear as self-given and in part at least as *given in a primordial* [*originärer*] *sense.*"—Eds.

41. Allusion to John 8:12.—Eds.

42. See Descartes, *Meditationes*, Meditatio 6, *Oeuvres de Descartes*, ed. Charles Adam and Paul Tannery, 12 vols. (Paris: L. Cerf, 1896–1913), vol. 7, pp. 79f. *The Philosophical Writings of Descartes*, trans. J. Cottingham et al., 2 vols. (Cambridge: Cambridge Univ. Press, 1984), vol. 2, pp. 50ff.—Eds.

43. See "Monadology" in Leibniz, *Discourse on Metaphysics, Correspondence with Arnauld and Monadology*, trans. George K. Montgomery (LaSalle, Ill.: Open Court, 1902), p. 252: "The Monads have no windows through which anything may come in or go out."—Eds.

spiritual "media"). They are the windows of our knowledge of reality, that through which reality opens up to us.

Basis phenomena do not give us access to external beings that we, with effort, have to "draw into our circle." They are the look that we cast on the world. They are the eye, so to speak, that we open up. In this first opening of the eye the phenomenon "reality" discloses itself to us.

We follow this out here according to the three basic directions or dimensions which also are separated out for us in Goethe's characterization. (We hereby begin by simply taking this three-dimensionality as a fact and hence do not ask about its "possibility" or its "foundation," although in a later stage of our investigation this "possibility" will also have to concern us.)[44]

[FIRST ASPECT:][45] THE PHENOMENON OF THE "*I*," OF THE *MONAS*, OF "LIFE" ITSELF.

This cannot be inferred from something else, but instead lies at the basis of everything else. This is apparent if we describe this phenomenon in a biological and vitalistic way (Bergson's intuition of the *durée vécue*),[46] if we grasp it psychologically (as the phenomenon of self-consciousness of the *cogito* in the broadest sense, as it was originally intended by Descartes), or in the transcendental sense (as the phenomenon of "consciousness in general").[47]

For the present we will ignore all these differences. We take the *monas* in the sense that Goethe gave to it. Here we find only the one, essential thing (essential for all three forms of description—the biological, the psychological, the transcendental), that it is not being (οὐσία as permanence), but

---

44. No discussion of the possibility of this three-dimensionality was found among the manuscripts.—Eds.

45. The enumeration of the "three Aspects" is not uniform: here "1)" is used. All others are written out.—Eds.

46. First formulated in Henri Bergson, *Essai sur les données immédiates de la conscience* (Paris: Félix Alcan, 1889), p. 149. Bergson, *Time and Free Will*, auth. trans. F. L. Pogson (New York: Macmillan, 1913), p. 154: "As we are not accustomed to observe ourselves directly, but perceive ourselves through forms borrowed from the external world, we are led to believe that real duration, the duration lived by consciousness, is the same as the duration which glides over the inert atoms without penetrating and altering them."—Eds.

47. Cf. here esp. the discussion in Paul Natorp, *Einleitung in die Psychologie nach kritischer Methode.*—Cassirer. See Natorp's *Einleitung* (Freiburg i. B.: J. C. B. Mohr [Paul Siebeck], 1888), pp. 1–13, 112.—Eds.

rather a stream and motion, which knows neither rest nor quiet, is bound to no particular "state," to nothing stationary, but is something moving (something in transition from perception to perception, Leibniz: *status ipse praesens, dum tendit ad sequentem, seu sequentem praeinvolvit*).[48] This "monadic" being is therefore not contained in the simple present. In fact, it is not even describable in terms of a present. It is not bound to a particular moment, but rather encompasses the totality of all aspects of life, the present, past, and future—"*chargé du passé et gros de l'avenir.*"[49] By experiencing "myself" as present, I do not experience myself as "being" (ontologically; fixed in different positions in time one after another and to this extent "enduring"). I experience myself as present, as past and as going-to-be.[50]

SECOND ASPECT: THE BASIS PHENOMENON OF "ACTION"

The "monad" as an isolated individual is an abstraction. If we remain within the phenomenological "findings," then we discover that we are never alone, enclosed within the walls of our intrasubjective "consciousness." We not only experience ourselves in "perception" in transition from state to state, but we experience ourselves as having an influence and acting. This influencing and acting is a second essential, constitutive aspect in all our "consciousness of reality." [There is] no consciousness of reality without this original, nondeducible consciousness of action. We do not

48. See Leibniz's letter to de Volder, January 21, 1704, no. 29, in *Die philosophischen Schriften von Leibniz*, ed. C.J. Gerhardt, 7 vols. (Berlin: Weidmann, 1875–1890), vol. 2, p. 262: "Vis autem derivativa est ipse status praesens dum tendit ad sequentem, seu sequentem praeinvolvit, uti omne praesens gravidum est futuro." Leibniz, *Philosophical Papers and Letters*, ed. and trans. Leroy E. Loemker, 2 vols. (Chicago: Univ. of Chicago Press, 1965), vol. 2, p. 869: "Derivative force is itself the present state when it tends toward or preinvolves a following state, as every present is great with the future."—Eds.

49. See Leibniz, "Nouveau Essais sur l'entendement par l'auteur du systeme de l'harmonie preestablie," in *Philosophische Schriften*, vol. 5, p. 48: "On peut même dire qu'en consequence de ces petites perceptions le present est gros de l'avenir et chargé du passé." Leibniz, *New Essays Concerning Human Understanding*, trans. Alfred Gideon Langley, 3d ed. (LaSalle, Ill.: Open Court, 1949), p. 48: "We may even say that in consequence of these minute perceptions, the present is big with the future and laden with the past."—Eds.

50. In this sense as "Life," as a Subject, with a "history," which was and will be; cf. on this Ortega "History as a System," in the Festschrift cit.)—Cassirer. José Ortega y Gasset, "History as a System" in *Philosophy and History: Essays Presented to Ernst Cassirer*, ed. Raymond Klibansky and H. J. Paton (Oxford: Clarendon Press, 1936), pp. 283–322.—Eds.

"experience" ourselves, but rather we experience something that stands in opposition to us, that is different from us, and out of this opposition grows our consciousness of the "object."[51]

This "standing in opposition," this "resistance" is originally encountered in the experience of the will, but not a merely impersonal "It." Rather, we find it originally as a "You." It is not so much something existing on its own, an object, that is merely "different" from us. It is something with a stubbornness of its own and a will of its own, something that limits and disputes the space of our action (not merely something that is or "is found" somewhere "outside," at some other location in space). The "being" of things "in space" is another, more complicated, and later problem. Here we are concerned with a different, more primitive one, with action in a shared action-space.

Biologically we can follow this phenomenon into the animal world. It occurs throughout the animal world, wherever we find a form of "life together," of "living-with-another" (in abstract terms: "social" life). We want to emphasize this one point, that this form of being-with-one-another in the form of having influence-on-one-another is a genuine Basis Phenomenon; it can be derived from nothing else, but is originally constitutive. We find "us" always characterized this way, not just as "living," that is, in transition from one state to another, but also as acting and reacting, as linked and bound to others through action and reaction. This "bond" (in action and reaction) is therefore an original phenomenon, without which there would be no "consciousness of objectivity." A core of this thought [is found] in Fichte's "deduction" of the non-ego from the "moral law."[52] In any case the experience of action is a genuine original experience of access—a "window to being."[53] All "pragmatist" theories of "knowledge" have here their justified root.

---

51. "Voluntaristic" theories of knowledge of reality—Schopenhauer, Being originally as Will; Dilthey's description and presentation of consciousness of reality.—Cassirer. See Dilthey, "Beiträge zur Lösung der Frage vom Ursprung unseres Glaubens an die Realität der Aussenwelt und seinem Recht," *Sitzungberichte der Königlich Preussischen Akademie der Wissenschaften zu Berlin* (1890): 977–1022.

52. See Fichte, "System der Sittenlehre," in *Sämmtliche Werke*, vol. 4, pp. 53–54.—Eds. Cf. also Max Adler's 'sociological' proof of reality.—Cassirer. See Max Adler, *Das Soziologische in Kants Erkenntniskritik: Ein Beitrag zur Auseinandersetzung zwischen Naturalismus und Kritizismus* (Vienna: Verlag der Wiener Volksbuchhandlung, 1924), esp. chap. 7, "Die intelligible Welt," and pp. 460–463.—Eds.

53. Cf. above.—Cassirer. Probably a reference to the "window" allusion in Leibniz's *Monadology*. See note 43 above.—Eds.

[THIRD ASPECT: THE SPHERE OF THE "WORK"]

In the third phase that Goethe describes we approach the "external world" in a new sense; it is the sphere of "works" that now opens up before us. The "work" appears, in contrast to the level of "action" as described in the second phase, as something objective and, to an extent, fixed. The work is the aim of "action"; but in this action it also comes to its end. The expression τελος encompasses both. The movement of action has come to a halt; it has found expression in a work. This involves distancing it from the "I," even alienation from it. But one would be mistaken and too quick to read into this expression of "otherness" only a negative sense, as so often happens (romanticism, mysticism, and so on). It is rather the beginning of a completely new position—of that "position" that only truly leads to an authentic consciousness of reality.[54]

The first step toward this "position" is the work that man "produces." This lasting "product" which is the "deposit" from his works, the "sphere of works," of creations provides the passage, the actual access, to the sphere of "objective" being. From the consciousness of works grows the consciousness of things. Here we first experience what the necessity of things means. The "object" makes its own independent requirements known. It demands and forces us to give it a particular kind of treatment, if it is successfully to become a "work." We must move beyond the sphere of mythic affect (mastery by means of wish)[55] to mastery by means of the work: *Natura non nisi parendo vincitur.*[56] Hence, it is also important that "being" not be given to us as a fully separate essence (being "outside us"), but rather that it be given to us in the medium of the work. Then it is (enduring) equipment for working or tool (Heidegger: "vorhandenes Zeug").[57]

---

54. Kant: "Being is . . . not a . . . concept of something which could be added to the concept of a thing. It is merely the positing of a thing, or of certain determinations, as existing in themselves."—Cassirer. A reference to Kant, *Critique of Pure Reason*, trans. Norman Kemp Smith (New York: St. Martin's Press, 1965), p. 504; Philosophische Bibliothek series: *Kritik der reinen Vernunft*, ed. Theodor Valentiner, 11th ed. (Leipzig: Felix Meiner, 1919), p. 516; see Kant *Werke*, vol. 3, p. 414 (A 598/B 626).—Eds.

55. This whole discussion of "works" is examined in greater detail in Cassirer's essay "Form und Technik," in Leo Kestenburg, ed., *Kunst und Technik* (Berlin: Wegweiser Verlag, 1930), pp. 32–35.—Eds.

56. See Bacon, *Novum Organum*, bk. 1, aph. 3: "Natura enim non nisi parendo vincitur." *Selected Writings of Francis Bacon*, ed. H. G. Dick, trans. J. Spedding et al. (New York: Modern Library, 1955), p. 462: "Nature to be commanded must be obeyed."—Eds.

57. See Heidegger, *Being and Time*, trans. John Macquarrie and Edward Robinson (New

The transition to the "enduring" work (product) and to the tool as something which is "always to be applied in the same way" is what actually opens up to mankind the "objective" sphere, the sphere of "things." It is important to be careful here not to interpret this sphere as some kind of "degradation," as a "falling away," as man's fall from the paradise of immediate feelings of life and from momentary, changing "primitive" activity. The sphere of things is, rather, the sphere of "objectivity." It is the "spirit" of objectivity which we attain to here and, with it, the final "advance" toward reality. Only now is the "window" to reality truly open. A "glimpse" of reality, of objectivity, is now opened up for us by spreading it out before us in the work and in objective, representational language. Here we agree with Noiré's thesis[58] that language and tools develop from a single basic disposition in mankind.

Here we have the three primary phenomena (basis phenomena) before us, for which we ourselves cannot give any further "explanation" and cannot want to:

(1) the I-Phenomenon [*Ich-Phänomen*]
(2) the Phenomenon of Action [*Wirkens-Phänomen*]
(3) the Phenomenon of the Work [*Werk-Phänomen*]

—or also: the Phenomenon of the I, of the You, of the It; the Phenomenon of the Self, the Phenomenon of the "Other" (the so-called problem of "other minds"), the phenomenon of the World ("Object," objective reality).

We can now make the same state of affairs more distinct from a different side, namely from the psychological perspective in the broadest sense. What can "psychological analysis" accomplish here, not of course in the sense of "explaining" the primary phenomena, the basis phenomena— for that would be an impossible undertaking, although it has been attempted often enough by dogmatic (especially "sensualistic") psychology. But what can it do, in order to make them "visible"? Not explanation, but elucidation is what psychology must accomplish if it is to do justice to its

---

York: Harper & Row, 1962), §15, pp. 95–102 (66–72). Here and throughout this discussion Cassirer plays on the word *Werk* (work) in the sense of a product and as a part of the German word for "tool" (*Werkzeug*). Citations of Heidegger's *Being and Time* give the German pagination in parentheses.—Eds.

58. See Ludwig Noiré, *Das Werkzeug und seine Bedeutung für die Entwicklung der Menschheit* (Mainz, 1880), esp. the sec. "Die Organprojektion," pp. 53–58. On Noiré, see Cassirer, "Form und Technik," p. 38 n.—Eds.

task. But do we find even an attempt in this direction in today's psychology, even the beginnings of such an elucidation?

We have to look long and hard, and in fact the whole "naturalistic" approach in psychology, which tries to break down the life of the soul into association mechanisms, remains mute when faced with our question. But the ideal of a descriptive psychology as Dilthey conceived of it, as Husserl presented it, and as Natorp attempted systematically to found it—together brought a new "breakthrough" to the basis phenomena, and we want now to turn to it.

[3.] Relation of Basis Phenomena to Psychology

If psychology is supposed to contribute anything to the resolution of the "basis phenomena," then it can obviously meet this task only if it subjects itself to a certain basic methodical requirement. It must adhere to its autonomy, that is, it must grasp each of these phenomena through its own specific "viewpoint" and not let this viewpoint be prescribed from outside. This latter has occurred whenever psychology conceived its highest task and its highest aspiration in competition with the "objectifying" sciences, in particular with the natural sciences. But it is clear that the "basis phenomena" cannot be brought into view that way because these phenomena lie in the opposite direction of that taken by the natural sciences. Natural science as such—no matter how undeniable and indispensable and enduring its cognitive value is—can never exactly subject these phenomena to its point of view, let alone exhaustively know and explain them. For its essential "pathos" and its methodological telos consist precisely in "disregarding" them more and more. We must look in the other direction, turn our gaze around, in order to obtain a view of the aforementioned "primary phenomena." The whole methodological development of psychology in the nineteenth century—and especially the clash between psychology as a natural science and psychology as a human science (Dilthey and his school, Hönigswald's "Denkpsychologie")[59]—proceeded from this state of affairs,

59. See Wilhelm Dilthey, "Ideen über eine beschreibende und zergliederende Psychologie," *Sitzungsberichte der Königlich Preussischen Akademie der Wissenschaften zur Berlin* (1894): 1309–1407. Dilthey, *Descriptive Psychology and Historical Understanding*, trans. R. M. Zaner and K. L. Heiges (The Hague: Martinus Nijhoff, 1977), pp. 21–120. See also Richard Hönigswald, *Die Grundlagen der Denkpsychologie: Studien und Analysen.* 2d rev. ed. (Leipzig and Berlin: B. G. Teubner, 1925).—Eds.

and seen from this point of view these methodological struggles immediately appear in a clear light.

The Ideal of objectifying science. Knowing is objectifying. All knowledge, insofar as it lays claim to any objective validity, insofar as it is more than a merely subjective "opinion" (*"Die 'Meinung' ist 'mein'"*—Hegel),[60] can only be knowledge of objects and about objects and objective relations. To know an object means here nothing other than determining in a definite fashion its place in space and time and thereby also establishing how it relates to other objects at other places in space and time and how it causally depends upon them.

If we follow this path of scientific explanation, of objective knowledge, what becomes of the "psychic" phenomena, especially of those primary phenomena of the "I," of "willing," and so on? The answer is simple: they disappear, because they are now behind our backs and the turn in viewpoint that would be necessary in order to make them visible again lies completely outside the methodological possibilities and the methodological competence of objective science.

This is immediately obvious in the phenomenon of the "I." For Descartes, the I in the *cogito* is still a genuine primary phenomenon, a basis phenomenon. It is not derived by inference;[61] it is intuitively grasped. But

---

60. Untranslatable pun: The opinion is mine. See Hegel, *Vorlesungen über die Geschichte der Philosophie*, vol. 1, *Sämtliche Werke*, vol. 17, p. 40: "Eine Meinung ist eine subjektive Vorstellung, ein beliebiger Gedanke, eine Einbildung, die so oder so, und ein Anderer anders haben kann;—eine Meinung ist *mein*, sie ist nicht ein in sich allgemeiner, an und für sich seyender Gedanke." *Hegel's Lectures on the History of Philosophy*, trans. E. S. Haldane, 3 vols. (London: Routledge & Kegan Paul, 1892), vol. 1, p. 12: "An opinion is a subjective conception, an uncontrolled thought, an idea which may occur to me in one direction or in another: an opinion is mine, it is in itself a universal thought which is existent in and for itself." Cassirer likely has in mind Hegel's famous play on *das Meinen* ("opinion") and *das Mein* ("mine," "what is mine") in the first chapter of the *Phänomenologie des Geistes*: "Die sinnliche Gewissheit; oder das Diese und das Meinen" ("Sense-Certainty: or the 'This' and 'Meaning'"). See *The Phenomenology of Spirit*, trans. A. V. Miller (Oxford: Oxford Univ. Press, 1977), secs. 90–110.— Eds.

61. Cogito ergo sum is only apparent, cf. esp. Objectiones.—Cassirer. See Descartes, *Objectiones, Secundæ Responsiones, Oeuvres de Descartes*, vol. 7, p. 140: "neque etiam cùm quis dicit, *ego cogito, ergo sum, sive existo*, existentiam ex cogitatione per syllogismum deducit, sed tanquam rem per se notam simplici mentis intuitu agnoscit." *The Philosophical Writings of Descartes*, vol. 2, p. 100: "When someone says 'I am thinking, therefore I am, or I exist,' he does not deduce existence from thought by means of a syllogism, but recognizes it as something self-evident by a simple intuition of the mind."—Eds.

this intuition dissolves in English empiricism. Of course Hobbes declares that of all phenomena τὸ φαίνεσθαι[62] is the most fundamental and admirable, but this means something quite different, even directly opposite, for him than it does for Descartes. For he does not put the emphasis on the phenomenon of perception as an act, but on that which "appears" in this act, on the phenomenon in an objective sense, and what "appears" according to him is necessarily a body.

The twofold nature, the dualism of *substantia cogitans* and *substantia externa*, is only an illusion. Only bodies are given to us, and "sensation" is nothing but a physical reaction. The I-experience is thereby eliminated without a trace. This is accomplished in a different way with Hume: "real" (datum) is just the individual sensation, the supposed "I" is nothing but a "bundle of perceptions,"[63] a mere name for a plurality of perceptions. It is well known how this radical elimination of the "I" affected all of nineteenth-century psychology.[64] This psychology was not merely a psychology without a soul, it was actually a "psychology without a 'subject.' "[65] The same "reduction" is suffered by the other "basis phenomena," especially the phenomena of feeling and of willing. They too, if they are to be made visible at all, if they are to "appear" before the gaze of psychology as a natural science, must first undergo a radical transformation. The program

---

62. Hobbes, *De corpore*, *Thomae Hobbes Malmesburiensis Opera Philosophica, quae Latine scripsit, omnia* (Amsterdam, 1668), vol. 1, pp. 147–261, pt. 4, chap. 25, pp. 192f.: "Phænomenôn autem omnium quæ propè nos existunt, id ipsum τὸ φαίνεσθαι est admirabilissimum." *Hobbes Selections*, ed. Frederick J. E. Woodbridge (New York: Scribner's, 1930), p. 105: "Of all the phenomena or appearances which are near us, the most admirable is apparition itself, τὸ φαίνεσθαι."—Eds.

63. See Hume, *Treatise of Human Nature*, ed. L. A. Selby-Bigge (Oxford: Clarendon Press, 1896), bk. 1, pt. 4, p. 252: "But setting aside some metaphysicians of this kind, I may venture to affirm of the rest of mankind, that they are nothing but a bundle or collection of different perceptions. . . ."—Eds.

64. Cf. esp. Mach's theory of the I.—Cassirer. See Ernst Mach, *Die Analyse der Empfindungen und das Verhältnis des Physischen zum Psychischen*, 2d ed. (Jena: Gustav Fischer, 1900), pp. 16–17: "Nicht das *Ich* ist das Primäre, sondern die Elemente (Empfindungen). . . . Das Ich ist unrettbar." Mach, *The Analysis of Sensations and the Relation of the Physical to the Psychical*, trans. C. M. Williams, rev. Sydney Waterlow (Chicago: Open Court, 1914), pp. 23f.: "The primary fact is not the ego, but the elements (sensations). . . . The ego must be given up."—Eds.

65. Friedrich Albert Lange coined this phrase in the second edition of his *Geschichte des Materialismus und Kritik seiner Bedeutung in der Gegenwart* (Iserlohn: J. Baedeker, 1875), p. 381. Lange, *The History of Materialism*, auth. trans. E. C. Thomas (New York: Arno Press, 1974).—Eds.

of this transformation has been most precisely and consistently developed by Münsterberg.⁶⁶

Here the goal [is] attained; the "psychical" is completely transformed into the physical, because it can only be exhibited and known as physical (that is, as capable of being ordered into spatial and temporal relationships). No other ideal of knowledge exists besides this causal ordering. In Münsterberg himself this "monism" [is] corrected through his theory of value.⁶⁷ But this "value" is something that cannot be grasped psychologically. It is an altogether different matter. Psychology is and remains a natural science, and as such it excludes everything mental, "noetic," and leaves it for a meta-psychological and "meta-physical" doctrine of value.

This process of exclusion goes further within psychology. "Naturalistic" psychology has been not exclusively, but essentially, a psychology of perception. All other phenomena were somehow "incomprehensible" for it and, because of this incomprehensibility, suspicious. It either left these phenomena aside, or it sought to describe them in the language of the psychology of perception, to translate them into that dimension.

In this way the phenomenon of "thought" was discovered in this psychology very late and by means of strange detours. See the beginnings of Külpe's *Denkpsychologie*, with its experiments using test subjects and the supposedly "objective" registering of their reports!⁶⁸ See Bühler's descrip-

---

66. On Münsterberg's Psychology and its methodical Program, see two essays by Jonas Cohn (Sep!). Cf. under Ausdrucksfunktion *MS*.—Cassirer. This is a reference to Cohn's essays "Münsterbergs Versuch einer erkenntnistheoretischen Begründung der Psychologie," *Vierteljahrsschrift für wissenschaftliche Philosophie* 24 (1900): 1–22, and "Der psychische Zusammenhang bei Münsterberg," *Vierteljahrsschrift für wissenschaftliche Philosophie und Soziologie* 26, N. F. 1 (1902): 1–20. Cassirer's parenthetical comment "(Sep!)" means that he had offprints (German: *Separata*) of these essays. The comment "Cf. under Ausdrucksfunktion *MS*" probably refers to the fifty-three-page manuscript with the heading "Ausdrucksfunktion" in Beinecke envelope 119. On p. 20 in section "Obj. Ausdr. VIII" of this manuscript Cassirer again makes reference to two essays by Jonas Cohn on Münsterberg in the "Vierteljahrsschr. f. wiss. Phil." and adds "(s. Separata)." Cassirer's collection of offprints is now in the library at the University of Illinois, Chicago. Hugo Münsterberg's psychology is oriented toward James' Pragmatism. See, e.g., Münsterberg, *Psychology and the Teacher* (New York: D. Appleton, 1909), p. 116: "The doings of man determine his possibilities of experience. . . . Our actions shape our knowledge."—Eds.

67. See Hugo Münsterberg, *The Eternal Values* (Boston and New York: Houghton Mifflin, 1909).—Eds.

68. See Oswald Külpe, *Grundriss der Psychologie: Auf experimenteller Grundlage dargestellt* (Leipzig: Wilhelm Engelmann, 1893), pp. 9–10: "Descriptions of the experiences must be determined exclusively through the objectivity of the observer."—Eds.

tion of *Denkpsychologie* and its "discovery."[69] It is difficult for us today to regard that as a discovery. It seems like a triviality. Thought [is] here characterized only negatively as a "non-intuitive experience."[70] This holds in a similar way for feeling and willing. The Lange-James theory of emotion [states]: We do not cry because we are sad; rather, we are sad because we cry.[71] [In] Münsterberg's theory of the Will, *Will* [is] reduced to the "sensations in muscles."[72]

We always find the same tendency: thought, feeling, willing are not primary phenomena, basis phenomena, that explain themselves, that simply "appear and are."[73] They can be truly grasped and understood scien-

69. See Karl Bühler, *Die Krise der Psychologie* (Jena: Gustav Fischer, 1927), p. 12: "A group of young Psychologists working with Külpe in Würzburg extended the sphere of their research to experiments dealing with thought and the Will. And see what they found! Even their first attempts revealed a twofold division in the manner and the lawfulness of thoughts. Thoughts ... follow—in well ordered, disciplined thought—not the law of association, but the demands of the objects of thought."—Eds.

70. [August] Messer, *Empfindung und Denken.*—Cassirer. From 2d ed. (Leipzig: Quelle & Meyer, 1924), p. 5: "If we talk about objects perceived through the senses or are concerned with such things in thought, it is by no means always so that they appear to us before the mind's eye. And how much of that about which we speak or think cannot be made intuitive at all! Nonetheless we can think of or 'mean' it, and this 'thinking' and 'meaning' is just as non-perceptual or non-intuitive as that which we are thinking of or 'mean.' "—Eds.

71. Perhaps a reference to the joint publication of their theories in Carl Georg Lange and William James, *The Emotions* (Baltimore: Williams & Wilkins, 1922). Cassirer is paraphrasing James' discussion in his *Principles of Psychology*, vol. 2, p. 450: "The hypothesis here to be defended says that ... the one mental state is not immediately induced by the other, that the bodily manifestations must first be interposed between, and that the more rational statement is that we feel sorry because we cry, angry because we strike, afraid because we tremble, and not that we cry, strike, or tremble, because we are sorry, angry, or fearful, as the case may be."—Eds.

72. See Hugo Münsterberg, *Die Willenshandlung: Ein Beitrag zur physiologischen Psychologie* (Freiburg i. B.: J. C. B. Mohr [Paul Siebeck], 1888), p. 109, where he upholds the view "that the order of conscious phenomena is conditioned by the lawful course of material events."—Eds. Cf. also Russell, The analysis of 'desire' and 'will' in the *Analysis of Mind*. On this, Main-MS!—Cassirer. Cassirer refers in another part of this manuscript (184c) again to Russell's *Analysis of Mind* with respect to James (see below, the section entitled "Significance of Basis Phenomena for Theory of Knowledge). This could be the "Main-Manuscript" insofar as it presents the "basis phenomena."—Eds.

73. The manuscript reads "erscheinen und sind"; see Goethe, *Zur Farbenlehre*, *WA*, Abt. 2, vol. 1, p. xxxvi: "Vom Philosophen glauben wir Dank zu verdienen, dass wir gesucht die Phänomene bis zu ihren Urquellen zu verfolgen, bis dorthin, wo sie bloss erscheinen und sind, und wo sich nichts weiter an ihnen erklären lässt." Goethe, "Theory of Color: Didactic Section" (pp. 155–298), *Goethe's Collected Works*, vol. 12, *Scientific Studies*, ed. and trans. Douglas Miller (New York: Suhrkamp, 1988), p. 166: "We believe we have merited recogni-

tifically only by making them into something completely different, for which they are immediately "given," so they are [understood] as mere epiphenomena of physical, bodily processes.

How are we to expect a turnabout here, a μετανοεῖν?[74] We must first note that nineteenth-century psychology did not in its entirety swim in this same stream of naturalistic, experimental psychology. There were thinkers who opposed it, who acutely grasped the problem and declared that primary phenomena could not be made visible by following this course and hence called for a return to simple observation, to "immediate experience." Theodor Lipps in particular upheld such a psychology of experience. In opposition to natural-scientific psychology he urged with increasing sharpness the primordial right of introspection and sought to bring it to bear in all his writings.[75] He was the psychologist who most decisively prepared the way for Husserl's phenomenology. Thus he was led far beyond a mere psychology of perception. He distinguished among the phenomena of feeling, willing, and thinking as different underived classes of psychical phenomena which cannot be reduced to mere sensation. (An old division, which was already clear in the eighteenth century, especially in Tetens,[76] but which Lipps fills with new content. The clearest and briefest presentation is in his work: *Vom Fühlen, Wollen und Denken*.)

In his unusual and often quite self-willed descriptions of these basic phenomena, Lipps takes nonetheless a very significant step that is in contrast to the psychology of the time. For he brings a whole aggregate of phenomena bit by bit back into view for psychology, which it had lost sight of. Feeling, willing, thinking is a division taken without special concern, and without any previous scientific preparation, from everyday, prescientific language and yet—perhaps because of this—it opens up again a new, deeper dimension for psychology that it had overlooked and underestimated all too greatly in its "sensualistic" form.

---

tion by the philosopher for our attempt to trace the phenomena to their origins where they simply appear, exist, and allow for no further explanation."—Eds.

74. "a change of mind."—Eds.

75. See, e.g., Theodor Lipps, *Vom Fühlen, Wollen und Denken: Eine psychologische Skizze*, Schriften der Gesellschaft für psychologische Forschung, vols. 13 and 14 (Leipzig: Johann Ambrosius Barth, 1902), p. 5: "As regards feeling, we are only concerned . . . with whatever appears to me, or, to be more precise, with how I *appear* to myself."—Eds.

76. The feeling, willing, thinking distinction is outlined in Johann Nicolaus Tetens, *Philosophischer Versuch über die menschliche Natur und ihre Entwickelung* (Leipzig, 1777), as *Gefühl, Willenskraft*, and *Denkkraft*.—Eds.

Feeling, willing, thinking:[77] we could go so far as to use these as chapter titles for the three primary phenomena that Goethe speaks about (Maxims 391–393).[78]

Feeling could serve as the expression of "life," the *monas*, *willing* as the expression of action or influence on others, and finally *thinking* as expression of that objectification or creation of distance that has its visible expression in the "work" (*Opus operatum*). From here, Lipps finds the way back to the "buried" problems of psychology, especially the way back to the "I." He fights against and ridicules the "psychology without an I." The I regains its central position and it becomes the particular focal point of Lipps' entire doctrine of feeling. According to Lipps, feelings constitute the I — namely the I as it is immediately experienced by me at every moment of my life—while the contents of sensations constitute the perceptual image of the objective world. It is the same if I say: "I feel" or "I feel myself."[79]

We can follow psychology's turn back to the true basis phenomena from yet another side. This time it did not emerge from within itself and its own immanent work but rather through the work of the thinkers who were the sharpest critics of psychologistic claims to unity, a claim set forth in an extreme way, for example, by Lipps, for whom even logic, ethics, aesthetics, and so on, are all only subdivisions of psychology. Here the decisive criticism of Husserl took effect—a criticism which Lipps recognized and which plays an essential role in the last phase of his work. The transition from "psychologism" to phenomenology is characteristic of this phase.

But even prior to this, an essential impetus came from quite a different side, from critical or "transcendental" philosophy. It began (with Cohen) by following the path shown by Kant. Transcendental philosophy had initially asked primarily about the "possibility" of mathematics and mathematical natural science and sought to construct a "system of axioms" for both. But with Natorp's *Einführung in die Psychologie nach kritischer Methode* [Intro-

---

77. *Marginal note:* For "Feeling" / cf. also Cohen's concept of F[eeling]! / Kant's Concept of the Aesthetic, / cf. 53ff. etc. / For the Kantian Division into faculty of knowledge, the feeling (of Lust and Unlust) / and faculty of desire / cf. ibid. p. 159.—Cassirer. Hermann Cohen's *Kants Begründung der Ästhetik* (Berlin: Dümmler, 1899) contains a discussion (pp. 153–155) of the concept of feeling as the effect of the nervous system itself upon consciousness. On p. 159, feeling is defined in the sense of pleasure and displeasure as a capacity of the soul which mediates between cognition and desire.—Eds.

78. Cf. Blatt [sheet] B1) B2!).—Cassirer. The manuscript of this text (184c) contains pages marked Blatt B1 and B2, the introduction to the notion of "basis phenomena."—Eds.

79. Cf. Lipps above, p. 2 and passim.—Cassirer. The quotation in *Vom Fühlen, Wollen und Denken*, p. 2: "So ist es auch Dasselbe, ob ich sage 'Ich fühle', oder 'Ich fühle mich'."—Eds.

ducton to psychology according to the critical method] a new kind of question was raised giving distinct expression to this characteristic "transformation." Psychology is now principally regarded as outside the sphere of objectifying knowledge, especially the sphere of natural science. Its path and its goal are diametrically opposed to those of natural science. It does not proceed forward toward things but turns backward: to "subjectification" instead of "objectification"—"minus"-direction instead of "plus"-direction. New and original in Natorp's foundation of psychology is that he opposes the one-sidedness of the objectifying method of natural science and on the other hand that he fully recognizes the rigorous and in a sense exclusively scientific character of this method. He does not therefore set up a method of his own, so to speak, a self-sufficient "human scientific" method which is supposed to be based on pure "introspection" or "intuition." According to him it is an error to think that the "immediate" in life can also be *known* immediately in the sense of the "philosophy of life," intuitionism, and so forth.

Life, the subject, and so on, may be πρότερον τῇ φύσει,[80] but it is in no way πρότερον πρὸς ἡμᾶς.[81] It can be made visible only indirectly—by asking about the "objective" structure's "subjective" sources and "origins." That is the unique "reconstructive" method of Natorp's psychology.[82] It prevents us from immediately "seeing" the primary phenomena, for no science can arise from seeing, since it requires proof and reasoned justification. But it stresses and recognizes that the founding of subjectivity must always take place in a very different way from objectivity. Knowledge of the subjective is by no means immediately given knowledge. It is, rather, knowledge which we must acquire and whose attainment can only be achieved by the indirect means of a detour through objectivity. Only by means of a reconstructive analysis from "factual knowledge," objective knowledge, can we attain knowledge of the forces that generate this knowledge and have brought it forth.

The complete plan of Natorp's psychology was never carried out; it remained a torso. It never had a direct influence on the development of psychological thought; it remained a completely foreign element, an

---

80. "by nature." See Aristotle *Physics* 184a16ff., *Metaphysics* 1029b 3–13, *Posterior Analytics* 71b33, *Nicomachean Ethics* 1095b 2–4.—Eds.

81. "previous with respect to us."—Eds.

82. On this see my Natorp essay and *The Philosophy of Symbolic Forms*, vol. 3.—Cassirer. See "Paul Natorp," *Kant-Studien* 30 (1925): 273–298, esp. 286–288; and *PSF*, vol. 3, pp. 51–57, 203 n. 12, 346–348.—Eds.

achievement on the periphery. Only Husserl recognized its fundamental value. In the whole of psychology it went almost completely unnoticed. Even those modern psychologists who stand under the decisive influence of the newer phenomenological approach have not recognized the significance of Natorp's "transcendental" approach. Yet there are important, indirect signs in the development of modern psychology that Natorp's call for reconstruction is also beginning to make headway there. We call attention here to a single characteristic example, to the turn which has taken place in the thought of Karl Bühler. It can be found in his work *Die Krise der Psychologie* and in his *Sprachtheorie*.[83] These two works belong together and explicate each other.

What does Bühler perceive to be the "crisis of psychology," and how does he describe it? Essential is the circumstance that psychology fails in the description of simple and fundamental elements of mental life, that it is not able to do them justice with the means at its disposal. This is demonstrated by means of the example of language. Language is a multidimensional structure containing completely different functions and encompassing them in a unity. It is "expression" or "announcement," "evocation," and "representation" all in one.[84]

But psychology in its present state is incapable of doing justice to this unity because it always selects only one of the aforementioned three aspects and considers it in a one-sided manner isolated from the rest. It cannot really grasp and exhaust the whole of language or of *meaning* in language. According to Bühler, the correct way would be to go from this analysis of meaning and its recognized multidimensionality back to the multidimensionality of the "psychical" itself.[85] A comparison with Kant's question of the possibility of mathematics, of pure natural science is found in Bühler himself.[86]

83. See Bühler, *Die Krise der Psychologie*, pp. 29–62, on "die drei psychologischen Aspekte"; Bühler, *Sprachtheorie*, pp. 24–33, on the three functions of language.—Eds.

84. The term "announcement" is used to translate Bühler's *Kundgabe*, and "evocation" for *Steuerung. Kundgabe* is sometimes translated "expression," but this is used here for Cassirer's term *Ausdruck.*—Eds.

85. Cf. the particular discussions in the *Krise* and the *Sprachtheorie.*—Cassirer. See note 83. Bühler, *Theory of Language: The Representational Function of Language*, trans. D. F. Goodwin (Philadelphia and Amsterdam: John Benjamins, 1990), pp. 30–39.—Eds.

86. See Bühler, *Die Krise der Psychologie*, p. 57.—Cassirer. "The goal of our investigation was a deduction, a derivation of the three psychological aspects from the tasks before which our science stands and from the means at our disposal to investigate them. Whoever is used to Kantian terminology might compare the character of this modest project in a particular

But what has actually occurred here—and what psychological method has been applied? Bühler did not take his starting point either from the psychology of language or from investigations into the psychology of thought in the usual sense, and he leaves the methods of purely "natural scientific" psychology far behind. Rather, his contribution is truly "reconstructive" in Natorp's sense. He begins with what language in fact is, that is, the unity and totality of its meaning, how it brings about meaning, and he distinguishes among the different "aspects" of this meaning (he asks about the "conditions of their possibility"). For each of the aspects he identifies—announcing, evocation, representation—he seeks a particular mode of mental representation, that is, the classification of mental phenomena is derived from them directly, not through pure "introspection." Instead, this classification is indirectly inferred from particular features of the structure of "language." This structure must be somehow "inherent" in the basic mental phenomena, for without this inherent "predisposition," it could not "develop"; it could not become what the functional analysis of the content of language says it is.

This is clearly a new turn in our perspective, and according to Bühler it is the only way to help escape the present "crisis." Another aspect of the results of Bühler's analysis is still more significant for our observations as a whole. For what does this division of "language" into three basic aspects—expression, evocation, representation—signify, and to what does it finally direct us? If we consider it more closely, then we find to our surprise that it refers to the three classes of basis phenomena that we distinguished before and that, for example, occur in Goethe's outlook. The phenomenon of "expression"—that is the way in which the pure "inwardness" of the subject testifies to its own *monadic* being and life. "Expression"—that is the only way in which this inwardness can "appear" or "reveal" itself to the "outside." *Evocation* corresponds to the aspect of an action-situation. No such action-situation [is] possible without "evocation" through sensory "signs" of some kind. These [are] even found in the animal world and [form] the foundation and presupposition of social life as we find it there. Finally, there is the third aspect: representation, the assertion of objective "being" and of objective "states of affairs," or, to put this into the earlier terminology of Lipps: announcement or expression belongs to the sphere of "feeling,"

---

science with the great epistemological attempt to provide a justification of mathematics and 'pure natural science.'"—Eds.

evocation to the sphere of "willing," representation to the sphere of "thinking." The latter, "thinking," should not be understood here merely to mean "abstract" thought. It is concrete thought, that is, the content of all cognitive acts in general, the content of all that leads to the "positing" of something objective (not only a sphere of the I and the You, but also an It-Sphere) and for which it is the indispensable condition. This includes every instance of "perception" insofar as it is not merely subjective sensation but involves a relation to an object, hence, to every genuine perception (for "sensation" without a relation to an object, without an intention to an object is a mere abstraction) as well as to all sensory intuition. Perception, sensory intuition, and thought form an undivided unity in the shaping of the "world of objects" as it comes about through—among other things—language. Language is "saturated" with all three, and on the other hand it is one of the most important vehicles for bringing the object function of perception to complete development.[87]

Here all the different problems we followed out in the critique of knowledge, in Goethe's "primary phenomena," in psychology and the theory of language come together in the question of the functions that disclose and make "reality" accessible to us at all, in the question of their systematic totality and their systematic organization. To this question we must now turn.

[4.] Relation of Basis Phenomena to Metaphysics

We must now make clear the "stratification" of the basis phenomena from the side of metaphysics and its historical development. First, a general comment about the relationship between metaphysics and experience. There is an interpretation and a definition of metaphysics that locate its essence in independence from experience, that see it as making a general statement about the essence of being which is not drawn from experience and which can be neither proven nor refuted through experience. Metaphysics is virtually defined for Kant by its going beyond everything that can be deter-

---

87. Cf. my Congress lecture and Jour. de Psychol.—Cassirer. Probably a reference to Cassirer's "Die Sprache und der Aufbau der Gegenstandswelt," *Bericht über den XII. Kongress der deutschen Gesellschaft für Psychologie* (Jena: G. Fischer, 1932), pp. 134–145, and the French translation ("Le Langage et la construction du monde des objects") in *Journal de Psychologie normale et pathologique* (1933): 18–44. This translation by Paul Guillaume contains four sections (4.2 to 8) not included in the German version.—Eds.

mined through "possible experience," that it in principle "transcends" experience.[88] But if we consider the historical forms of metaphysics, we see that in them this claim to absolute freedom from experience is nowhere realized. They all are rooted somehow "in the fruitful bathos of experience."[89]

How could it be otherwise? How could a generally valid, completely universal statement about reality be attained if we break off every bridge to experience, if we separate ourselves from the earthly kingdom of experience? We do not find such a separation therefore in any real metaphysics—in Parmenides, in Heraclitus, in Aristotle, in Leibniz, in Spinoza, in Hegel. What we find is, rather, that in each case a certain aspect of experience has been posited as absolute and then taken in isolation, whereupon this absolute positing is declared to be primordial, being in itself. It is always a particular feature of experienced reality that is hypostasized this way as *Ens a se* and *Ens per se*.[90] Now it is being, now becoming, now unity, now plurality, now it is nature, now God, now the soul (the mind), now matter, that are posited in this way as "absolute," as fundamentally original. But in all these positings the umbilical cord that connects the metaphysical concept with "reality" is never broken; a particular experience is always kept in store, which now is given not a merely relative, but an absolute, character.

Hence, metaphysics only then stands in radical opposition to experience if this latter itself is defined through a completely arbitrary narrow interpretation of its concept: as the sum of sense-data, impressions, or the like. But in and for itself metaphysics is in no way a turning away from experi-

88. See, e.g., Kant, *Prolegomena zu einer jeden künftigen Metaphysik die als Wissenschaft wird auftreten können*, §1, *Werke*, vol. 4, pp. 13f. *Prolegomena to any Future Metaphysics*, trans. Paul Carus, rev. Lewis White Beck (Indianapolis: Bobbs-Merrill, 1950), §1 "Of the Sources of Metaphysics," p. 13: "First, as concerns the sources of metaphysical knowledge, its very concept implies that they cannot be empirical. Its principles (including not only its basic notions) must never be derived from experience. It must not be physical but metaphysical knowledge, namely, knowledge lying beyond experience."—Eds.

89. Kant, *Prolegomena zu einer jeden künftigen Metaphysik die als Wissenschaft wird auftreten können*, *Werke*, vol. 4, p. 129 n. *Prolegomena to any Future Metaphysics*, p. 122 n. 2: "My place is the fruitful bathos of experience."—Eds.

90. On this method of metaphysics, cf. e.g., Georg Simmel, *Hauptprobleme der Philosophie* [Leipzig: G. J. Göschen, 1910], esp. pp. 30ff., and *Die Probleme der Geschichtsphilosophie [Eine erkenntnistheoretische Studie*, 5th ed. (Munich and Leipzig: Duncker & Humblot, 1923)].—Cassirer. The reference in the latter is probably pp. 196–199, "Metaphysik und Empirie der Historik." Simmel, *The Problems of the Philosophy of History*, trans. Guy Oakes (New York: Free Press, 1977).—Eds.

ence, from the phenomenon per se. It seeks, rather, to give a reading, interpretation, understanding of phenomena, a "reading" which of course in traditional metaphysics usually proceeds such that a phenomenon or a particular kind of phenomena is taken up and then in this isolation is treated as truly essential and primordial, as the "ground of all being." "Metaphysics" errs here not by turning away from experience per se but by screening out certain basic aspects of it. By virtue of this screening out it is not able to make good on its own claim, the claim to provide a total vision and a total interpretation of reality. It always has to repress certain aspects of reality in order to make others visible. It must be "monism" or "pluralism," "materialism" or "spiritualism," idealism or realism, voluntarism or intellectualism.

But each of these theses has to certify itself through some original view of things, must exhibit the source from which it flows, and its claim to certainty, its *quid juris*, consists in this exhibiting of this source. If this is so, then we may assume that the analysis of metaphysics in its historical form can divulge something to us about the structure of knowledge of reality, even though only indirectly, that the forms, the types of metaphysics as they have actually come forth in history result in an indirect representation of this structural relationship— a kind of map of the entire territory of knowledge of reality. This assumption is in fact confirmed: an overview of the types of metaphysics leads us back again to those typical "basis phenomena" that we have sought to distinguish.

Characteristic of the method of metaphysics is the circumstance that it is not satisfied with making "visible" the relevant primary phenomenon, basis phenomenon, that it rests upon; rather, it strives to unravel it, it wants to unveil the veiled image of Sais,[91] it wants to find "the clue" to the riddle of life, of nature, and so on. It believes that it can attain this goal only by establishing that this phenomenon is all-encompassing, is "reality" itself, the core of being, so that there is room for nothing else except as its mere shell, as a completely unessential "empty" appearance—as illusion, as the veil of Maya. But the roles can be completely turned around; what for one thinker is the core of being is mere appearance for another and vice versa. What for the one is the authentic, deep reality is mere illusion for another.

91. Allusion to Friedrich Schiller's poem "Das verschleierte Bild zu Sais," in *Sämtliche Werke*, vol. 1, pp. 207–210. "The Veiled Statue at Sais," in *The Poems of Schiller*, trans. E. A. Bowring (Chicago: Hennebery, 1873), pp. 188–190.—Eds.

So for Parmenides becoming is illusion, for Heraclitus being is illusion; for Plato the "Idea" [is] ὄντως ὄν,[92] while for strict nominalism and empiricism it is an empty fiction, a *flatus vocis*.

Let us trace this through the three classes of basis phenomena:

[FIRST TYPE:][93] THE "MONAD";
THE FIRST: "LIFE, THAT KNOWS NO REST NOR CALM"

It is "a mystery to us and others," but metaphysics presumes to be able to "take down the gates." It wants to open the holy shrine of life, the *mysterium tremendum* of life.[94] This is how the different varieties of the philosophy of life arise. [In] the vitalistic dynamism of the Renaissance (Campanella, *vita, vis*,[95] Giordano Bruno): nature is the realization of divine life, and God is nothing other than this life itself: Deus non est intelligentia exterior etc., but rather *internum principium motus*.[96] From here the way leads directly via mysticism to Schelling.[97]

---

92. "true being."—Eds.

93. This division is not uniform. The MS has "a)" and then "*Second Type*" and then "3/." The headings have been standardized.—Eds.

94. See Rudolph Otto, *Das Heilige: Über das Irrationale in der Idee des Göttlichen und sein Verhältnis zum Rationalen* (Breslau: Trewendt & Granier, 1917), chap. 4, "Mysterium tremendum."—Eds.

95. Tommaso Campanella, *Universalis philosophiæ seu metaphysicarum rerum, iuxta propria dogmata, partes tres, libri 18, duce Deo* (Paris, 1638), pt. 3, bk. 18, chap. 1, art. 1: "Vita dicitur à vi, hoc eft essendi virtute potestateque: ea igitur ratione, qua sunt Entia cuncta, vivunt: et ubi sunt, et de quo sunt" (Life [vita] comes from force [vis], that is, in the sense of effectiveness: and all things live in the same way: no matter where they may be and wherever they may go).—Eds.

96. See Giordano Bruno, *De Immenso et innumerabilibus, Jordani Bruni Nolani Opera Latine Conscripta*, ed. F. Fiorentino et al., 3 vols. (Naples, 1879–1891), vol. 1, pt. 2, p. 158: "Non est Deus vel intelligentia exterior circumrotans et circumducens; dignius enim illi debet esse internum principium motus, quod est natura propria, species propria, anima propria quam habeant tot quot in illius gremio et corpore vivunt" (God is not an external intelligence rolling around and leading [the universe] around; it is more worthy for him to be the internal principle of motion, which is his own nature, his own appearance, his own soul, than that as many entities as live in His bosom and body should have motion).—Eds.

97. *Marginal note:* immediate connection with the *Renaissance*, cf. the dialogue Bruno.—Cassirer. See Schelling, *Bruno oder über das göttliche und natürliche Princip der Dinge: Ein Gespräch, Sämmtliche Werke* (Stuttgart and Augsburg: J. G. Cotta, 1859), Abt. 1, vol. 4, pp. 213–332.—Eds.

Jakob Boehme; cf. Leese, *Von Jakob Böhme zu Schelling*, 1927.—Cassirer. Kurt Leese, *Von Jakob Böhme zu Schelling: Zur Metaphysik des Gottesproblems*, Weisheit und Tat, vol. 10 (Er-

[His] founding of the philosophy of nature [is] based on the concept or, rather, on the intuition of life. What life "is" cannot be grasped abstractly in a concept, for concepts only serve to abstract, isolate, deaden, "mechanize." But there is an intellectual intuition of life that goes beyond all the divisions of the concept, which makes visible [the] unity and fundamentality of the process of life.[98] The mind emerges from it, not as life's opposite, but as its culmination and completion. "What we call 'nature' . . . [is] only the odyssey of the mind. Could the riddle be solved . . . who miraculously fools himself, flees from himself."[99] This is the same basic type of metaphysics as in Bergson: his concept of intuition and of "creative evolution."

SECOND TYPE: THE PRIMARY PHENOMENON OF THE "WILL"

The primary phenomenon of the "will" is found in two different basic forms, according to whether the will is grasped as a "blind drive"[100] or as

---

furt: Kurt Stenger, 1927). This was Leese's doctoral dissertation, written in Hamburg in 1927 under Cassirer.—Eds.

98. *Marginal note:* [The] *starting point* [is] completely monadic: Vom *I* als Prinzip der Philosophie—but then [comes a] *Projection* of the I into the whole of the 'World', of 'Nature' and of 'Mind'. Most developed in the *System des transz[endentalen] Id[ealismus]*. [*An arrow points from* "Philosophie" *to page numbers added later:* 366, 368.] cf. Traest. 94f.—Cassirer. Schelling, *Vom Ich als Prinzip der Philosophie*, *Sämmtliche Werke* (Stuttgart and Augsburg: J. G. Cotta, 1856), Abt. 1, vol. 1, pp. 149–244, and *System des transzendentalen Idealismus*, *Sämmtliche Werke*, Abt. 1, vol. 3, pp. 327–634.—Eds.

99. See Schelling, *System des transzendentalen Idealismus*, *Sämmtliche Werke*, Abt. 1, vol. 3, p. 628: "What we call 'nature' is a poem, which lies hidden in secret, wonderful form. But if the riddle could be solved, we would recognize in it only the odyssey of the mind, and he who miraculously fools himself while seeking himself, flees from himself: for through the world of the senses we only catch a glimpse of that which we seek, the way that meaning appears in words, like the way the land of fantasy appears through a half-transparent fog."—Eds.

100. See Schopenhauer, *The World as Will and Representation*, trans. E. F. J. Payne (New York: Dover Books, 1969), vol. 1, bk. 4, sec. 54, p. 275: "The will, considered purely in itself, is devoid of knowledge, and is only a blind, irresistible urge, as we see it appear in inorganic and vegetable nature and in their laws, and also in the vegetative part of our own life. Through the addition of the world as representation, developed for its service, the will obtains knowledge of its own willing and what it wills, namely that this is nothing but this world, life, precisely as it exists."—Eds.

Schopenhauer—Primacy of Will. Will as Ens a se. Modern Forms: Life as the life of drives—Drives as the foundation of all Being and all Differentiation in Being—economic drives (historical "Materialism"), Sexual drive (Freud). *Marginal note:* This under "History."—Cassirer. Cassirer often brings Schopenhauer together with Freud and the latter together with Marxian historical materialism; see *An Essay on Man* (New Haven: Yale Univ. Press, 1944), p. 21; *The Myth of the State* (New Haven: Yale Univ. Press, 1946), p. 32.—Eds.

something on its own, independent, autonomous, opposed to the mere drives which it governs and shapes. The metaphysics of ethics—as it is most clearly seen in Fichte[101]—emerges from this.

Consciousness of duty, "conscience," breaks through the merely "monadic" form of self-consciousness. It leads to the "reality of the You"[102] as the subject of ethics with equal rights and equal autonomy—individuality [is] only illusion. There is only one divine life,[103] but it is conceivable only as the unity of ethical life. "Nature" itself [is] only a means to the realization of the final ethical goal. Hence, its being is also only to be understood as something mediate, as the sensualized material of duty.[104]

The totality of being is concentrated in a highly unusual way into a single point, "devoured" by the phenomenon of the will, so that even the I-You problem is visible only in terms of pure ethics.

[THIRD TYPE:] THE BASIC PHENOMENON OF THE "WORK"—THE PROBLEM OF CULTURE AND "HISTORY"

The stockpiling of "works" as a persisting remainder of activity gives rise to that kind of being which we call culture or history. "Culture" is distinguished from "nature" (φύσις) by the fact that it is not something which has merely "grown" (φύω, φύεσθαι).[105] It is something "effected"[106] as

---

101. Fichte's *System der Sittenlehre.*—Cassirer. See Fichte, "System der Sittenlehre nach den Prinzipien der Wissenschaftslehre," in *Sämmtliche Werke*, vol. 4, pp. 1–365.—Eds.

102. *Marginal note:* On this cf. Basis phen. (theory of knowledge).—Cassirer. See the section below, "The I-Aspect; the 'Monadic Aspect.'"—Eds.

103. Cf. Bestimmung des Gelehrten and others.—Cassirer. See Fichte, "Einige Vorlesungen über die Bestimmung des Gelehrten," *Sämmtliche Werke*, vol. 6, pp. 289–346. See "Ueber das Wesen des Gelehrten, und seine Erscheinungen im Gebiete der Freiheit," *Sämmtliche Werke*, vol. 6, pp. 347–448, esp. the second lecture: "Nähere Bestimmung des Begriffs der göttlichen Idee," pp. 360–371. "Some Lectures Concerning the Scholar's Vocation," in Fichte, *Early Philosophical Writings*, ed. and trans. Daniel Brezeale (Ithaca, N.Y.: Cornell Univ. Press, 1988), pp. 144–184.—Eds.

104. See Fichte, "Ueber den Grund unseres Glaubens an eine göttliche Weltregierung," *Sämmtliche Werke*, vol. 5, p. 185: "Unsere Welt ist das versinnlichte Materiale unserer Pflicht." Fichte, "On the Foundation of Our Belief in a Divine Government of the Universe," trans. Paul Edwards, in *Nineteenth Century Philosophy*, ed. Patrick Gardner (New York: Free Press, 1969), p. 24: "Our world is the sensualized material of our duty."—Eds.

105. "produce, let grow."—Eds.

106. Here Cassirer plays on *Gewirktes* (something woven) but in reference to *Wirken* (doing or effecting). "Weaving" (*Weben*) is a favorite metaphor of Goethe's for the inner organization

human handiwork, something brought forth by the human spirit. Historical being can be made visible only in this process of bringing forth.

The structure of effects in history "exists" and is understandable for us only by virtue of its manifesting itself in enduring creations. These creations do not need to have a physical "existence," as is the case in the "plastic arts" (the canvas on which the painting appears, the wood or marble of a sculpture). They also can be quite "immaterial," as in the case of the law or the state. The essential thing is that they have somehow "become flesh" (as the law and the state are both "incarnated" customary ethics). The fleeting, temporary, transitory must somehow be held fast; it must become "objective spirit" in Hegel's sense.[107] This occurs only when it becomes condensed and expressed in a system of works—the works of politics (constitutions, law books), works of art, literature, philosophy, and science.

This work-sphere places metaphysics before new tasks. These cannot be dealt with (1) by approaching them through purely monadic being—for every work is as such not that of an individual, but proceeds from cooperative, correlative action. It bears witness to "social" action. "History" and "culture" can be understood only as social phenomena. (2) Nor can the metaphysics of will fully grasp them. For all of these particular creations are not what they are because some conscious beings wanted them to be that way, because we deliberately produced them.

It is of course always tempting to interpret them in this way, to take them as "products," things made according to specific "plans," to find an explanation of "works" by tracing them back to acts of the will. In this sense, for example, myth traces all these works back to "gifts from above." They are all (language, writing, law, the constitution, and so on, but also the various individual tools and knowledge of how to use them) brought to man through saviors (Prometheus and fire) or implanted in man through divine revelation. The question of the "author" of "works" is also answered mythically by projecting it into a higher world, a world of gods, demons, heroes. As soon as this mythical world is lost, as soon as an "immanent"

---

of reality, an ancient notion found, e.g., in Plato's Myth of Er (*Republic* 616–617; *Collected Dialogues*, pp. 840f.).—Eds.

107. Encompasses law, individual and social morality. See G. W. F. Hegel, "Die Philosophie des Geistes," *System der Philosophie*, *Sämtliche Werke*, vol. 10, §488–502. *Encyclopedia of the Philosophical Sciences in Outline*, ed. Ernst Behler, trans. A. V. Miller and Steven A. Taubeneck, part C, "The Philosophy of Spirit," sec. 2: "The Objective Spirit," pp. 241–256.—Eds.

explanation of these "works" or "creations" is demanded and the explanation is limited to the human domain, nothing appears to be left but to trace them to the acts of single persons, to individuals, which join together in their production. This is how contract theories arise, which are applied in different ways to the origin of language, society, law, and the state. This [is] the general answer of the Enlightenment, of classical "Rationalism." But its weakness is obvious; such "works" cannot be grasped this way as the sum of individual acts. They are not based upon reaching agreements, stipulations, contracts, and so forth. Hence, Romanticism rejects in principle the Enlightenment's solution, as we see both in organological theories as well as in a fundamentally different way in Hegel. Yet the Romantics and Hegel share one feature in this act of rejection; they call for a different solution that goes beyond the sphere of individual consciousness and "subjective spirit" because this is the only way the "objectivity" of the "works" can be really understood and guaranteed. They cannot be the results of mere "conventions" and mere "contracts"; they cannot have arisen from the individual's will or from a mere external association of such wills. They must have a different and firmer footing.

But where do we find this footing? In order to find it, both Romanticism and Hegel must move the basis of their solutions into the superempirical and supersensual. Romanticism goes directly back to myth. It conceives of a world of spirits that these works belong to and which they are supposed to stem from. The "spirits of the peoples" in their variety, particularity, and irreducible uniqueness are the creators of poetry, art, law, the state, customary morality, and so on. What is envisioned here is less an overworld than an underworld. At work here are "underworld" forces and out of their volcanic activity the mountain of human "works" rises up. The forces of the earth, the soil, the chthonic gods permit all this to boil forth. This solution is repugnant to Hegel. He strives to liberate this whole process—and here he is in agreement with the Enlightenment—from the darkness of Romanticism and raise it into the bright light of knowledge, of philosophy, the "absolute idea." He wants to make it completely transparent, although he does not seek to grasp it in the sense of a mere philosophy of the understanding, the philosophy of reflection. From this grows his conception of the "Idea" as that agency whose self-development hammers out these works with an immanent, dialectical necessity.

But both the Romantic "spirits of the peoples" and Hegel's "world spirit" are subject to the same objection. Neither has a satisfactory answer. All they do, basically, is to give the question back to us in a different form (the question of the "origin" of "works"). They do not solve the problem but rather give it a new name. For the notions of the spirit of a people or the world spirit, and so on, commit the same fundamental mistake of metaphysical substantialization and hypostatization.

They act like "explanations," but their explanation consists in nothing other than in referring the phenomena, which are to be explained, to some unknown X as their final "underpinning." This concept of substance proves to be just as inadequate when applied to cultural phenomena as does the concept of "substance" in natural science when applied to particular phenomena of nature. Hence, after the downfall of Hegel's metaphysics, a new approach was needed. Once again, the attempt was made to give a purely immanent solution to the problem. The human world—as it is known and given empirically—should be investigated and principles of explanation found in it alone, in the history of mankind.

This is the decisive step taken by Dilthey.[108] He is the decisive opponent of "Rationalism," of the Enlightenment, the philosophy of reflection. He points out again and again that history cannot be conceived through abstract concepts; rather, the only access to it is through the richness of "lived experience" in all its forms. The world of history can only be derived from the structure of lived experience. This is the only way to gain an "understanding" of historical reality.

But according to Dilthey, on the other hand, this "understanding" is to be sharply and radically distinguished from all the different types of metaphysical explanation, all of which he criticizes and rejects.[109] They all move in a sphere of seeming explanations; none of them accomplishes what they promise to do. So Dilthey strives to begin again from below, to show us historical structures *in concreto*, to analyze them and identify their particular conditions so as to make them "understandable." The step from immediate "lived experience" to the work, put simply, is the great, general theme of Dilthey's philosophy of history. In this way, through this synthesis and through this correlation, Dilthey liberates the psychological concept of

---

108. On Dilthey: cf. Spranger's Dilthey lecture.—Cassirer. See Eduard Spranger, *Wilhelm Dilthey: Eine Gedächtnisrede gehalten in der Societas Joachimica zu Berlin* (Leipzig, 1912).—Eds.

109. See Wilhelm Dilthey, *Einleitung in die Geisteswissenschaften: Versuch einer Grundlegung für das Studium der Gesellschaft und der Geschichte*, vol. 1 (Leipzig: Duncker & Humblot, 1883), chap. 4. Dilthey, *Introduction to the Human Sciences: An Attempt to Lay a Foundation for the Study of Society and History*, trans. Ramon J. Betanzos (Detroit: Wayne State Univ. Press, 1988), pp. 303–323: "Final Consideration Concerning the Impossibility of a Metaphysical Status of Knowledge."—Eds.

"lived experience" from its narrow limits, from its merely psychological subjectivity, from which there is no way to gain access to the objective world of history as a κοινός λόγος (Heraclitus)[110] and, in addition, he keeps history as a fruitful bathos of experience, rejecting every merely conceptual metaphysics of history.

This is decisive for Dilthey; for him "lived experience" is neither a psychological nor a metaphysical conception, although it is applied to the problems of both psychology and metaphysics. Dilthey's basic problem is that of creative activity, that is, the activity that gives birth to the "work," to what is deposited, manifested in works and is revealed in them—and *only* in them. The analysis of merely subjective lived experience in the sense of a psychology of lived experience can therefore never be sufficient. It must be supplemented through the structural analysis of the work, of things produced, because only in this way is it possible, indirectly, through reflection on things created, for productive activity to understand itself and to attain clarity about the different directions it takes. Dilthey carries this theme through first in the area of poetry. He is particularly interested in the "personality" of the poet, and he believes that this is the only way to "understand" the work, the poetic work (his characterization of Lessing, Goethe, Novalis, Hölderlin).[111]

But this form of reconstruction from a "lived experience" does not treat it as something merely psychological, as a biographical peculiarity. There is something merely coincidental, accidental, and purely subjective which cannot make the objectivity and particular nature of the work understandable. "Understanding" means, rather, to appropriate the inner process of creation, which is based as much on the conditions of the personality producing a work as on the (teleological) conditions of the structure of what has been produced, or, to put it a better way: of what is to be produced. The work of art, for example, has a structure of its own that can be

---

110. "common notion." Heraclitus frag. 12 B 2 (Diels, vol. 1, p. 77; Freeman, p. 24): διὸ δεῖ ἕπεσθαι τῶι [ξυνῶι, τουτέστι τῶι] κοινῶι· ξυνὸς γὰρ ὁ κοινός. τοῦ λόγου δ' ἐόντος ξυνοῦ ζώουσιν οἱ πολλοὶ ὡς ἰδίαν ἔχοντες φρόνησιν ("Therefore one must follow [the universal Law, namely] that which is common [*to all*]. But although the law is universal, the majority live as if they have understanding peculiar to themselves").—Eds.

111. Reference to Wilhelm Dilthey, *Das Erlebnis und die Dichtung: Lessing, Goethe, Novalis, Hölderlin* (Leipzig and Berlin: B. G. Teubner, 1906); translations of the Goethe and Hölderlin essays appear in Dilthey, *Selected Works*, vol. 5, *Poetry and Experience*, ed. Rudolf A. Makkreel and Frithjof Rodi (Princeton: Princeton Univ. Press, 1985), pp. 235–384.—Eds.

objectively distinguished, for example, from the structure of a work of philosophy or of science.

The individual process of creation by a great artist takes place within this particular general structural regularity. We can imaginatively put ourselves into this productive process; we can creatively witness it because these structural regularities are accessible to us. We can grasp them here indirectly, as through a prism in a great artistic personality. "Lived experience" does not mean for Dilthey a passive, mere re-experiencing; it means a creative sharing in lived experience.[112]

Only by virtue of this creative sharing in lived experience is there such a thing for us as the factum or phenomenon of "history." The possibility of all historical "understanding" rests upon it. To understand historically means to make visible the forces that have left their mark as, or have been condensed into, the works of history. According to Dilthey, political history works no differently. In order to understand its *"res gestae"* we must immerse ourselves in the creative process from which they originally stemmed. By regarding Roman law and the Roman Empire[113] in this way, we can explain the particular direction taken by the Roman will to power and order, not *in abstracto*, but in the way they both are found concretely in a great personality, for example, in Caesar.

Gundolf's analyses[114] are an example of this "personalistic"[115] view of

---

112. *Marginal note:* On this see also Bühler, *Krise*, pp. 23ff.—Cassirer.

113. On Dilthey and Roman law, see Dilthey, "Der Aufbau der geschichtlichen Welt in den Geisteswissenschaften," *Abhandlungen der Königlich Preussischen Akademie der Wissenschaften zu Berlin* (1910), Philosophisch-Historische Klasse, pp. 1–123.—Eds.

114. Cf. Scheler, "Philosophische Weltanschauung," p. 46.—Cassirer. See Scheler, "Mensch und Geschichte," in *Philosophische Weltanschauung* (Bonn, 1929), p. 46. "Philosopher's Outlook," in *Philosophical Perspectives*, trans. Oscar A. Haac (Boston: Beacon Press, 1958), p. 93: "What does history mean to this anthropology? Kurt Breysig has attempted to answer this question in his recent work on historiography. Even if one considers his answer erroneous (as does this author), one must say, in recognition, that here the historical and categorical personalism of being and values has been considerably deepened. Collective forces in history are not simply denied as, e.g., by Treitschke and Carlyle ('men make history'), but recognized. Still, they are always reduced again to *personal causality*. The actual effect of such an anthropology on historical writing proper is most clearly illustrated by the members of the circle around Stefan George who concern themselves with historical questions. The best examples are the works of Friedrich Gundolf on Shakespeare, Goethe, Caesar, George, Hölderlin, and Kleist."—Eds.

115. See esp. his essay "Dichter und Helden," in Friedrich Gundolf, *Dichter und Helden* (Heidelberg: Weiss, 1921), pp. 23–58.—Eds.

history. His works in modern literary criticism have provided the purest, most perfected applications of Dilthey's program. This gives us a new possibility for understanding history as an interweaving of acts and of works, or better: as the correlation of both, the immersion of the one in the other. Personalities live not in their coincidental acts, but in their works, their efforts become the works, the *monumenta,* which as such bear witness *aere perennius* to these creative personalities. Documentation through the products generated,[116] that is the theme of historical understanding, whether this product is a work (*opus*) of art, science, politics, the history of religion, or whatever.

A concluding, fundamental way to try to understand the "works" of culture—their peculiar kind of objectivity—is the method that Kant introduced into philosophy. It calls for the change in viewpoint, the fundamental turnabout in standpoint and viewpoint that Kant illustrated with the example of the Copernican revolution. It does not begin with the analysis of things but rather asks about the specific mode of knowledge[117] in which things alone are "given" to us and through which they can be made accessible to us. This concept of the "mode of knowledge" should be understood in the broadest sense; there is a particular mode of knowledge, the *modus cognoscendi* of theoretical knowledge, in which the lawfulness of "nature" and objects of experience in space and time is disclosed. There is another mode of knowledge (practical knowledge, practical reason) that discloses for us the lawfulness of morality, the "autonomy of the will." Finally, there is a third (the mode of knowledge of judgment) that makes the field of art and its specific "truth" and objectivity transparent to us and its constitutive principles understandable. None of these termini—understanding, reason, judgment—are to be understood here in terms of a faculty psychology but only in a strictly transcendental sense. They are not conceived as "facts of consciousness" but are derived and called for as the "conditions of the possibility" of natural science, of morality, and of art. They cannot be understood in any way as "things," neither in external nor in internal experience, in the "outer world" or "inner world." They must always be thought of as having the character of pure "conditions of experience."

Their validity, their objective dignity may not be confused with the

---

116. An untranslatable pun: "Das Zeugnis durch das Gezeugte, Erzeugte." This line of thought is developed in Cassirer, *The Logic of the Humanities*, pp. 89ff., and *An Essay on Man*, pp. 196–197.—Eds.

117. See Kant, *Kritik der reinen Vernunft, Werke,* vol. 3, pp. 48f. and 606 (A 10–11/B 24–25). *Critique of Pure Reason,* p. 59.—Eds.

existence of any kind of object, be it empirical or transempirical ("transcendental"). Kant does not investigate directly the being of things in the sense of the older ontology. He investigates the factum of specific "works" (the "work" of "mathematical natural science," and so on), and he asks how this work was "possible," that is, on what logical presuppositions and principles it is based. This is quite different from any kind of "psychology," also quite different from Dilthey's human science of psychology. But it agrees with him in that here too structural questions are the focal point, yet these are not, as for Dilthey, particular structures which are actually realized here and now at a particular historical point in being and which must be understood in this particular realization. They must be understood as universal forms—the form of natural science, the form of art.

This is where the final way of inquiring into the "structure" of works begins—the approach of the philosophy of symbolic forms. It goes back to Kant's "critical" question, but it gives it a broader content. All the "works" of culture are to be investigated in regard to their conditions and presented in their general "form." This "form" can be found only through immersion in the empirical material, but this is accessible to us—and here our analysis agrees with Dilthey—only in a historical form.

But as the philosophy of symbolic forms regards things, history is only the starting point, not the end—*terminus a quo* not *terminus ad quem*, a phase, not the goal of philosophical knowledge. The history of language, the history of myth, the history of religion, the history of art, the history of science, all provide the "material" for the philosophy of symbolic forms, and without this material, which it takes from the particular sciences, it would not be able to take a single step forward. Now a turn toward the general takes place that leads it neither to psychological generalities (basic forces of the "psyche") nor to metaphysical generalities ("phenomenology of spirit" in Hegel's sense of showing the dialectical steps of its development and self-evolution), but to an interpretation of "language" in general—its "inner form"—of myth in general, of natural science and mathematics in general. That is no mere abstraction, which would remain a mere *flatus vocis*; it is genuine constitution. (That the question in this sense [is] quite justified [has] now been recognized and acknowledged among psychological researchers; the most important example of this is Bühler's theory of language.)

What the philosophy of symbolic forms claims is that this [turn toward the general "inner form"] is what truly gives us access to the sphere of "works." Now we no longer need to explain these "works" as something from an "overworld" (Hegel) or an "underworld" (Romanticism, spirit of a people), nor do we need to trace them directly to creative personalities in order to give a reading of them and "understand" them. This form of understanding cannot be regarded as unnecessary, but it must be preceded by another, more general understanding, a knowledge of τί ἐστι[118] (of "eidos" or "telos") of language, of art, and so on, as specific yet truly universal and original (because originary) forms of giving meaning.

[5.] Significance of Basis Phenomena for Theory of Knowledge

The different dimensions of the basis phenomena are also valid in the organization of the theory of knowledge, for within each dimension the problem of knowledge acquires a different shape and "meaning," that is, another teleological structure. Something different is understood by "knowledge" in each case because something different is "meant" or wanted in each case. The various "theories of knowledge" that have emerged in the history of philosophy explicate these different "meanings or opinions" concerning the concept of "knowledge." The theory of knowledge is basically nothing other than a hermeneutics of knowledge, but a hermeneutics that in each case takes up a particular "direction" of knowledge and makes it the foundation of interpretation. These different forms of exegesis take in each case a specific basis phenomenon to be the central, indeed the only one. They seek analytically to constitute and so to reduce everything that we call "knowledge' to it. This determines the various basic directions taken by the theory of knowledge.

The task of a truly universal theory of knowledge would be to grasp the relative character of all these different interpretations, that is, to comprehend how each of them is related to a particular fundamental kind of basis phenomenon and how they provide its "interpretation" or "reading." It would then synthetically unite them in such a way that justice is done to every aspect of our knowledge of reality. But the historical course of the theory of knowledge has been quite different; it consisted in taking some aspect to be the truly legitimate, the sole foundation of knowledge and then, by reconstruction (reduction) or derivation (deduction), lending the others surrounding it their relative truth and validity, their "*quid juris.*" But this results everywhere in one-sided perspectives.

---

118. "what it is." See Aristotle *Metaphysics* 1025b9–18; see *Posterior Analytics* 89b23–94a19.—Eds.

In presenting this state of affairs, we may not allow ourselves to be led astray by those conventional schemes according to which it is customary to characterize the different "directions" and "schools" of the theory of knowledge. Here our concern is not with the traditional opposites of realism and idealism, of empiricism and rationalism, but with a distinction that lies much deeper, compared to which these oppositions are merely superficial categories.

Categories such as "empiricism" or "rationalism" relate to the question of the "origin" of knowledge, not in the genetic sense, but in the sense of their "dignity." Must we look for the "origin" of knowledge and the criterion of its truth in "reason" or strictly in "experience"? Is "sense" or the "understanding" the foundation of certainty and of validity, and to which does truth originally belong? The different schools of thought in the theory of knowledge part company according to how they answer this question.

Different from this question of the "mode" and various qualities of certainty and evidence ("sensory" evidence; logical, mathematical evidence) is the question of the *basis* of knowledge. For each of the three basis phenomena that we have distinguished from one another can itself be seen and interpreted in terms of a different mode of knowledge. A specific characterization of the theory of knowledge results from each of these modes. These two aspects—the basis of knowledge (that is, the primary phenomenon that is its basis) as the "source" from which all certainty springs and flows, and the mode of knowledge in which this phenomenon must be "comprehended" and "interpreted"—must therefore be distinguished from each other if we are to attain a systematic overview of the possible forms of the theory of knowledge. If we begin with the definition of the basis of knowledge, then in accordance with our earlier discussions we can begin with a threefold basis, which accords in each case with a particular primary phenomenon. For brevity we call them the I-basis, the you-basis, the it-basis. Each of them is associated with a particular, characteristic form of knowledge: the form of "intuition," of "action," of "contemplation."

A. [The "First Dimension":] The I-Aspect; the "Monadic Aspect"

How can we characterize the original giving of knowledge that goes with and corresponds to the I? What kind of knowledge is [it] that opens up the world of the I as a whole to us and that makes it possible for us to distinguish different structures within it? To this we can at first give only a negative answer: the mode of knowledge that alone comes in question here is specifically different from the kind that is valid in the objectifying sciences, and this includes both the sciences of "outer" and "inner" experience. Objectifying knowledge—knowledge of objects—is directed toward "data" or "states of affairs," toward "matter of fact" or "relations of ideas." Those are the two basic contents of this kind of knowledge. We cannot take a single step beyond them.

This ideal of objectifying knowledge was proposed and established in Hume's *Enquiry*—what cannot be traced to this source must not be anything other than pure fiction or illusion. "*Does it contain any abstract reasoning concerning quantity or number?* No. *Does it contain any experimental reasoning concerning matter of fact and existence?* No. Commit it then to the flames: for it can contain nothing but sophistry and illusion."[119]

Once we take this criterion of (objectifying) knowledge as fundamental, then even the (basis) phenomenon of the I is subject to the same judgment: it is "sophistry and illusion." For the I is neither given to us as a factum (matter of fact) nor can it be demonstrated as "general truth" (relations of ideas). It is not "accessible" to us in either way. "Facts" are accessible to us inductively through observation and comparison. They must be able to corroborate themselves through "perceptions" (impressions). But while there are perceptions of particular contents (red, hard, sour), there are no perceptions of the I.[120]

The I is not given through any particular perception; it is merely a collective name for a bundle of perceptions[121]—a name to which no independent reality of its own corresponds. Even the inductive comparison of perceptions cannot make this reality accessible to us, for where in their mere sum could we find what was not contained in any one of the perceptions itself?

There is also just as little a rational way to push foward to the I. All the general concepts typical of the metaphysics of the "psyche," all "rational"

---

119. II, 135 Ess.—Cassirer. This is a reference to David Hume, "An Enquiry Concerning Human Understanding," in *Essays: Moral, Political, and Literary*, ed. Thomas Hill Green and Thomas Hodge Grose (London: Longmans, Green, 1889), vol. 2, sec. XII, pt. III, p. 135.—Eds.

120. Cf. Treatise.—Cassirer. See Hume, *Treatise of Human Nature*, bk. 1, pt. 4, sec. 6, p. 252: "For my part, when I enter most intimately into what I call *myself*, I always stumble on some particular perception or other, of heat or cold, light or shade, love or hatred, pain or pleasure. I never can catch *myself* at any time without a perception, and never can observe any thing but the perception."—Eds.

121. See Hume, *Treatise of Human Nature*, p. 252.—Eds.

psychology, with its logical demonstrations of the substantial soul, are completely empty; they are also nothing but mere names. So the phenomenon of the I is negated and dissolved in a nominalistic fashion—unless it is possible to find another "access" to the I, different from that offered by (psychological) "induction" or in metaphysical-logical deduction or demonstration. If we are unsuccessful in turning up such an access (outside induction or deduction), then there is no truth in the notion of the I, and we must recognize it to be a "sophistic" illusion.

But there is such an access, and this is the course taken by all the philosophical theoreticians who have built upon the phenomenon of the I in their doctrines of knowledge. The designation that they chose for it is *intuition*. They believed that with this they had named a source of knowledge which is specifically correlated to the I, that reveals the new, unique "figure" ("visage") of the I in a unique, unparalleled way of seeing. This "visage" is primordial, original, but this original can be taken in different ways, differently interpreted in different "modes" of knowledge whereby each modus is indicative of a different level or "elevation" of knowledge, a certain "niveau" of knowledge.

Let us next attempt to distinguish more closely between these "elevations," these "plateaus" of knowledge. Common to them all is their δός μοί ποῦ στῶ, their I-basis, on which they rest and which they take to be given originally (= intuitively). The "*mode* of knowledge" that interprets and renders this originally given original intuition is different. We distinguish here among three levels, which can be designated with the names Bergson, Descartes, Husserl. They all appeal to intuition as a source of knowledge, and for them it is indispensable as the foundation of certainty. For Bergson, the intuition of the I melts into the universal intuition of "life" or of "lived duration" of *durée vécu*. The original form of life and of the I is given to us in this "duration."

This kind of duration is inaccessible and closed off in principle to objectifying observation, to scientific conceptualization. This latter does not grasp duration—it kills it—and all so-called science is nothing other than such a fixation and killing of "duration." We must liberate ourselves from this form of scientific "conceptualization" in order again to obtain a view of the I or of life in its specific significance and in its entirety. That is the character of metaphysical intuition, as compared to empirical "induction" and rational "deduction."

With Descartes it is different. He completely disengages the bond that joins the phenomenon of the I with the phenomenon of life. He attains the phenomenon of the I in pure isolation, in sharp opposition to the phenomenon of life. "Nature" and the "I" cannot be brought under a common denominator. They stand opposed to each other as unbridgeable opposites in a strict methodological distinction. "Nature" is given up to mechanism and mathematicism. What we are used to calling the "life" of nature is merely an illusion (the animals are "automatons" and have no souls).[122] The phenomenon of life shrinks to the phenomenon of the I and thereby to the phenomenon of thought, of "*cogitatio.*" Only in thought and by the power of thought do we grasp our "life," our "existence," our "I": "cogito ergo sum."

This proposition is to be interpreted here in such a way that it does not eliminate the original intuition of the I (its "self-certainty"), but expresses it. For Descartes too the certainty of the I is a certainty *sui generis*, which can in no way be traced back to discursive (logical) certainty but, as something independent, must be "made the ground" of the latter. The I of the *cogito* is for Descartes therefore not found or proven through the *cogito*, through a logical process of inference. In the *Meditations*, Descartes had explicitly rejected this kind of proof.[123] Here he explicitly goes back to "intuition." But once we have found this original intuition, this "source" of all certainty, this δός μοί ποῦ στῶ, then deduction comes in for its due. Then we can, should, and must trace everything else that lays claim to certainty back to it by means of a rational procedure of proof. "Seeing" the variety of life and immersion in its many forms cannot give us certainty.

This (Bergsonian) view provides us in Descartes' sense with nothing but mere phantasmagoria. From it we can never ever attain "knowledge of being" as called for by philosophy. The *cogito ergo sum*, the *sum cogitans* as the "program of rationalism," claims something quite different. It claims that the primary phenomenon of the "I," reduced to its essential component—which is secured and given through intuition as an "absolute" phe-

---

122. See Descartes, *Discours de la méthode, Oeuvres de Descartes*, ed. Charles Adam and Paul Tannery, 12 vols. (Paris: L. Cerf, 1896–1913), Vol. 6, pp. 58–59. *The Philosophical Writings of Descartes*, trans. J. Cottingham et al. (Cambridge: Cambridge Univ. Press, 1984), vol. 1, p. 141: "It is also a very remarkable fact that although many animals show more skill than we do in some of their actions, yet the same animals show none at all in many others; so what they do better does not prove that they have any intelligence, for if it did then they would have more intelligence than any of us and would excel us in everything. It proves rather that they have no intelligence at all, and that it is nature which acts in them according to the disposition of their organs."—Eds.

123. See Descartes, *Objectiones, Secundæ Responsiones, Oeuvres de Descartes*, vol. 7, p. 140, lines 18–23. *The Philosophical Writings of Descartes*, vol. 2, p. 100.—Eds.

nomenon—consists in the mode (in the way it is explicated) of logical (deductive, demonstrative) knowledge. Only that possesses "truth" or "certainty" which is permeated by these two (totally different) forms of knowledge, what participates (μετέχει)[124] simultaneously in the phenomenon of the origin—I, *ego cogito*—and in the different forms of inference of the *cogitatio*. The *cogito* and the *mathesis universalis* are the two poles of Cartesian philosophy. The certainty of the "world of bodies" is something mediate, requiring "proof" and a phenomenon capable of proof.

Yet another way of intuition is found in Husserl. He too is a "rationalist," but in a broader sense than that of the Cartesian "mathesis universalis." His "ratio" embraces the whole area of *noesis* and *noema*, the whole variety of possible intentions of meaning, of possible *noeta*. But this is all based for Husserl as for Descartes in the original, "transcendental" vision of the I, of the *ego cogito*. The entire reality of things is swept aside, "put in brackets," put out of view through the ἐποχή.[125] All that remains is the reality of the stream of consciousness, of the "pure I," to which all so-called being, all truth is related and in which it is "founded."[126] This Husserlian standpoint [is] the most consistent statement of the pure I-aspect, of "transcendental idealism," in modern philosophy.

We must keep in mind in this characterization of the monadic "perspective" that no real doctrine of knowledge can limit itself to a particular aspect. It has to do justice to the different aspects, "dimensions" of being, to somehow express and encompass them. It does not therefore deny these aspects and cannot do without them, if it is to fulfill its task to make visible and accessible the whole of knowledge (of "possible experience" in the broadest sense, experience of the I, the You, the World—which encompasses the "sensory" world as well as the "supersensual" world).

But the question is which relational system should [be] chosen here [and] where should we set the middle point of the coordinates toward which all knowledge is directed and oriented, what therefore is to count as "immediate" (self-certain, per se *notum*, evident) and what as mediated. The "monadic" interpretations possess this coordinate center in the "pure intuition"

---

124. See Plato *Phaedo* 100D, *Parmenides* 130C–131A.—Eds.

125. On "Epoché" in Husserl's sense, see Husserl, *Ideen*, §31. Husserl, *Ideas*, pp. 96ff.—Eds.

126. [*MS has on a line by itself*]: Further described in Husserl's *Cartesian Meditations.*— Cassirer. See Husserl, *Méditations Cartésiennes: Introduction à la Phénoménologie*, trans. from German by Gabrielle Peiffer and Emmanuel Levinas (Paris: A. Colin, 1931). Husserl, *An Introduction to Phenomenology*, trans. Dorion Cairns (The Hague: Martinus Nijhoff, 1960).— Eds.

of the I from which everything else (the "You," the "It") must then be deduced in order to attain its mediate evidence. This explains the methodology of the particular epistemological systems, which represents a truly universal feature in them—a genuine structural form which extends beyond all the "material" differences, no matter how great.

Let us consider, for example, the three "monadic" theories of knowledge of Bergson, Descartes, and Husserl. They are, from the standpoint of their content and their inferences, completely different, even divergent and irreconcilable, for example, Descartes' mechanism and Bergson's vitalism, Bergson's "realism" contrasted with the transcendental idealism of Husserl, and so on. But in the manner in which they work out, attain, and secure their center ("pure intuition" of the I), they follow a very specific course in which they coincide. What course is this? No "theory of knowledge" stands alone or consists only of itself. It always starts with some specific factual content of the entity that it presupposes as "given," but this presupposition is not something absolute, which cannot be expunged, but is relative and provisional. It is made with the particular proviso of self-correction.

The "technic" of the theory of knowledge consists in taking a specific body of knowledge, the content of cognitions, in order then to put it hypothetically in suspension and to see what follows from this suspension. This is the only way it can move ahead to its "center," to the middle point of coordinates, to the "unconditioned" (that is, incapable of suspension) evidence (to the "Archimedean point"). This method, as closer inspection shows, is common to all theories of knowledge of a certain type, despite all the divergencies in their results which stem from material that they take as their starting point.

We can follow this distinctly in the opposition Descartes—Bergson—Husserl; they are all directed toward the same point (the pure "intuition" of the I), but they attain it in completely different ways. They all share the characteristic form of "disregarding," which is something quite different from ordinary "abstraction," for it consists instead of a positive looking at or attention to, with the characteristic intention, or aim of meaning,[127] of establishing a particular view. In order to do justice to this intention, we

127. Seeing = sequi cf. Bühler.—Cassirer. Bühler discusses the etymology of "Sinn" in *Die Krise der Psychologie*, p. 133: "It is remarkable that even 'Sinn' = sensus (Sinnesorgan) [sense organ] and the verb for the most important activities of sense still make use of teleological concepts. Consider how 'Spur' [a trace] and 'spüren' [to sense] or 'Sehen' [to see], which is related to the Latin sequi = to follow and originally meant 'to follow with the eyes.'"—Eds.

must not only ask what is being disregarded but also what this disregarding and intention are directed toward. It is essential here for the "monadic" theories of knowledge that they "disregard" the "You" and the "It," not in the sense that they are declared to be ontologically unreal or invalid, but in the sense that they direct and orient them toward the pure I. This orientation (direction toward something) at first truly has the character of a real execution or death penalty[128] that "gets rid of" the other aspects, at least insofar as they are claimed to be something independent—to be an absolute being or an "absolute" truth outside the relationship to the "I" (as the middle point of coordinates, of "evidence").

This is an illusion that must be eliminated, and this is accomplished through the characteristic method of reduction, of bracketing, which encompasses the entirety of the material we start out with. Material of some kind, stemming from the scientific methods of "induction" or "deduction," must always also be assumed (for how else is the theory of knowledge to obtain its subject matter), but this "also assuming" should not be confused with an absolute "presupposition." The absoluteness of presuppositions is, rather, put in abeyance in order to attain to the ἀρχὴ ἀνυπόθετος.[129] Plato is the first to conceive this as the essence of philosophical knowledge, which he for this reason understands as dialectical knowledge (as assuming in canceling and canceling in assuming). Let us pursue this in the examples of Bergson, Descartes, and Husserl.

Bergson. The most obvious thing about Bergson's program for "metaphysics" is that he wants strictly to separate metaphysics in principle from science. "Metaphysics" is for him actually nonscience. The opposition between metaphysics and science is complete. All true evidence is denied to science. It belongs exclusively to metaphysics and to its original intuition. On the other hand, Bergson's doctrine of being and life is based upon very comprehensive and diverse material from biological inductions. The makeup of *Évolution créatrice*, with its series of steps of *torpeur*, *intelligence*, *instinct*, and so on—all this is inconceivable and cannot be understood without taking biology into account, whose empirical truth and accuracy are presupposed. Bergson's "tactic" consists here in the fact that, while he accepts all this biological and psychological material, he at the same time invalidates it, that he gives it no ontological, but only a symbolic significance, that is, that he takes it in the sense of a mere indication, an indication

---

128. Cassirer plays here on the German *Hinrichtung*, which literally means "direction toward something," as well as "death penalty."—Eds.

129. "presuppositionless principle." See Aristotle *Metaphysics*, 1005b14.—Eds.

of the primary phenomenon of the pure I, of *durée vécue*. Absolute (real) value is sacrificed—the "factual" (the rigid "facts" of psychological or biological science) become an "analogy" for the metaphysician, an indication that points us toward the original intuition. The facts acquire a meaning only in this "loosened" way; they are not the final goal of knowledge, they are ways to something else, something new, to something "beyond" mere "science," namely to real, genuine "evidence."

This method of Bergson emerges clearly in his first work, the *Données immédiates*.[130] From the usual "inductive," "scientific" method of empirical psychology he wants here to attain by means of a "turn" (the "turn toward the light" in the Platonic cave)[131] the genuine, true theory of the I, to "metaphysical" psychology, which makes visible the basic fact of the life of consciousness, the *durée vécue*. This basic fact, this basic intuition, is then used in Bergson's later works as the key for unlocking the secret of the I. "Life" cannot be "explained" through the mere piling up and abstract comparison of "biological" facts, for *bios* does not submit to the *logos*, the logos remains a completely inadequate form for it. As soon as the logos with its "rigid" forms comes forth, the particular character, the "flow" of life, disappears while on the other hand the pure intuition of this stream of life lets us understand how it divides into different directions, into different typical basic forms, whose "development" remains, however, always pure creation (*évolution créatrice*).

[*Descartes.*] Let us contrast this procedure of Bergson with that of Descartes. At first [there is] an extreme opposition: for Bergson everything is directed toward life, for Descartes, toward the turn away from it, the complete elimination of the psyche from reality; for Bergson, the split, the unhealable separation between "metaphysics" and "science," for Descartes the call and urge to make metaphysics a science, to raise it to the level of scientific knowledge. The ground of its being and its justification consists in this very elevation.

Yet [there is a] deep analogy in method between the two that derives from their belonging to the same "type," the "monadic" type. The scientific material that Descartes "also assumes" and presupposes (see above) belongs to the field not of inductive but of deductive science. Deduction is the only scientific type of certainty. Besides it, there is no "truth," no "knowledge,"

130. Bergson, *Time and Free Will.*—Eds.
131. See Plato *Republic* 518B; cf. 521C.—Eds.

no certainty. The "material" that Descartes starts with is therefore taken not from the "sciences of fact" but from the "sciences of the ideal." It consists not in *"vérités contingentes,"* but rather in *"vérités universelles,"* not in sensory objects, but in the objects of mathematics, in extension, number, quantity. But now the same typical turn sets in regarding these objects and the universal "truths" accruing to them, a turn whose aim is, rather than to declare them "invalid," to "turn them around," to direct them to another light source, the only one that is accessible and adequate, the light source of the *cogito.* This is what the Cartesian method of doubt consists in, "doubt in order to be certain," and this is its explanation, negation for the sake of a breakthrough to a new position.

Descartes assumes the universal truths, the axioms and principles of mathematics—just as Bergson assumes the inductive facts of biology and psychology. He constructs propositions deductively on the basis of his "material," just as Bergson constructs propositions inductively on the basis of his, but both of them consider this first assumption only a "springboard" (ἐπίβασις καὶ ὁρμάς), in order to attain to ἀρχή ἀνυπόθετος.[132] This ἀρχή can be attained only through a commitment to a "turn" accomplished by putting in abeyance what is (inductively or deductively) "given." That is what Cartesian doubt does, and the paradoxical notion of "God as a deceiver"[133] can only be cleared up this way. It is Descartes' violent tearing himself away from the type of mathematical certainty, from the "objective," unquestionable truth of mathematics, by "calling into question the unquestionable," in order to attain the actual original source of certainty, the *cogito.* This violent negation is the only way to open up the new, truly originary and original position.

[*Husserl.*] We find this procedure of the "monadic" theory of knowledge perhaps still more sharply, more pointedly and characteristically expressed in Husserl, who is quite conscious of his relationship to Descartes, who sees in Descartes the radical renewer of philosophical thought, the thought that received its complete development in "phenomenology."[134] Husserl's "universe" of thought is related to Descartes', but they do not completely coincide. Just as Descartes had emphasized the *one "sapientia humana"* in

132. See Plato, *Republic* 511B3–C2. *Collected Dialogues,* p. 746, where he speaks of how dialectic uses assumptions as springboards and not absolute beginnings.—Eds.

133. See Descartes, *Meditationes,* Meditatio 1, *Oeuvres de Descartes,* vol. 7, pp. 22f. *The Philosophical Writings of Descartes,* vol. 2, pp. 15f.—Eds.

134. Cf. *Cartesian Meditations.*—Cassirer.

contrast to the dispersion of knowledge in the various particular sciences, as he had contrasted pure knowledge of reason to mere knowledge of facts, which always remained in doubt, and just as he had opposed "induction" and "deduction," so Husserl wants to found "philosophy as a rigorous science"[135] by freeing it from psychologism, by distinguishing knowledge of "pure form" radically and in principle from knowledge that is based on mere matter of fact and on "inductive generalizations." He wants to show a fundamentally new way that leads to the "pure forms," the pure *Wesenheiten*. This way is not that of inductive generalization, but the way of intuiting essences, of eidetic intuition. It is absurd to try to attain or derive an eidetic intuition from inductions. Such an attempt is complete *ignoratio elenchi*.

This [is] the core of the *Logical Investigations*:[136] the *theme* of pure logic and of *mathesis universalis*, the theme of a general doctrine of meaning and theory of form is to be developed and guarded against "psychologistic" mistakes and misinterpretations. This world of pure (logical) forms is the "objective" presupposition, which is also assumed in Husserl's phenomenology, just as Bergson also implicitly assumed the realm of biological facts and Descartes the realm of mathematical truths about number, quantity, and extension. But now, in the same sort of turning around, this assumption is assumed to be in suspension. It is "bracketed out," must submit to the "transcendental reduction," and this reduction is what really makes visible the true center of phenomenology, of the *cogito*, the *ego cogito*, of "monadic" self-certainty.[137] *All* intentions, intention toward the "You" as well as toward "It," toward the empirical objects of nature as well as toward the ideals of mathematics, every view toward the empirical, mathematical, metaphysical cosmos, all this lies enclosed in *noesis*, in the pure ego's meaning-giving acts, its directions of meaning; it must in the end all be traced back to it and understood through it. That is "transcendental idealism," as Husserl understands it.

---

135. Reference to Husserl, "Philosophie als strenge Wissenschaft," *Logos* 1 (1910): 289–314. Husserl, "Philosophy as Rigorous Science," in *Phenomenology and the Crisis of Philosophy*, trans. Quentin Lauer (New York: Harper & Row, 1965), pp. 71–147.—Eds.

136. Edmund Husserl, *Logische Untersuchungen*, 2 vols. (Halle: M. Niemeyer, 1900, 1901). Husserl, *Logical Investigations*, 2 vols., trans. J. N. Findlay (London and New York: Routledge & Kegan Paul and The Humanities Press, 1970).—Eds.

137. Cf. esp. the *Cartesian Meditations*.—Cassirer. What Cassirer calls "'monadic' self-certainty" in Husserl's *Cartesian Meditations* refers to Meditation I: "The Way to the Transcendental Ego," pp. 7–26.—Eds.

B. The "Second Dimension": The Action and Will-Aspect

The theory of knowledge takes a new turn as soon as it reaches beyond the monadic basic scheme and decides to make a radical turn outward away from the monadic turn inward (introspection). Expressed in the language of consciousness, this turn toward outside is most evident and unmistakable in the phenomenon of the will, in will as unlimited by mere "possibility" but pressing forward toward effectiveness, reality, "energy." This is what distinguishes the phenomenon of will in principle from that of pure "intuition," in which we grasp our ego in the form of the *cogito*. There we have a closing off from all outer reality and an exclusion from it, a withdrawal into the pure isolation of the ego, a compression of all "world" and the whole breadth of existence into a single point: the extreme concentration of the whole "periphery" into the single central datum of the self. In the will, by contrast, we have the opposite direction: an urge to expansion, a turn to the world, and the conquering of this world. The will is characterized by this "endlessness," by this urge to "further and further" expansion to the *plus ultra*; in fact, this is what fundamentally constitutes it. It overshoots every goal and its essence lies in this "over." It is essentially centrifugal.

What type of "theory of knowledge" will correspond to this centrifugal tendency? We must here again make clear the difference between the distinction of types as such and the modal differences within a specific type.[138] Both can deeply influence and change the features of a specific, concrete theory of knowledge, but the "modal" change belongs to a different dimension from the change in type, and the two must be carefully kept apart in our analytic observations. If we remain with the general "typic of the phenomena of will," we meet with various kinds of theories of knowledge, depending upon whether the intepretations focus on the "elementary" or "higher" forms of the will—the "inner" drives or the "spiritual" ones—the dull "unconscious" will or the "rational," conscious will. Both forms are represented in the history of the theory of knowledge.

The will as a completely blind drive of life, as totally unfounded, unreasoned will, brings forth the intellect from itself. The intellect then stands opposite the will and views it through its own forms of space, time, causality, but in this form of observation it cannot tear itself away from the will, cannot really emancipate and liberate itself; it always remains adhered to

---

138. See above.—Cassirer. Cassirer refers to his discussion of types.

the will as its servant and slave. New forms of this "voluntaristic" theory of knowledge include modern Pragmatism and Fictionalism. Just as there is no intellect independent of the will, so too there is no truth independent from it, no being or validity sitting on a throne above it which it must respect and act in accordance with. Such "truth" is mere illusion. Truth is not objective; it has a merely instrumental character. It stands in the service of the will, it is a *tool* that the will [has] created in order for it to serve its ends.

All truth, in order to be really "understood" and epistemologically justified must be traced to this single source (coordinate middle point). In this way a whole new system of relations arises that differs characteristically from the monadic system of relations, the system of the *cogito*. Even the phenomenon of pure self-consciousness, of I-consciousness, upon which Descartes and Husserl sought to build their theories of knowledge, is now swallowed up. This turn emerges conspicuously, for example, in James, one of the main representatives of Pragmatism. He finally denies the very "existence," reality, and truth of self-consciousness, declaring that this truth is only a useful fiction.[139]

This is highly characteristic; it indicates nothing other than that, in order to bring the pragmatic aspect fully to bear, the other—the I-aspect, the monadic aspect, that we are directed toward by the concept of consciousness in Descartes, Husserl, and Kant ("pure apperception")[140]—is now blacked out, put out of commission.

This might seem paradoxical, for one could ask in reply: is then the basic phenomenon that is here the middle point, that of "drive" and of "will" and the categories that go with them—means-aims—even understandable without an "I" that wills, without a subject that posits aims? Doesn't Pragmatism fall into a bottomless pit when it robs itself of this foundation in the "I," in "consciousness"? But the answer here is that

---

139. Cf. the Essay [by William James] "Does consciousness exist?," cit. in Russell, *Analysis of Mind*, p. 22.—Cassirer. Russell cites on pages 22–24 various passages from James' "Does Consciousness Exist?" as published in William James, *Essays in Radical Empiricism* (New York: Longmans, Green, 1912), pp. 2, 3, 4, 9, 10, 36–37.—Eds. *Marginal note:* H[ei]d[e]g[ger], Fichte, Nietzsche, Marx—Fasc[ism], θέοσ[ις].—Cassirer. On the Sophists' θέσις *theory, see* below, note 146.—Eds.

140. See Kant, *Kritik der reinen Vernunft, Werke*, vol. 3, pp. 114–117 (B 134 n.). *Critique of Pure Reason*, p. 154 n.: "The synthetic unity of apperception is therefore the highest point, to which we ascribe all employment of the understanding, even the whole of logic, and conformably therewith, transcendental philosophy. Indeed this faculty of apperception is the understanding itself."—Eds.

"drive" and "will" are taken in a much broader sense, that they do not stem from the aspect of consciousness. Rather, they belong to another, purely vital level. Drive, will, these are those "blind" potencies that assert themselves as "primordial being" in Schopenhauer's metaphysics of the will, as that "being driven" that stands before us in total objectivity in certain kinds of actions that lie completely outside the field of consciousness, in so-called instinctive actions. These actions exhibit a particular directedness, that we can read off in purely behavioristic fashion, without having to attribute any sort of "consciousness" to them or even to assume any. This is the explanation of this apparent paradox; it is essentially the aspect of action, not the (subjective, phenomenological) aspect of will, that governs and directs the theory of knowledge in Pragmatism. To this extent James proceeds consistently when he eliminates consciousness as "pure consciousness," pure apperception, as the *cogito* and includes it among other fictions.[141]

This same blacking out, as applied here to the I-sphere, also is brought to bear on the sphere of objective values, objective being, and objective truth. They all must submit to the means-end scheme in the sense discussed above—they are means to an end (preservation of life, preservation of power, increase of power). There are no objective "autonomous" values. All so-called values serve a foreign purpose (stemming from the will to power). That is the conclusion already drawn by Nietzsche, who is the most persistent and consistent representative of this pragmatic leveling of the value of truth. (What if error were better than truth? and so on.)[142] All fictionalism amounts to this: why should there not be errors that further life, that increase power; is not perhaps everything that we call truth and value such an error? Is it not born from the drive to life, which seeks protection and support for itself, which out of fear of the uncertainties of becoming and the dynamism of life itself wants to flee to the harbor of a secure being and a secure truth? Is not being, is not the Platonic realm of Ideas, the realm of eternal forms just such a phantasmagoria, which we must see through if we are to grasp its origin? That [is] Dewey's thesis.[143]

---

141. See James, "Does Consciousness Exist?" p. 37: *"That entity [consciousness] is fictitious, while thoughts in the concrete are fully real."*—Eds.

142. See Nietzsche, *Jenseits von Gut und Böse*, Erstes Hauptstück: Von den Vorurtheilen der Philosophen, *Nietzsches Werke* (Leipzig: C. G. Naumann, 1896), Abt. 1, vol. 7, p. 9; Nietzsche, *Beyond Good and Evil*, trans. Walter Kaufmann (New York: Vintage Books, 1966), "On the Prejudices of Philosophers," pp. 7–32.—Eds.

143. Studies (cf. Cit. Leander).—Cassirer. Probably a reference to John Dewey, *Studies in Logical Theory* (Chicago: Univ. of Chicago Press, 1903); and to Folke Leander, *The Philosophy*

All theories that treat objective "being" and objective "values" as dependent upon a "positing" by the will, as derived from the will's claim to power, go the same route: *Sic volo, sic jubeo*;[144] *Stat pro ratione voluntas*.[145] That is the earliest form of sophistic θέσις theory—which came from the sphere of *action* and was calculated for it—which let itself here τὸν ἥττω λόγον κρείσσωνα ποιεῖν,[146] and saw in this very being "stronger" the character of "greater importance," of the better and the true.[147] [This theory] came from the sphere of the rhetorician, who is concerned not with the truth in itself, but with effectiveness, who wants to *move* things with words, λόγοι. For him the logos that "moves" is the true logos; effectiveness is a criterion of value.

This reduction of truth to effectiveness is characteristic therefore of all theories that make the "Will to Power" their highest principle, of fascist theories as well as of the Marxist theory of the superstructure. What we call truth is really nothing but the superstructure, that is, it is fundamentally an alibi for a particular "interest" that is "behind it" and that we need to debunk. The theory of knowledge is nothing but this technique of debunking, not the uncovering of a truth that exists "in itself," but the discovery of an original force that is *hidden* behind this supposed truth (for example, religious or philosophical truth) or [is] "symbolized" in it. Turned toward the viewpoint of the subject, this process of discovery, of exposing or unmasking, is the guiding principle of psychoanalysis.

As soon as we enter into this second *type*, every claim made in the name of the "theory of knowledge" takes on all at once a completely different meaning and another color. A marked example of this is the turn that phenomenology has taken from Husserl to Heidegger. All the technical

---

of John Dewey, Göteborgs Kungl. Vetenskaps- och Vitterhets-Samhälles Handlingar, femte följden. ser. A, vol. 7, no. 2, 1939. Dewey touches on Plato's doctrine of ideas, but Leander does not cite this work in his study. Folke Leander received his doctorate under Cassirer in 1937 in Göteborg.—Eds.

144. "As I will, so I command." See this phrase in Kant, *Kritik der praktischen Vernunft, Werke*, vol. 5, p. 36. *Critique of Practical Reason*, trans. Lewis White Beck (Indianapolis: Bobbs-Merrill, 1956), p. 31.—Eds.

145. See Leibniz, *Méditation sur la notion commune de la justice, Mittheilungen aus Leibnizens ungedruckten Schriften*, ed. Georg Mollat (Leipzig: H. Haessel, 1893), p. 41: "Et de dire 'stat pro ratione voluntas,' ma volonté me tient lieu de raison, c'est proprement la devise d'un tyran" (If someone said, "stat pro ratione voluntas," my will alone serves as my reason, this would be the motto of a tyrant).—Eds.

146. "to make the weaker argument the stronger." See Plato *Apology* 195B5–C1.—Eds.

147. Protagoras's speech in *Theaetetus*.—Cassirer. See Plato *Theatetus* 166A–168C.—Eds.

particularities aside, the definitive and decisive thing about this turn can be put this way: here the step is made from the first type (monadic theory of knowledge) to the second type (theory of will and action). Immediately, all the basic categories are changed: the pure I, "being for itself," now becomes "being in the world." Intuition (the seeing of essences) disappears. "Persistence in the self" becomes being driven to the outside, being driven forward. "Dasein" falls into "care," and so on.[148] In all this the characteristic turn becomes evident.

We meet with another form of theory of knowledge, the "theory of science," if we, remaining within this second type, turn to another mode of understanding. [We meet with this] if we retain the primacy of the will before knowledge but do not begin with the will as a dull, dark, unconscious "drive," but see in it rational, reasoned energy conscious of itself—not merely a "being driven," but as something actively, consciously, "freely" reaching beyond itself. [We accomplish this] if we move on from the "vital" to the "intellectual"—in short, if we conceive the imperative directing the will as an ethical imperative ("authority of reason"). This turn is represented historically in the purest form by Fichte.

Fichte is considered on the traditional view to be a "subjective idealist," κατ' ἐξοχήν.[149] His doctrine is usually understood as perfecting and as excessively radicalizing the I-standpoint. It is the I that by itself here makes or produces the world as if by magic. So he seems to belong fully to the first, the purely monadic type. But this way of looking at it is deceiving. Fichte does not take Descartes' or Husserl's *cogito* in any sense as his starting point. He begins with Kant's doctrine of the "transcendental apperception"; he also sees in it the "highest point," to which all transcendental philosophy must be "secured." But the main point of this transcendental apperception has been shifted for him from the logical to the ethical, from the intellect to the will. It does not rest in the pure intuition of the I; this is not for him some final given, a final fact. Indeed, it cannot even be "shown" (in the sense of phenomenological showing) as such a fact—at rest, static. It must be produced, demonstrated through a *Tathandlung*. Therefore, as soon as we even speak the word "I," we were already in the midst of the sphere of action. Characteristic of this is also that the old expression θέσις returns again. For the I finds neither itself nor the "world" receptively as a

---

148. *Marginal note:* On Heidegger cf. the material for vol. IV—more there!—Cassirer. The material mentioned here is in folder 184a. See below in Part 3: "'Geist' and 'Life': Heidegger."—Eds.

149. "the most noble."—Eds.

simple datum. It "posits" the world and posits itself in an originary, spontaneous act.

How does this positing come about and what does it depend upon? That is the question that Fichte's *Theory of Science* seeks to answer. It returns, significantly, to an original drive of consciousness, not to a drive toward "something" (to some concrete individual object or individual goals), but to the drive to action per se, to action in general. This drive is the first "spur" to positing the I, and it initiates the whole series of *Tathandlungen* that follow. This spur, as Fichte explicitly emphasizes, cannot be inferred or explained theoretically; it must be explained practically.[150]

At the apex of the Fichtean creation of the world, therefore, there stands no pure ego, reflecting upon itself, thinking itself and, so to speak, immersed in this (static) self-observation. When he writes of "intellectual intuition," he means something completely different. In the first and second *Introduction to the Theory of Science*, his decisive, convincing example for this intellectual intuition is the categorical imperative.[151] Intuitions of the I, the You, and the World are all born from the categorical imperative: intuition of the *I*, because it is I only insofar as it is practical and it is practical only insofar as it submits to a general, completely universal commandment of reason; of the You, because the "recognition" of the You comes about only through the "ought";[152] of the World, because this is nothing other than "duty's material made sensible," and so on.

C. The "Third Dimension": The Starting Point of the "Work"

The borderline between this and the earlier dimension—the dimension of "willing" and "action"—appears at first glance to be difficult to draw. For

---

150. *Marginal note:* "Cit. s. Erkprol III und Kuno Fischer zur Lehre von 'Anstoss'."—Cassirer. A reference to the discussion of Fichte's doctrine of "Anstoss" in Cassirer, *Das Erkenntnisproblem in der Philosophie und Wissenschaft der neueren Zeit* (Berlin: Bruno Cassirer, 1920), vol. 3, pp. 153–155; and to Kuno Fischer, *Fichtes Leben, Werke und Lehre*, vol. 6 in his *Geschichte der neueren Philosophie*, 3d ed. (Heidelberg: Carl Winter, 1900), pp. 370–372: "Die Deduktion des Anstosses."—Eds.

151. See Fichte, "Zweite Einleitung in die Wissenschaftslehre," in *Sämmtliche Werke*, vol. 1, p. 463–468. The "Second Introduction" to J. G. Fichte, *Science of Knowledge*, ed. and trans. Peter Heath and John Lachs (Cambridge: Cambridge Univ. Press, 1982), pp. 38–42.—Eds.

152. Cf. System der Sittenlehre. *Marginal note:* V, 185: The compulsion, by which the reality of a world forces itself upon us, is a *moral* compulsion.—Cassirer. This is a quotation from Fichte, "Ueber den Grund unseres Glaubens an eine Göttliche Weltregietung," *Sämmtliche Werke*, vol. 5, p. 185. The emphasis is Cassirer's.—Eds.

is not every work also something willed and actuated? Doesn't it belong exclusively to the world of willing, and is it not exhausted in this sphere? Yet there is a sharper distinction to be drawn here. There are "works" whose content, whose meaning, whose "sense" does not consist exclusively in their bringing about a specific "effect," their making any physical or psychical changes in things, or their intervening in the physical or psychical causal order. Rather, in addition to the many particular changing effects they have (besides their "technical" usefulness and their effects on the "souls" of men), they also possess a particular content of their own, an enduring "being." It is this "being" that "outlives" the moment which is not dragged into the turmoil of physical and psychical activity as it changes from moment to moment—this is the basic determining factor in the make-up of a "work." We can make this clearer by considering it in the work of language and the work of art, and generally in the whole area of the "poetic" in contrast to the merely and exclusively practical.[153]

The poetic and the practical differ in the varying "temporal shapes" they create. The practical is directed toward an effect in the present, as something momentary, toward an "influence" on physical nature or on the human will. The poetic is different because its being is not limited *only* to such works. The poetic "arises" and "endures" outside every "intention" (as "aiming at a goal" taken as a specific, momentary, individual action). It is "without interest." It dwells within itself and is "blessed in itself." This "absence of interest" makes obvious how it differs from the "second dimension." This absence of interest is not confined to the work of art alone, but holds equally for works of language, philosophical works, works of science, and pure knowledge in general. Here we move from the sphere of intuition

---

153. On the concept of "Poesie" cf. Aristotle; see also the comment in Bühler's book on language.—Cassirer. This probably refers to the passage in Bühler's *Theory of Language*, p. 62, in which Bühler, referring to Aristotle's distinction between theory and praxis, distinguishes between an "act of speech" and a "work of language": "Aristotle supplies the categories and the child at play the clearest observational data for a conceptually sharp distinction between the speech action and the language work. Aristotle prepares for us the division of human behaviour into *theoria* and *praxis* in the first step of an important series of concepts, and then in the second step separates *poesis* from *praxis* in the strictest sense. . . . Looking back at what is finished or at what has been finished by chance is a stimulus for the child at play, and the decisive phase follows, the phase in which the result of the activity is anticipated in a conception and thus begins to regulate the operation on the material prospectively and in which finally the activity does not come to rest before the work is completed." In regard to the "poetic" in contrast to the practical, see Aristotle *Nicomachean Ethics* 1140a2–5, 1140b4, 6.—Eds.

(first dimension) and of action (second dimension) to the sphere of pure contemplation.[154]

In the history of philosophy it is Socrates who discovers this sphere, who puts it forth and establishes it as a central object for philosophical investigation and "marvel." Among the paradoxes of the figure of Socrates which make him so "utopian" (ἄτοπος) for the Greeks and so "incomprehensible" for philosophical interpretation from then on, so "contradictory," is that we cannot clearly classify him as belonging either to the theoretical or practical world. Every attempt at such a classification immediately turns dialectically into its opposite. As soon as we believe that we have grasped the "true" face of Socrates and of Socratic thought, then this "truth" dissolves. Our "knowledge" is transformed into "ignorance." Socrates seems to defy every attempt to "pin him down"; his every aspect immediately turns into its opposite. This [is] a fundamental part of Socratic irony. This "irony" has been borne out again and again in the historical interpretations of the figure of Socrates.

Above all, where does he belong in the basic opposition between "theory" and "practice"? Is Socrates a theoretician or a practician? Is he most concerned with a problem of knowledge or is he only concerned with practical action? Is he the teacher and master of conceptual analysis, the art of *diaeresis*, or is his purpose solely and exclusively directed toward willing and doing, to ἀρετή? To this question there can be many answers: (1) Socrates can be proclaimed as the first discoverer of the logos, of ratio, of the concept, as the first great "artist of reason." This is how he appears in Plato's early dialogues, where he asks about the concept of ἀνδρεία,[155] the concept of the ὅσιον,[156] and so on. This is how Aristotle conceives him—as the "discoverer of the concept."[157] [(2)] Sharply opposed to this we have Xenophon's figure of Socrates—Socrates as the pure practician, as a "moralist," his teaching a "practical wisdom."[158] But this resulting dialectical cancellation is only a symptom of the fact that the real question of Socrates

---

154. On the history of the word cf. Boll: Contemplatio.—Cassirer. See Franz Boll, *Vita contemplativa, Sitzungsberichte der Heidelberger Akademie der Wissenschaften*, Philosophisch-Historische Klasse, XI (1920), 8. Abhandlung, pp. 1–34.—Eds.

155. "courage." See Plato *Laches* 190D–E.—Eds.

156. "holy." See Plato *Euthyphro* 5D7.—Eds.

157. Aristotle *Metaphysics* 987b3; see 1078b19.—Eds.

158. Heinrich Maier.—Cassirer. See Heinrich Maier, *Sokrates: Sein Werk und seine geschichtliche Stellung* (Tübingen: J. C. B. Mohr [Paul Siebeck], 1913); on Xenophon's Socrates, pp. 13–77.—Eds.

has not yet been raised, that the unique problem Socrates poses has not yet been fully undestood. This problem consists in the fact that the opposition between theory and practice—the opposition between knowledge and action—has been denied and overcome by Socrates, raising it in a synthesis to a new level.

Socrates seems to reject the opposition; for him all knowing is doing. Virtue (ἀρετή) is knowledge.[159] But that seems paradoxical and outrageous, for are there not countless forms of acting that lead to specific results in which immediate proof and certification can be found without any corresponding specific, clear, distinct knowledge? Doesn't the poet, the politician, the craftsman produce something "unconsciously" and yet with complete "instinctive" security? But do we not undermine this security when we raise the Socratic question of what it "is" that is produced and what rules and norms it is subject to? Do we not threaten and even completely undermine the free, uninhibited nature of human "praxis" when we pester it with this question? Are these "active" individuals—the poet, the politician, the shoemaker—not right when they indignantly and angrily dismiss it?

Here is where we find Socrates' "originality"; he always starts with such productive action, with practical, technical matters, with a craftsman's efforts. But he finds in all this a new "aspect," he discovers a new "view" of productive action—θέαμα,[160] which [forms] the kernel of all genuine θεωρία[161]—a view that never occurs to us as long as we consider productive action merely in terms of its immediate, "unconscious" performance, but only when we "turn back" to it from what has been produced, the work, and grasp it in this turning back in this "reflection." The reflection of productive activity in the work is what creates the new sphere that is characteristically to be distinguished from that of mere "theory" and from that of mere "praxis." In this sense Socrates' observation is neither one-sidedly theoretical nor practical, neither intuitive nor active, but genuinely *contemplative*. In this contemplation the realm of form—of εἶδος and of ἰδέα—is discovered. Socrates begins with the Delphic oracle's call of γνῶθι σεαυτόν,[162] but as Goethe correctly saw, he grasped this in a quite different sense. He does not call for "self-knowledge" in the sense of some pure

---

159. See Plato *Meno* 98D.—Eds.
160. "aspect, look."—Eds.
161. "theory, seeing."—Eds.
162. "know thyself." See Plato *Phaedrus* 230A.—Eds.

(monadic) looking inward (intro-spection, intuition of the I in the pure act of the *cogito*); instead, it means something completely new and unique for him. This call now means: know your *work* and know "yourself" *in* your work; know what you do, so you can do what you know. Give shape to what you do; give it form by starting from mere instinct, from tradition, from convention, from routine, from ἐμπειρία and τριβή[163] in order to arrive at "self-conscious" action—a work in which you recognize yourself as the sole creator and actor.[164] Ask not, in what you do and accomplish, about its mere "influence," but about the "work." Submit to the imperative of the work.

The discovery of this imperative of the work—its autochthonic and autonomous sense,[165] its "binding character"[166]—that is Socrates' real deed. With this he accomplishes the "turn to the Idea";[167] this contains the synthesis of theory and praxis.[168] The "Idea" is no mere "concept" (abstract-logical), but it is also no mere "doing" (empirical, technical-practical, con-

163. "experience" and "habituation."—Eds.

164. *MS has in angle brackets:* cf. Goethe, Max. 657, 663 etc.—Cassirer. See Goethe, *Maximen und Reflexionen*, no. 657; Goethe, *Wisdom and Experience*, p. 209: "If then we examine the significant adage, Know Thyself, we must not put an ascetic interpretation upon it. It does not point to the self-probing of our modern hypochondriacs, humorists, and self-tormenters. It means very simply: Keep a moderate watch upon yourself in order that you may become aware of your relations as regards your fellow-men in the world. For this no psychological self-tormenting is needed. Every worthwhile individual knows and experiences what it means. It is a good piece of advice, of the greatest practical benefit to everyone." See also Goethe, *Maximen und Reflexionen*, no. 663: "Just as Socrates called the people of the community to himself, so that he could to this extent become enlightened about himself, in the same way Plato and Aristotle approached nature as individuals, the one with the spirit and attitude of assimilating it, the other hoping to attain it with the eye and method of the scientist. And so it is then with every approach which makes it possible for us, generally and in detail, to attain to these three, an event which we feel with the greatest happiness as it serves to greatly further our education.— Eds.

165. Simmel speaks of the "autochthonic meaning" and "autonomous objectivity" of works of culture as things in contrast to their subjective cultural value. See Simmel, "Vom Wesen der Kultur," *Österreichische Rundschau* 15:1 (1908): 39f.—Eds.

166. (Simmel, Freyer).—Cassirer. According to Freyer, the "binding character" (*Bündigkeit*) of an objective content is torn apart by the activity of the understanding subject. See Hans Freyer, *Theorie des objektiven Geistes: Eine Einleitung in die Kulturphilosophie*, 3d ed. (Leipzig and Berlin: B. G. Teubner, 1934), pp. 117f.—Eds.

167. Simmel; Cf. Lebensanschauung, chap. II, "Die Wendung zur Idee."—Cassirer. Published in 1918 by Duncker & Humblot.—Eds.

168. See above.—Cassirer. Reference is to p. 184.—Eds.

crete productive activity). It is rooted in both, but it goes beyond them both; it has a peculiar "transcendence." Above the realm of abstract thought and conceptualization and above the realm of immediate activity and performance it erects a "third realm,"[169] the "realm of pure forms," that is given to us in a pure vision (πᾶσα ψυχὴ φύσει τεθέαται τὰ ὄντα).[170] What we call truth, goodness, and beauty rests upon and derives from this realm of form.

Truth. [Let us consider truth as] emergence from and opposition to the sphere of productive activity. "Truth" is not bound to productive activity and it is not to be measured by its criteria. That was the basic error of the Sophists, that they looked for truth in this pragmatic sphere and sought to limit it to it and measure it with such criteria. Πάντων χρημάτων μέτρον ἄνθρωπος[171]—that means for Protagoras, that the criterion of truth is pragmatic, that it is to be measured by its "usefulness."[172] But truth is not a matter of usefulness; it is a formal value. There is an εἶδος of truth, *αὐτὸ καθ' αὑτό*. The recognition of this purely formal value of truth "itself in itself" is what distinguishes the "philosopher" from the "Sophist," the "dialectician" from the "rhetorician" and "eristic." For the sophist and the rhetorician, "truth" is exhausted by the sphere of action. True is whatever is effective on the audience, whatever influences it in accordance with the concrete goal of the speaker and inclines it in a certain direction. For the dialectician, it is something that "rests within itself"; it is formed according to its own, autonomous rules—the rules of the "logos itself"—and which can be recognized, held fast, and grasped in this purely formal character.

Plato invokes, develops, and systematically describes this realm of "forms," the ἰδέαι as λόγοι, as the completion of Socrates' claim. And with this the new sphere of contemplation stands before us, opposed to the world of the I (the subjective world of perception and opinion, δόξα) as well as to the world of "productive activity." According to Plato the I as

---

169. See Cassirer, "The Problem of the Symbol and its Place in the System of Philosophy," trans. John Michael Krois, *Man and World* 11 (1978): 420: "Thus language proceeds from expressive meaning to pure representative meaning and from this it is constantly directed towards the third realm of pure significance."—Eds.

170. See Plato *Phaedrus* 249E: πᾶσα μὲν ἀνθρώπου ψυχὴ φύσει τεθέαται τὰ ὄντα ("every human soul has, by reason of her nature, had contemplation of true being").—Eds.

171. See above, note 34.—Eds.

172. Cf. above; Protagoras's speech in *Theaetetus* [166A–168C].—Cassirer. See above, note 147.—Eds.

such belongs to the Heraclitean flux of becoming. There is no "Archimedean point" in it; it is pulled along ἑλκόμενα ἄνω καὶ κάτω[173] in the flux of mere images, of "phantoms." So too all productive activity as mere activity also passes away. It is not able to discern itself as something fixed and objective. Only the pure form endures. To put productive activity under the guidance and protection of pure form and knowledge of pure form—that is the goal that Plato also sets for himself as a politician. Politics is supposed to be delivered from the sphere of power and productive activity; it is to be taken up into the sphere of knowledge, of "contemplation." The "philosophers," the masters at seeing the Ideas, of contemplation—not the mere "practicians," the active individuals striving for power—are the ones who should govern. The "imperative of the pure form" is supposed to permeate and determine the actions of the individual as well as of the populace, the πολιτεία. As with truth, "just law" can arise from this alone. For such "just law" can be nothing other than the inner "objective" definiteness of form that Plato compares with the definiteness found in geometry. It is "geometrical equality."

In modern philosophy this cognitive ideal of "pure form" was most clearly realized by Kant. Kant's "idealism" is not "subjective" idealism in the sense of Descartes. As Kant explicitly emphasizes, in order to distinguish it from every kind of subjective idealism, it is a "formal idealism."[174] How does this "formal" idealism proceed and how is it distinguished from mere subjective idealism? It too begins with the "work," and it uses this work in order to find out, through retrospective "reflection" on the structure of the work, what forms are invested in it. This is initially the case with natural science. It is first taken as a "factum," but it is not simply taken for what it is—an aggregate of truths and knowledge; rather, inquiry is made into its systematic "form," into the principles, basic rules, and axioms that "constitute" it and the "conditions of its possibility." In the

173. "fluctuating back and forth." See Plato *Cratylus* 386D8–E4. *Collected Dialogues*, pp. 424f.: Socrates: "But if neither [Protagoras and Euthydemus] is right, and things are not relative to individuals, and all things do not equally belong to all at the same moment and always, they must be supposed to have their own proper and permanent essence; they are not in relation to us, or influenced by us, fluctuating according to our fancy, but they are independent, and maintain to their own essence the relation prescribed by nature."—Eds.

174. See Kant, *Prolegomena zu einer jeden künftigen Metaphysik die als Wissenschaft wird auftreten können*, *Werke*, vol. 4, p. 131; *Prolegomena to any Future Metaphysics*, pp. 124f. See also Kant, *Kritik der reinen Vernunft*, *Werke*, vol. 3, p. 349 Anm (A 491/B 519 n.); *Critique of Pure Reason*, p. 439 n.—Eds.

same way the question is raised about the "conditions of the possibility" of morality, or art, and so on. Even the question of morality is traced back to a pure form. The "categorical imperative" can only be a "formal imperative." That is what links Kant—through the centuries, over Descartes and Leibniz—again with Plato.

In this way the paradoxical nature of Kant's ethics becomes understandable. For what is it that is so paradoxical about this ethics, that has caused it again and again to be met with incredulity and to cause offense? It is that Kant set forth a purely "formal" ethics instead of a "material" ethics, that he had to deprive action of all content and of every object in order to legitimize and justify it ethically. But what is acting without content? What is a deed that is not done in the service of some particular goal, without regard and care concerning its effects and its success, but rather is to be done only "for its own sake"? Is not this "pure" ought—an ought only for the sake of the ought—a completely empty ought, something to which no force can be attributed? Does not this force, through which only can the will be set in motion, come solely from the object that the will is directed toward and which acts as the concrete motive, the moving force, hence, from the will's matter, from what is willed, not the will's "form"?

This contradiction is resolved if we pay attention to the basic tendency of Kantian ethics, which consists in nothing other than to liberate ethics the same as logic from the despotism of merely material aims, that is, from the despotism of mere action, to purify it in the process of simple contemplation, knowledge of the ought, knowledge of what duty "is," of ἀγαθόν as αὐτὸ καθ' αὐτό.[175] This purification is conceived along Socratic and Platonic lines: the rejection of all "Utilitarianism," of all "outside" "heteronomous" determination and the call for "purity," that is, for autonomy, the determination of the will through its own pure form.

The "philosophy of symbolic forms" grows out of this critical, transcendental question and builds upon it. It is pure "contemplation," not of a single form, but of all—the cosmos of pure forms—and it seeks to trace this cosmos back to the "conditions of its possibility." We must remember here that this turn to "contemplation," to pure "objectivity" as a turn toward the Idea in the broadest sense—to "objectivity" as a recognition of things and as a value in opposition to the "will" as subjective and arbitrary—was not a breakthrough occurring for the first time in the discovery of the Socratic-Platonic world of Ideas or Forms. We find it already, merely in a different

---

175. "good [as] in and for itself." See Plato *Phaedo* 100B.—Eds.

"mode"[176] of interpretation, in the "discovery of nature." This could not come about in any other way except by "objective" perception—the experience of "nature" as embodying forms and following rules—taking the [place of] the sphere of mythic perception, which everywhere sees "forces" at work, concentrations of the will of gods and demons. This first occurs in Greek culture and originally only in it. This discovery of nature in objective "perception" is then confirmed, furthered, and supplemented, in a sense "transcended," in the discovery of the realm of Ideas, as the realm of "pure forms."

176. Cf. above!—Cassirer. See above, pp. 167–169.—Eds.

PART III

*Symbolic Forms:
For Volume Four
c. 1928*

Section One

For the Introduction

[1. The Concept of the Whole]

WE start with the concept of the whole: the whole is the true (Hegel).[1] But the truth of the whole can always only be grasped in a particular "aspect." This is "knowledge" in the *broadest* sense—"seeing" the whole "in" an aspect, through the medium of this aspect. With this, the problem of representation becomes the central problem of knowledge. Knowledge is "organic" insofar as every part is conditioned by the whole and can be made "understandable" only by reference to the whole. It cannot be composed of pieces, of elements, except to the extent that each part already carries in itself the "form" of the whole. The concept of "form" εἶδος, μορφή[2] was already grasped in this way in Greek philosophy and goes through the whole history of Western philosophy.[3]

TRANSCENDENTAL PHILOSOPHY

"Fact" and "Theory": the highest thing would be to recognize that all fact is already theory.[4]

1. Preface to Hegel, *Phänomenologie des Geistes*, *Sämtliche Werke*, Jubiläumsausgabe, 20 vols., ed. Hermann Glockner (Stuttgart: F. Frommann, 1927), vol. 2, p. 24. *The Phenomenology of Spirit*, trans. A. V. Miller (Oxford: Oxford Univ. Press, 1977), p. 11: "The True is the whole."—Eds.

2. "form, gestalt." See Aristotle, *Metaphysics* 1045b18.—Eds.

3. A development (negative) against the *false* concept of an element: Mach etc., cf. Introduction.—Cassirer. Mach's concept of elements is criticized in the introduction to *PSF*, vol. 3, pp. 24–28.—Eds.

4. See Goethe, *Maximen und Reflexionen*, Schriften der Goethe-Gesellschaft, 21, ed. Max Hecker (Weimar: Verlag der Goethe-Gesellschaft, 1907), p. 125, no. 575: "Das Höchste wäre: zu begreifen, dass alles Faktische schon Theorie ist." Goethe, *Wisdom and Experience*, ed. Ludwig Curtius and Hermann Weigand, trans. H. Weigand (New York: Pantheon, 1949),

"Concept" and "experience": every particular experience is an aspect of a whole of meaning. This [is] the theoretical concept of meaning expressed in Kant's notion of *synthesis a priori*. Every empirically given particular is already determined through the form of the whole of experience. This [is] the solution to the question: How are synthetic judgments a priori possible? The form of experience can be anticipated:[5] *anticipatio mentis*. The "particular" always also represents the "context of experience."

[There are] defects in the definition of the correlative relationship between matter and form in Kant. They stem from the fact that a question concerning matters of meaning has again been reinterpreted in an unacceptable way as a genetic question about origins. From the standpoint of meaning, of knowledge in the essential sense, there is only matter and form, the particular in the general, the individual in the whole. But Kant also asks: Where does the matter come from; where does form come from? The answer is: matter comes from the thing in itself, form comes from the mind. But we cannot ask about the separate origin of aspects taken in abstraction, about where they came from. The unity of representation, the unity of meaning, cannot be composed of isolated *pieces*. If this were the case, then the parts would exist *prior* to the whole. There would be no synthesis a priori, only synthesis a posteriori.

The separation of sensation (intuition) and concepts of the understanding makes sense therefore in Hume, but it no longer does so for Kant. The concept of mere conjunction (*conjunctio*) was overcome by that of synthesis.

Synthesis a priori would never have been possible if experience were an aggregate of the given in sensation and the forms of the understanding; it comprehends this given in its determination through the pure form itself (logic of facts).[6]

[2. The Problem of Knowledge as the Problem of Form]

To be developed: The problem of knowledge as a problem of form.

---

p. 94: "It were the height of insight to realize that everything factual as such is, in a sense, theory."—Eds.

5. Cf. Leibniz, Klem. d. Th.—Cassirer. Perhaps a reference to Leibniz's *Theodicy.*—Eds.

6. On this concept of Synthesis as Synthesis of the whole, cf. now also [Josef] König, *Der Begriff der Intuition* [Halle: Max Niemeyer, 1926], further: [Hans] Heyse, *Begriff der Ganzheit [und die Kantische Philosophie: Ideen zu einer regionalen Logik und Kategorienlehre* (Munich: E. Reinhardt, 1927)].—Cassirer.

The whole problem of knowledge turns, also taken historically, on two axes:

a) around the axis of the problem of form
b) around the axis of the problem of the symbol (the problem of representation).

One could in fact distinctly characterize and define every "theory of knowledge" that has emerged in the history of philosophy through its relationship to these two basic problems. Their basic philosophical attitudes are determined by the meaning and the place that they give to (a) the concept of form and (b) the concept of representation.

The basic problem since ancient Greek philosophy consists in understanding how it is possible for the form of being to be pictured in the form of knowledge such that both appear as specifically *different* worlds and yet in this very difference remain one and the same in their *meaning*, so that the cosmos of "reason," of λόγος, and the cosmos of being, φύσις, "correspond" to each other. The battle of the systems concerns the meaning that is to be attributed to "correspondence"—here every solution is attempted.

[a) The] first, most "primitive" solution consists in claiming that a relationship of identity exists here. There are not really two forms but rather only one—the relationship of knowledge, of thought, to being is an *analytic* relationship: αὐτὸ γὰρ ἐστι νοεῖν τε καὶ εἶναι.[7] A "representation" of being in thought does not therefore take place. The relationship of representation is declared actually to be that of coinciding.

b) [The second solution:] transformation into a causal relationship. Being "effects" thought, enters with its form or a portion of it into thought. Representation [is traced] back to uniformity and [to] the effect of something on the same sort of thing. As Empedocles says: "We see Earth by means of Earth, Water by means of Water."[8]

Preformation System: Identity, as the unity of the Microcosm and Macrocosm, makes possible the relationship that we possess in knowledge—or as a system of *epigenesis*: being penetrates into knowledge.

---

7. Parmenides frag. 18 B 5 (Diels, vol. 1, p. 152; Freeman, B 3, p. 42): τὸ γὰρ αὐτὸ νοεῖν ἐστίν τε καὶ εἶναι ("For it is the same thing to think and to be").—Eds.

8. Empedocles frag. B 109 (Diels, vol. 1 p. 262): γαίηι μὲν γὰρ γαῖαν ὀπώπαμεν, ὕδατι δ'ὕδωρ, αἰθέρι δ' αἰθέρα δῖον, ἀτὰρ πυρὶ πῦρ ἀίδηλον, στοργὴν δὲ στοργῆι, νεῖκος δέ τε νείκεϊ λυγρῶι. Freeman, p. 63: "We see Earth by means of Earth, Water by means of Water, divine Air by means of Air, and destructive Fire by means of Fire; Affection by means of Affection, Hate by means of baneful Hate."—Eds.

εἴδωλον[9] *Theory*: "Representation" [is] "explained" here as similarity (original) or as a picturing (mediate)—from Epicurus'[10] εἴδωλ[ον] theory to all the variations of the picture theory.

c) [The third solution:] *representation* as μέθεξις.

The new turn consists in now shifting the problem into a new sphere or dimension. In all previous theories, in the identity theory as well as the picture or causal pictures, the aim is always to interpret knowledge as a part of being, which on the other hand, however, is supposed somehow to "embrace in itself" the whole. This containing of "the part in the whole," of the Microcosm in the Macrocosm, gave rise to ever new puzzles. For how is what is comprehended able at the same time to be comprehensive, the comprehending? Knowledge is supposed to be comprehending and comprehended.[11] The metaphysics of knowledge draws constant sustenance from this antinomy and aporia. This metaphysics contains, as its most recent development in Nikolai Hartmann[12] shows, the kernel of Skepticism. In all the dogmatic systems that begin with the concept of being, which proceed from the notion of "substance," this aporia makes itself felt again and again. So it is in Spinoza's conception of attributes.[13] Being has infinitely many attributes—including among others the attribute of *cogitatio*.[14]

But how does *cogitatio* come to know about infinity and to express it? The expression (*expressio*) of extension in thought remains the real prob-

---

9. "image, phantom."—Eds.

10. See *Epicurea*, ed. Hermann Usener (Stuttgart: B. G. Teubner, 1887), Epistvla Prima, 46a, 47a, 48, 50. *Epicurus: The Extant Remains*, ed. Cyril Bailey (Oxford: Clarendon Press, 1926), Ep. I, 46a, 47a, 48, 50; Frag. xxiv; Vit. 28.—Eds.

11. The German is "Umfangend-umfangen," which is from Goethe's poem "Ganymed," *WA*, Abt. 1, vol. 2, p. 80: "Umfangend umfangen! / Aufwärts an deinen Busen, / Alliebender Vater!" This phrase is translated as "Embraced embracing!" in "Ganymede" in *Goethe's Collected Works*, vol. 1, ed. Christopher Middleton, various translators (Boston: Suhrkamp/Insel, 1983), p. 33: "Embraced embracing! / Upward to your sweet breast, All-loving father!"—Eds.

12. See Nikolai Hartmann's "metaphysics of knowledge" in his *Grundzüge einer Metaphysik der Erkenntnis* (Berlin: Walter de Gruyter, 1921).—Eds.

13. See Spinoza, *Ethica*, pt. 1, def. 4, *Opera quotquot reperta sunt*, ed. J. van Vloten and J. P. N. Land, 3d ed., 4 vols. (The Hague: Martinus Nijhoff, 1914), vol. 1, p. 37. *The Ethics*, trans. Samuel Shirley, ed. Seymour Feldman (Indianapolis: Hackett, 1982), p. 31: "By attribute I mean that which the intellect perceives of substance as constituting its essence."—Eds.

14. See Spinoza, *Ethica*, pt. 2, prop. 1, *Opera*, vol. 1, p. 74. *The Ethics*, p. 64: "Thought is an attribute of God; i.e. God is a thinking thing."—Eds.

lem. For now it is immediately clear that the relation of substance to the attributes of being as *ens a se* and of thought cannot be that of the (extensive) whole to the (extensive) part. For this relation retains an element of fundamental non-homogeneity: *cogitatio* expresses *extensio*, but *extensio* is not *cogitatio*. Here every "Parallelism" fails—the proposition "ordo et connexio rerum *idem est atque ordo et connexio idearum*,"[15] the bare relation of identity, is not sufficient to characterize the relationship of *expressio repraesentatio*. That is the decisive point at which Leibniz departs from Spinoza. He places the *expressio repraesentatio* at the middle point of his concept of the monad, which is his designation for primordial being. For the monad in its essence is *repraesentatio*—is *multorum in uno expressio*. Put differently, in the concept of representation we have moved from the level of simple reality to the level of meaning: meaning is the basic category through which we are able to define "being" and "reality."

The relation of "being" to "thought" is now neither a (real) relation of parts nor a (real) causal relation (microcosm, inference, and so on); rather, it is a purely *significative* relation, a meaning relation, or, as we would say, a symbolic relation. This turn emerges historically for the first time in Greek philosophy. With the Pythagoreans both motifs struggle against each other. The number is what has being, and beings "imitate numbers," "participate in the number."[16] The two expressions appear for them, according to Aristotle's report, not yet distinguished from each other.

Not until Plato's conception of μέθεξις is this distinction clearly drawn.[17] "Idea" and "phenomenon" are both unmistakably different in their being. They can never "coincide," nor does a "phenomenon" reproduce the "idea" in the sense that a part of the idea "enters into" the phenomenon. These are all inadequate expressions of the relation. "The same" (stones and sticks) are in fact never "sameness" (the idea of sameness), but nonetheless a relationship of μέθεξις holds between the phenomenon and the idea, between the same and sameness, a relationship which goes beyond the fundamental ἑτερότης. Things that are same express sameness, beautiful things, πράγματα, express the idea of beauty.

Here in the idea of "participation" [we have] a new relation of "part" to "whole"—an "intensive" instead of an "extensive" relation. The problem of knowledge is the problem of μέθεξις. "Knowledge" and "being" are dif-

---

15. See Spinoza, *Ethica*, pt. 2, prop. 7, *Opera*, vol. 1, p. 77. *The Ethics*, p. 66: "The order and connection of ideas is the same as the order and connection of things."—Eds.

16. See Aristotle *Metaphysics* 13.6.1080b16 and 1.5.985b23–986a.3.—Eds.

17. See, e.g., Plato *Parmenides* 132D3, 151E8.—Eds.

ferentiated and yet even in this differentiation they are necessarily and correlatively related to each other. The concept of εἶδος itself is capable thereby of a twofold definition which is given expression in typical clarity by Plato and Aristotle. Plato proceeds from εἶδος as pure meaning; *the* triangle, its τί ἐστι, is "present" in all triangles, stands in common with them—μέθεξις as παρουσία and κοινωνία.[18] The meaning, the sense of a triangle "lights up," "appears," is always given for us only in "the" triangles. The universal is never otherwise *there*, never otherwise present than in the particular, in the single "case" of its realization, but *through* this case we can *grasp* the universal as καθόλου, according to what it is in itself as an αὐτο καθ αὐτό.

This [is] the basic relationship in Plato: the universal is grasped in the particular, the meaning "in itself" is grasped in the particular case of its realization. Through the particular case of its realization we "look at" the universal, the εἶδος. This kind of "viewpoint" defines the relation of idea to appearance.

See also Nicholas of Cusa: in the triangle as something particular and quantitatively limited, something appears, an entity, that itself is not subject to any further quantitative limitation—in the finite there appears something infinite—in the Quantum a "Quid" and "Quale," in "existence" something 'essential': *dum trigonum depingit quantum*, and so on.[19]

The concept of εἶδος is different in Aristotle, for here εἶδος is not primarily a mathematical essence; rather, it is the organic form. The form as realization of the possible—as the totality of configuration. Each particular configuration has its basis in this totality. The form as a whole explicates itself in the serial order of becoming. It is the dynamic form which can "appear" only in the process of becoming.

All knowledge is founded on this. Knowledge means: to see the whole of the "form" in the individual, which comes, or has come, into being. The *meaning* of becoming emerges only when we see it in this way *sub specie* of form, when we take every particular configuration as a phase of the whole

---

18. "participation as presence and community." See Plato *Phaedo* 100D5.—Eds.

19. See *Complementvm theologicvm figvratum in complementis mathematicis Nicolai de Cvsa Cardinalis, Nicolai Cusae Cardinalis Opera*, vol. 2 (Paris, 1514), cited from reprint (Frankfurt am Main: Minerva, 1962), chap. V, fol. 95b: "Nam dum trigonú depingit quantú: non ad trigonum respicit quátum / sed ad trigonum simpliciter absolutum ab omni quátitate / & qualitate / magnitudine & multitudine" (For while he [the mathematician] draws a quantitatively specific triangle, he does not look to this, but to a triangle absolutely free of all quantity and quality, magnitude and multitude).—Eds.

and when every particular phase symbolically embodies the whole. This is expressive meaning, not significative meaning as in Plato. There are clearly two *types* of knowledge set against each other here, but both are in agreement in their grasp of the form relation as a relation of μέθεξις—not of identity or of sameness.[20]

[The] *whole* of experience of science is only one level of the whole. We distinguish among the following:

Hermeneutic:	a) Expression = "Understanding"—"Life"
	b) Representation = "Perception"—"Gestalt"
interpretatio naturae:	c) Significance = "Knowledge"—"Law"

"Experience" in the sense of objectifying science is only one form of the whole. We distinguish from it:

α) the life-whole, found in the primary phenomenon of *Expression*—something "sensory" appearing as expression, that is, as a manifestation of a felt whole to which it belongs as something individual. Every gesture, and so on, is an expression of a soul and also is historical and belongs to the history of ideas. The entire history of ideas rests upon hermeneutics. Interpretation in a physiognomic sense—in Spengler, the "morphology of culture"—[is], however, always only *one* side.

β) "Representation." Representation in the construction of the empirical image of the world, representation as "shading." (cf. Helmholtz.)[21]

γ) pure knowledge. The system of "ideal" "Signification" (Mathematics).

Concerning α) In all "hermeneutics" the concern is also to grasp "totalities" (life-totalities, "biographies") in particulars—the average "character." Transindividual unities (cultures, and so on) also have character in this sense.[22]

ad β) Grasping an "object" in a particular perspective or "viewpoint."

20. There follow several lines of unfinished notes, which are not reproduced here.—Eds.

21. The influence of shading (*Abschattung*) on the representation of forms is briefly discussed in Helmholtz, *Handbuch der physiologischen Optik*, 2d rev. ed. (Hamburg: L. Voss, 1896), pp. 773, 792f.—Eds.

22. Wach, Problem of *Understanding*.—Cassirer. Joachim Wach, *Das Verstehen: Grundzüge einer Geschichte der Hermeneutischen Theorie im 19. Jahrhundert*, 3 vols. (Tübingen: J. C. B. Mohr [Paul Siebeck], 1926–1933). A brief discussion of these matters can be found in "The Meaning and Task of the History of Religions," in *Understanding and Believing: Essays by Joachim Wach*, ed. Joseph M. Kitagawa (New York: Harper & Row, 1968), pp. 125–141.—Eds.

ad γ) Every particular "proposition," whether mathematical or physical in kind, is valid only within a system of truths. We grasp the "system" in it as an aspect. Every experience is based upon a theory.[23]

There is also a way of grasping "nature," as exemplified by Goethe, which remains entirely within the limits of the expressive whole and the perceptual whole—"Willst Du Dich am Ganzen erquicken, so muss Du das Ganze im Kleinsten erblicken!"[24]

This direction of our "glance" at the whole (of phenomena, at the primary phenomena) defines a specific way of regarding things which must be strictly distinguished from having a view of the "system" ("signification," Newton).[25]

Section Two

["Geist" and "Life"]

[1. "Geist" and "Life": Heidegger]

For Heidegger, who comes not from biology but from the philosophy of religion, the problem of "life" and "geist" also poses itself differently. His view of "existence" [*Existenz*] and "temporality" is not determined, like

---

23. Duhem—Here the concept of the symbol in physics.—Cassirer. See Pierre Duhem, *La théorie physique: Son objet et sa structure*, Bibliothèque de philosophie expérimentale, II (Paris: Chevalier & Rivière, 1906), chap. 5, §1, "Les lois de Physique sont des relations symboliques," pp. 269–273. Duhem, *The Aim and Structure of Physical Theory*, trans. Philip P. Wiener (New York: Atheneum, 1962), pp. 165–179, "The laws of physics are symbolic relations." See also Cassirer, *Substance and Function* and *Einstein's Theory of Relativity* (two books bound as one), auth. trans. W. C. Swabey and M. C. Swabey (New York: Dover Books, 1953), p. 281 n.—Eds.

24. See Goethe's collection of sayings in verse, "Gott, Gemüth und Welt," *WA*, Abt. 1, vol. 2, p. 216: "Willst Du Dich am Ganzen erquicken, / So musst Du das Ganze im Kleinsten erblicken" (If you wish to enjoy the whole, then you must find it in the smallest part).—Eds.

25. Problem: Goethe and Newton.—Cassirer. Cassirer discusses the controversy between Goethe and Newton, in "Goethe und die mathematische Physik: Eine erkenntnistheoretische Betrachtung," in *Idee und Gestalt: Fünf Aufsätze* (Berlin: Bruno Cassirer, 1921). On the distinction between "the whole" and a "system," see the comment in Cassirer's "Zur Logik des Symbolbegriffs," *Theoria* 4 (1938): 173: "The 'Philosophy of symbolic Forms' cannot and does not want . . . to be a 'System' in the traditional meaning of the word."—Eds.

Bergson's, through the contemplation of the natural phenomenon of *life*—the phenomenon of natural "coming to be" and "passing away"; rather, for him all temporality has its roots in the "present moment" seen in a religious sense—for it is constituted through "care" [*Sorge*] and through the basic religious phenomenon of death—and "anxiety" [*Angst*] (cf. Kierkegaard).[26]

He does not seek to derive the region of the geist from "nature"—the ontology of existence from the being of "things," from reality. On the contrary, he recognizes that this whole world of things, the world of "reality," is a secondary phenomenon.[27] Here is the root of Heidegger's "Idealism." "The world is neither present-at-hand nor ready-to-hand, but temporalizes itself in temporality. It 'is', with the 'outside-of-itself' of the ecstases, 'there'. If no Dasein exists, no world is 'there' either" (365).[28] Dasein as the dasein of geist—for care is also of course a basic phenomenon of "intelligence"—is the πρότερον τῇ φύσει[29] of any positing of reality in the sense of the "thing-like."

But even this starting point itself is now limited by Heidegger, quite in the manner of Kierkegaard, to the moment as "this here" and constantly restricted to it. Everything "general," all giving in to the general is for Heidegger a "fall"[30]—a disregarding of "authentic" *dasein*—a giving in to the inauthenticity of the "they" [*das "Man"*].

Here, essentially, is where there is a parting of the ways between his path and ours. The ontological cannot be separated from the ontic nor the

26. See the commentary on the innocence of anxiety, in Søren Kierkegaard, *The Concept of Anxiety: A Simple Psychologically Orienting Deliberation on the Dogmatic Issue of Hereditary Sin*, ed. and trans. Reidar Thomte, in collaboration with Albert B. Anderson (Princeton: Princeton Univ. Press, 1980), p. 41: "In this state there is peace and repose, but there is simultaneously something else that is not contention and strife, for there is indeed nothing against which to strive. What, then, is it? Nothing. But what effect does nothing have? It begets anxiety. This is the profound secret of innocence, that it is at the same time anxiety."—Eds.

27. [*MS has on a line by itself*]: On this see esp. pp. 350ff.—Cassirer. Cassirer's citation refers to the pagination in Martin Heidegger, *Sein und Zeit, Jahrbuch für Philosophie und phänomenologische Forschung* 8 (1927): v–xii, 1–809. These numbers have been retained (cited here in parentheses), since they are also reproduced in the margins of the English translation: *Being and Time*, trans. John Macquarrie and Edward Robinson (New York: Harper & Row, 1962).—Eds.

28. *Marginal note:* Also especially 277: "Because the kind of being that is essential to truth is of the character of Dasein, all truth is relative to Dasein's Being."—This is dubious!—Cassirer.

29. "first things."—Eds.

30. Heidegger, *Being and Time*, §38: "Falling and Thrownness," pp. 219–224 (175–180).—Eds.

individual from the "general" in the way that Heidegger tries to—rather, the one is only from within the other.[31]

We understand the general not as the mere they, but as "objective spirit and objective culture." For Heidegger, thought has no access to such objectivity. So even the *logos*, language, now becomes a merely social phenomenon which as such—similar to Bergson—carries no genuine intelligent content. Discourse is not grasped as λόγος, as embodying reason; rather, it hardens into mere "talk about," into superficial "idle talk" (160ff., 167ff.).[32] Here giving in to the world of the "general" is again considered to be a mere looking away from oneself, a kind of "fall from grace."

Here, basically, is where we depart from him, because for us objective spirit is not exhausted by nor does it degenerate into the structure of everydayness. The "impersonal" does not consist merely in the pale, diluted social form of the average, the everydayness of the "they," but in the form of transpersonal meaning. For this transpersonal, Heidegger's philosophy has no access.

To be sure, it has a sense for historical life, but it takes all historical understanding as but mere repetition, the bringing-up-again of personal dasein, personal destinies, personal fate. This feature of history [is] very deeply and very well comprehended. See what is said about historiology and fate, 384ff.[33]

The deliberating resoluteness that comes back to itself turns into a repetition of a received possibility of existence (385).[34] Here one feature of historicality is deeply and clearly recognized, but it is always a religious-individualistic comprehension of history that confronts us here. History as

---

31. See Heidegger, *Being and Time*, §27: "Everyday Being-one's-Self and the 'They,' " pp. 163–168 (126–130), esp. p. 165 (128): "The '*they*', which supplies the answer to the question of the '*who*' of everyday Dasein, is the '*nobody*' to whom every Dasein has already surrendered itself in Being-among-one-other [*Untereinandersein*]."—Eds.

32. See Heidegger, *Being and Time*, §34: "Being-there and Discourse: Language," pp. 203–211 (160–167), and §35: "Idle Talk," pp. 211–214 (167–170).—Eds.

33. Perhaps a reference to Heidegger, *Being and Time*, p. 438 (386): "*Authentic Being-towards-death—that is to say, the finitude of temporality—is the hidden basis of Dasein's historicality.* Dasein does not first become historical in repetition; but because it is historical as temporal, it can take itself over in its history by repeating. For this, no historiology is as yet needed."—Eds.

34. Heidegger, *Being and Time*, p. 437 (385): "The resoluteness which comes back to itself and hands itself down, then becomes the *repetition* of a possibility of existence that has come down to us. *Repeating is handing down explicitly*, that is to say, going back into the possibilities of the Dasein that has-been-there."—Eds.

the history of culture, the history of meaning, as the life of the objective spirit is *not* thereby disclosed. This is especially clear: "This interpretation of the concept of 'meaning' is one which is ontologico-existential in principle (according to it all meaning stems from our 'caring' or engagement)[35], if we adhere to it, then all entities whose kind of Being is of a character other than Dasein's must be conceived as *unmeaning* [*unsinniges*], essentially devoid of any meaning at all. Here 'unmeaning' does not signify that we are saying anything about the value of such entities, but it gives expression to an ontological characteristic" (152).[36]

For us meaning is by no means exhausted by dasein; rather, "there is" [*es gibt*] impersonal meaning which, of course, is only experienceable for an existing subject—for instance, mathematical meaning; there is objective meaning in the sense of significance (= "geist").

There is finally a breaking away from the *merely* ontological, without actually severing the bond with it.

Heidegger moves through the sphere of life to that of personal existence, which he utilizes unremittingly for a religious purpose, but on the other hand he is also confined by this sphere. His religion draws its power and depth from the individualistic tendency it takes from Luther[37] and Kierkegaard.

In opposition to it, we uphold, despite everything, the broader, more universal, *idealistic* meaning of religion and the idealistic meaning of history. In *it* we behold liberation and deliverance from the "anxiety" which is the signature, the basic "state-of-mind" of finite dasein.[38] But this anxiety

35. Cassirer's interpolation.—Eds.
36. Heidegger, *Being and Time*, p. 193 (152).—Eds.
37. In notes for a lecture on Heidegger given at the second Davoser Hochschulkurse in 1929 (Beinecke envelope 94; in the text with the heading "Das Todesproblem"), Cassirer compares Heidegger's view of death with Martin Luther's and cites *Being and Time*, p. 282 (239): "And even if, by thus Being there alongside, it were possible and feasible for us to make plain to ourselves 'psychologically' the dying of Others, this would by no means let us grasp the way-to-be which we would then have in mind—namely, coming-to-an-end. We are asking about the ontological meaning of the dying of the person who dies, as a possibility-of-Being which belongs to *his* Being." Cassirer compares this with the following passage in Luther, cited here from "The Eight Wittenberg Sermons (1522)," trans. W. A. Lambert, *Works of Martin Luther*, 6 vols., various translators (Philadelphia: Muhlenberg Press, 1943), vol. 2, p. 391: "The challenge of death comes to us all, and no one can die for another. Everyone must fight his own battle with [the devil and] death by himself, alone. We can shout into one another's ears, but everyone must be prepared finally to meet death alone. I will not be with you then, nor you with me." Translation emended.—Eds.
38. Cf. Kierkegaard's concept of *dread* and pp. 342ff., 184ff.—Cassirer.

signifies only the beginning, not a final, inevitable constraint on our finite *dasein*. Here Schiller's words about the world of "form" and the "ideal" apply:

> But free from the ravages of time . . .
> Would'st thou freely soar on her wings on high,
> Throw off earthly dread,
> flee from narrow, stifling life
> into the realm of the ideal![39]

For *us* that is no bloodless, empty "Idealism" as it must seem for Heidegger. It is "life in the idea," liberation from the ontological confinement and dullness of dasein. For us "world history" in no way means to enter into the mere objectivity of an impersonal "they"—"inauthentic historicality," cf. 387ff, esp. 391,[40] but rather, in Hegel's sense, "the abode of the Idea." Here too Heidegger puts the ontological not only before the ontic, but also unconditionally before the "ideal." See 393: "Because *Dasein, and only Dasein*, is primordially historical, that which historiological thematizing presents as a possible object for research, must have the kind of being of *Dasein which has-been-there.*" For us, however, not only *dasein*, but meaning—the idea—is primordially historical.

For Heidegger, "dasein," as individual particular being, is always primordial. Everything else is a "degeneration," a falling away from dasein.

"Infinite time" is for Heidegger a mere fiction. He understands this as the "endlessness" whose subject is the "they," hence in the sense of bad infinity—accordingly as mere *inauthentic* time (330f.).[41] But is this infinite

---

39. See Schiller, "Das Ideal und das Leben," *Sämtliche Werke*, Säkular-Ausgabe, 16 vols., ed. Eduard von der Hellen (Stuttgart and Berlin: J. G. Cotta, 1904), vol. 1, p. 192: "Aber frei von jeder Zeitgewalt, / Die Gespielin seliger Naturen, / Wandelt oben in des Lichtes Fluren / Göttlich unter Göttern, die *Gestalt*. / Wollt ihr hoch auf ihren Flügeln schweben, / Werft die Angst des Irdischen von euch, / Fliehet aus dem engen dumpfen Leben / in des Ideales Reich!" In the Davos debate with Heidegger in 1929, Cassirer again quotes from this Schiller passage. See "Davos Disputation between Ernst Cassirer and Martin Heidegger," published as a supplement to Martin Heidegger, *Kant and the Problem of Metaphysics*, 4th ed., enl., trans. Richard Taft (Bloomington: Indiana Univ. Press, 1990), pp. 171–185.—Eds.

40. See Heidegger, *Being and Time*, p. 443 (391): "In inauthentic historicality, on the other hand, the way in which fate has been primordially stretched along has been hidden. With the inconstancy of the they-self Dasein makes present its 'today' . . . the temporality of authentic historicality, as the moment of vision of anticipatory repetition *deprives* the 'today' of its character as present, and weans one from the conventionalities of the 'they.' "—Eds.

41. Heidegger, *Being and Time*, p. 379 (330f.): "In what sense is 'time' endless? . . . The problem is not one of *how* the *'derived'* [*'abgeleitete'*] infinite time, in which the ready-to-hand

time not something more—and is it not something positive? For *us* it is not mere objective, physical time, but a time specific to mankind—a change of the subject of temporality. This time of "humanitas" is by no means limited to the "they."

But Heidegger's philosophy ultimately recognizes history only in *this* sense: as the totality of religious-individual destinies, each of which is in itself irrationally thrown, dispersed in itself. The *idea* of humanitas he would reject as a mere "concept" (cf. Herder against Kant's "Averroism").[42] But the "unity of the idea" should not be understood in an Averroistic sense; here we take a stand on the same ground as Hegel against Kierkegaard.

[2. Heidegger and the Problem of Death]

Heidegger's whole discussion [is] centered on the problem of death. The analytic of existence [*Existenz*] has its focal point here, for it lies in the meaning and essence of human existence that this existence has an end, that human beings die.

This dying is not an external fate, but must be understood through the *essential nature* of human being. cf. Simmel.[43]

Being thrown [*Das Geworfensein*], and so on.[44] (See Heidegger's discus-

---

arises and passes away, becomes *primordial* finite temporality; the problem is rather that of how the *in*authentic temporality arises out of finite authentic temporality, and how inauthentic temporality, as *in*authentic, temporalizes an *in*-finite time out of the finite. Only because primordial time is *finite* can the derived time temporalize as *infinite*."—Eds.

42. See Kant, *Idee zu einer allgemeinen Geschichte in weltbürgerlicher Absicht*, *Werke*, vol. 4, p. 153. "Idea for a Universal History," second thesis, *On History*, ed. Lewis White Beck, trans. Lewis White Beck et al. (Indianapolis: Bobbs-Merrill, 1963), p. 13: "*In man* (as the only rational creature on earth) *those natural capacities which are directed to the use of his reason are to be fully developed only in the race, not in the individual.*" Without mentioning Kant by name, Herder rejects this view and refers to it as "Averroistic," pointing out that according to Averroes' philosophy "the whole human species possesses but one mind; and that indeed of a very low order." See Johann Gottfried Herder, *Ideen zur Philosophie der Geschichte der Menschheit* (1785), pt. 2, *Herders Sämmtliche Werke*, ed. Bernhard Suphan (Berlin: Weidmann, 1877–1913), vol. 13, pp. 345f. *Outlines of a Philosophy of the History of Man*, trans. T. O. Churchill (New York: Bergman Publishers, 1966), p. 226.—Eds.

43. Heidegger refers in *Being and Time* §50, p. 249, n. vi (293), to Simmel's discussion of death in *Lebensanschauung: Vier metaphysische Kapitel* (Munich: Duncker & Humblot, 1918), pp. 99–153.—Eds.

44. See Heidegger, *Being and Time*, p. 135 (174): "This characteristic of Dasein's Being—this 'that it is'—is veiled in its 'whence' and 'whither', yet disclosed in itself all the more

sion and the report by Bréh[ier])[45] Here we find the essential statement: for an entity that is in time and which passes away in time, there can be no eternal truths.[46] The stigma of death is impressed upon *everything* human and on everything that man takes up—that "truth" [is] an object and content of human *consciousness*, that imprints with this stigma. For since this consciousness is necessarily finite, that makes it a finite, transitory consciousness. The thought of "eternal truths" seems therefore to Heidegger almost as a kind of hybris, a reaching beyond human limits, ignoring the primary phenomena of death. His whole analytic of existence has no other goal than to reverse this process—again to remove death from its "concealment" [*verdeckung*] to make it truly visible again.

Here—we do not deny—a genuine religious tone becomes audible, as with Kierkegaard. As with Kierkegaard the concept of anxiety [*Angst*] steps into the middle of this phenomenology—anxiety is essentially anxiety about finitude, about transitoriness, about annihilation. With Heidegger the problem seems to cut more deeply insofar as his posing of the question was quite determined by theological considerations (on this, see the com-

---

unveiledly; we call it the '*thrownness*' of this entity into its 'there'; indeed, it is thrown in such a way that, as Being-in-the-world, it is the 'there.' "—Eds.

45. Probably a reference to Emile Bréhier.—Eds.

46. See the formulation in Descartes, *Principia philosophiæ*, *Oeuvres de Descartes*, ed. Charles Adam and Paul Tannery, 12 vols. (Paris: L. Cerf, 1896–1913), vol. 8, p. 23: "Cùm autem agnoscimus fieri non posse, ut ex nihilo aliquid fiat, tunc propositio hæc: *Ex nihilo nihil fit*, non tanquam res aliqua existens, neque etiam ut rei modus consideratur, sed ut veritas quædam æterna, quæ in mente nostrâ sedem habet, vocaturque communis notio, sive axioma. Cujus generis sunt: *Impossibile est idem simul esse & non esse: Quod factum est, infectum esse nequit: Is qui cogitat, non potest non existere dum cogitat*: & alia innumera, quæ quidem omnia recenseri facilè non possunt, sed nec etiam ignorari, cùm occurrit occasio ut de iis cogitemus, & nullis præjudiciis excæcamur." *The Philosophical Writings of Descartes*, trans. J. Cottingham et al., 2 vols. (Cambridge: Cambridge Univ. Press, 1984), vol. 1, p. 209: "But when we recognize that it is impossible for anything to come from nothing, the proposition *Nothing comes from nothing* is regarded not as a really existing thing, or even as a mode of a thing, but as an eternal truth which resides within our mind. Such truths are termed common notions or axioms. The following are examples of this class: *It is impossible for the same thing to be and not to be at the same time*; *What is done cannot be undone*; *He who thinks cannot but exist while he thinks*; and countless others. It would not be easy to draw up a list of all of them, but nonetheless we cannot fail to know them when the occasion for thinking about them arises, provided that we are not blinded by preconceived opinions." See Heidegger, *Being and Time*, §44c, pp. 269f. (227): "That there are 'eternal truths' will not be adequately proved until someone has succeeded in demonstrating that Dasein has been and will be for all eternity. As long as such a proof is still outstanding, this principle remains a fanciful contention which does not gain in legitimacy from having philosophers commonly 'believe' it."—Eds.

ment by Rickert),[47] but the theological solution to the problem is rejected. He does not allow anxiety, as mankind's basic state of mind, to be pacified through either theological metaphysics nor a religious Gospel of salvation.

Yet this religious attitude toward death that reduces life as a whole to anxiety and dissolves it into care is not the only one possible—nor is it the authentically philosophical one.

Here we esteem more highly the ancient solution, which Heidegger rejects in the sharpest terms. Stoic ethics: ἀταραξία as the opposite of anxiety.[48] Let us not forget [from whence] this ideal of Stoic wisdom derives; it is essentially Platonic: philosophy is learning how to die.[49] But Plato draws the very opposite conclusion concerning eternal truth: because there are and must be eternal truths,[50] for this reason man too cannot completely die, hence is sure of his immortality.

This assures him of his eternal endurance (Goethe).[51] From the idea of truth, [*nous*], as subject, is also inferred, and, from this, immortality. With Spinoza, there is something else: no completely *individual* immortality—

---

47. See Rickert, "Die Logik des Prädikats und das Problem der Ontologie," *Sitzungsberichte der Heidelberger Akademie der Wissenschaften*, Philosophisch-Historische Klasse (1930–1931), pp. 1–236 (pp. 227–236 are on Heidegger). Probably a reference to the concluding comment in which Rickert criticizes the centrality of "Nothingness" as a topic in Heidegger, p. 236: "One no longer knows anymore what has an objective basis and what is a personal 'creed,' and such confusions, under every circumstance, mean trouble."—Eds.

48. See *Stoicorvm vetervm fragmenta*, collegit Ioannes ab Arnim (Stuttgart: B. G. Teubner, 1964), vol. 3, p. 109, no. 449, lines 18–20: "Unde Stoici hanc gulae et corporis libidinem criminantur, τὴν ἀταραξίαν τῆς ψυχῆς, *hoc est nihil timere nec cupere, summum bonum esse*." See the descripton of ἀταραξία as the liberation from fear, in Epistula prima, *Epicurea*, esp. sec. 81, pp. 30f.—Eds.

49. See Plato *Phaedo* 80E 3–81A 1–2. *Collected Dialogues*, p. 64: "If at its release the soul is pure and carries with it no contamination of the body, because it has never willingly associated with it in life, but has shunned it and kept itself separate as its regular practice—in other words, if it has pursued philosophy in the right way and really practiced how to face death easily—this is what 'practicing death' means, isn't it?" For Cassirer's interpretation of this doctrine, see *Die Philosophie der Griechen von den Anfängen bis Platon* (Berlin: Ullstein, 1925), pp. 115–116.—Eds.

50. On the view that there "must" be eternal truths, see Plato's doctrine of *Anamnesis*; see also Cassirer, *Die Philosophie der Griechen*, pp. 108, 111–114.—Eds.

51. The words "eternal endurance" (ewigen Bestand) come at the end of Goethe's poem "Zur Logenfeier des dritten Septembers 1825. Zwischengesang," *WA*, Abt. 1, vol. 3, p. 68: "Denn das Beständige der ird'schen Tage / verbürgt uns ewigen Bestand." "On the Lodge Celebration of September 3, 1825, *Poems of Goethe: A Sequel to "Goethe the Lyrist,"* trans. Edwin H. Zeydel (Chapel Hill: Univ. of North Carolina Press, 1957), p. 121: "For what we do on earth that has duration / Vouchsafes us our eternity."—Eds.

except as regarded *sub specie aeterni*.⁵² Whoever has learned to see things *sub specie aeterni* is elevated above the fear of death. Homo liber de nihilo nunc quam de morte cogitat.⁵³ The decisive thing is that to man and only to him knowledge of death is given. With this knowledge the mere factuality of death is overcome; the mere *factum* becomes a necessity which man knows and accepts.

Only man is capable of this *amor fati*. He is not completely subjugated to death; he does not just undergo it as does every other organic creature—rather, he proves here too his basic capability for distancing. He faces it as an opposite. He develops a concept of nature and of thinking of natural necessity and within this he gives the phenomenon of death its place. He interprets his own annihilation and thereby annuls it. Pascal: un roseau qui pense l'univers.⁵⁴

Cf. Schiller: Mit dem Geschick in hoher Einigkeit.⁵⁵

This might be a very ancient way of thinking, this might be found by some to be very heathen, but it is the truly philosophical solution, which takes death itself up among the realm of necessity, and through this thought of necessity, through *amor fati*, it is able to liberate us from anxiety about death. And with this, life itself is raised above realm of mere "care" [*Sorge*] (Heidegger).⁵⁶

---

52. "under a form of eternity." See Spinoza, *Ethica,* pt. 5, prop. 30, *Opera*, vol. 1, p. 264. *The Ethics*, p. 218: "Therefore to conceive things under a form of eternity is to conceive things in so far as they are conceived through God's essence as real entities."—Eds.

53. See Spinoza, *Ethica*, pt. 4, prop. 67, *Opera*, vol. 1, p. 232. *The Ethics*, p. 193: "*A free man thinks of death least of all things, and his wisdom is meditation of life, not of death.*"—Eds.

54. See Blaise Pascal, *Pensées*, ed. Léon Brunschvicg, *Oeuvres*, vol. 13 (Paris: Hachette, 1904), no. 347, pp. 261f. Pascal, *Pensées*, trans. W. F. Trotter and Thomas M'Crie (New York: Modern Library, 1941), p. 116: "Man is but a reed, the most feeble thing in nature; but he is a thinking reed. The entire universe need not arm itself to crush him. A vapour, a drop of water suffices to kill him. But, if the universe were to crush him, man would still be more noble than that which killed him, because he knows that he dies and the advantage which the universe has over him; the universe knows nothing of this."—Eds.

55. From Schiller's poem "Die Künstler," *Sämtliche Werke*, vol. 1, p. 186: "Mit dem Geschick in hoher Einigkeit, / Gelassen hingestützt auf Grazien und Musen, / Empfängt er das Geschoss, das ihn bedräut, / Mit freundlich dargebot'nem Busen / Vom sanften Bogen der Nothwendigkeit." See "The Artists," *The Poems of Schiller*, trans. E. A. Bowring (Chicago: Hennebery, 1873), p. 90: "Joining in lofty union with the Fates, / On Graces and on Muses calmly relying, / With freely-offer'd bosom he awaits / The shaft that soon against him will be flying / From the softbow Necessity creates."—Eds.

56. See Heidegger, *Being and Time*, pt. 1, VI: "Care as the Being of Dasein," §§39–45, pp. 225–273 (180–235).—Eds.

3. [Time in Bergson and Heidegger]

On the critique of Bergson's concept of time (future).
Still to be considered: that there appears here to be a particular dialectic between the metaphysical "essence" of duration and the intuition of duration. For in terms of its metaphysical essence, Bergson's time appears indeed to relate to the future and to be directed to it. It is none other than *élan vital*, which strives *forward* and lives wholly in the future—the life will, which constantly aims and strives to get beyond itself.

Cf. on this, the discussion in König, *Begriff der Intuition*.[57]

But Bergson's method of intuition, the way in which *durée* is *experienced* and scrutinized, does not correspond to this at all—for it is a return to the *past*, recollection. The future aspect of time is eliminated and devalued here—it is no longer part of the pure "theoretical" viewpoint of speculation, but only of the sphere of activity, and this view construes it too narrowly and misinterprets it *pragmatistically*.

On the General Problem of Time
Difference between ontic and ontological time—
 the time of "nature" and time of "dasein"
cf. the discussion in Heidegger.

Heidegger's understanding of time differs from Bergson's primarily in that it is not the past, but the "future" which is taken to be the essential aspect of time. Being as "having been" is itself understandable only with regard to the future. The image of death as the "end" of time discloses the authentic "historicality" of dasein.
On this, very perceptive and profound remarks:
cf. esp. Heidegger, 325ff.[58]
The *primary* sense of existence is the future, 327, 328, 329; "the primary phenomenon of primordial and authentic temporality is the future" (329).[59]

---

57. See König, *Der Begriff der Intuition*, sec. 2, chap. 5: "Die Intuition bei Bergson und ihr Verhältnis zur intellektualen Anschauung der speckulativen Philosophie."—Eds.

58. See Heidegger, *Being and Time*, pp. 372f. (325): If either authentic or inauthentic Being-towards-death belongs to Dasein's Being, then such Being-towards-death is possible only as something futural in the sense which we have now indicated, and which we have still to define more closely. By the term 'futural', we do not here have in view a 'now' which has not yet become 'actual' and which sometimes will be for the first time. We have in view the coming in which Dasein, in its ownmost potentiality-for-Being, comes towards itself."—Eds.

59. This whole sentence is italicized in Heidegger, *Being and Time*, p. 378 (329).—Eds.

This [is] the advancement beyond Bergson,
cf. H[eidegger]'s criticisms of "Bergson's interpretation of time—which is ontologically quite indefinite and inadequate," p. 333.[60]
Cf. esp. pp. 393ff. on historicality.
The ground on which authentic historicality is founded is temporality as the existential meaning of the Being of care (397).[61]

Only an "existence" directed to the future can have "historicality" (411).[62] cf. esp. pp. 372ff.[63] Dasein is not only something that has been in the sense of having been there (ontically); rather, it is something that has been in the sense of *something futural which is making present*, that is, in the temporalizing of its temporality (381).[64]
[This is] most explicit [on p.] 385.[65]

60. See Heidegger, *Being and Time*, p. 382 (333): "But time, as within-time-ness, arises from an essential kind of temporalizing of primordial temporality. The fact that this is its source, tells us that the time 'in which' what is present-at-hand arises and passes away, is a genuine phenomenon of time; it is not an externalization of a 'qualitative time' into space, as Bergson's Interpretation of time—which is ontologically quite indefinite and inadequate—would have us believe."—Eds.

61. See Heidegger, *Being and Time*, p. 449 (397): the *ground . . . temporality.*—Eds.

62. Perhaps a reference to the following passage in Heidegger, *Being and Time*, p. 464 (411f.): "Although one can concern oneself with time in the manner which we have characterized—namely, by dating in terms of environmental events—this always happens basically within the horizon of that kind of concern with time which we know as astronomical and calendrical *time-reckoning*. Such reckoning does not occur by accident, but has its existential-ontological necessity in the basic state of Dasein as care."—Eds.

63. See Heidegger, *Being and Time*, pp. 424–455 (372–404), chap. 5: "Temporality and Historicality."—Eds.

64. See Heidegger, *Being and Time*, p. 432 (381): "The antiquities which are still present-at-hand have a character of 'the past' and of history by reason of the fact that they have belonged as equipment to a world that has been—the world of a Dasein that has been there—and that they have been derived from that world. This Dasein is what is primarily historical. But does Dasein first *become* historical in that it is no longer there? Or *is* it not historical precisely in so far as it factically exists? *Is Dasein just something that 'has been' in the sense of 'having been there', or has it been as something futural which is making present—that is to say, in the temporalizing of its temporality?*"—Eds.

65. Probably a reference to Heidegger, *Being and Time*, p. 437 (385): "*Only an entity which, in its Being, is essentially* FUTURAL *so that it is free for its death and can let itself be thrown back upon its factical 'there' by shattering itself against death—that is to say, only an entity which, as futural, is equiprimordially in the process of* **having-been***, can, by handing down to itself the possibility it has inherited, take over its own throwness and be* **in the moment of vision** *for 'its time'. Only authentic temporality which is at the same time finite, makes possible something like fate—that is to say, authentic historicality.*"—Eds.

Only an entity which, in its Being, is essentially futural can exist as "having been" and as "in the moment" for "its time."

"History has its essential importance neither in what is past nor in the today and its connection with what is past, but in that authentic historizing of existence which arises from Dasein's *future*" (386).[66]

Section Three

For the Concluding Chapter

The Sphere of the Thing and the Sphere of Meaning

THE NATURE OF CONCEPTS OF PHYSICAL OBJECTS— TRANSFORMATION OF THE NAIVE "WORLDVIEW"

Physics creates a different kind of world of things. That is usually interpreted so that physics is taken to replace the reality of things as they merely "appear" to us with their "true" reality. It teaches us to recognize the "objective" features of things. The sensory qualities recede for physics into a realm of mere "illusory appearances."

This conflict can also be interpreted in the opposite way: physics diverts us from genuine reality, *mechanizes* this reality, separates us from *durée réelle*, from the view of "true being" which is found in the I, *prior* to all objectification.

For us, from the standpoint of the philosophy of symbolic forms, this competition and conflict do not exist. The philosophy of symbolic forms seeks out the *entirety* of the perspectival views in which reality is disclosed to us. It does not begin with a prejudice about the character of their reality, but seeks to understand *every view* according to its own norms. Each form or "view" carries in itself the measure of its reality. We must first find this measure and learn to understand it—the measure of lan-

---

66. See Heidegger, *Being and Time*, p. 438 (386): "But if fate constitutes the primordial historicality of Dasein, then history has its essential importance neither in what is past nor in the 'today' and its 'connection' with what is past, but in that authentic historizing of existence which arises from Dasein's *future*."—Eds.

guage, myth, science. For us true reality is the subject which is capable of all these "views."

PHENOMENOLOGY OF THE THING CONCEPT

[The] naive view [is]: reality is *in itself* organized in thing-like terms. The question now is: how does this world of *things* come to be "pictured" in knowledge? How do "representations" of things arise from things, which are real in themselves? But this question contains a πρῶτον ψεῦδος and a *petitio principii*, namely the assumption that the "thing character" of reality itself is objectively given. We uphold the contrary thesis that the *category* of the thing exemplifies a particular *phase* in the view of things, and is an outgrowth of what came before. The thing is not the final condition of all knowledge; rather, the thing itself is conditioned: it holds only relatively for a particular point of view.[67] It is a *mode* of having or understanding a world, not the presupposition or *foundation* of our understanding a world. To be precise: the "thing" is the specifically *human* category. It does not apply either in the perceptual world of animals or for an *intellectus archetypus*. Animal consciousness stands *beneath* the category of the thing, the divine stands above it.

We begin with the *first* point, the surrounding world and inner world of animals.[68] The animal is a life center—a circle of life which comes into contact with other circles of life, is receptive to influences from them, and exercises influences of its own. It is dangerous to attempt to portray this relationship in terms of consciousness. We can only begin with actions or behavior. We see how these living circles of action interact with one another.

Whatever is alive has its own circle of action for which it is there and which is there "for" it—both as a wall that closes it off and as a "viewpoint" that it holds "open" for the world.

This "attunement of the circles of life" to one another is the primary phenomenon of living nature. But we do not approach any closer to this

---

67. Cassirer engages here in an untranslatable play on the word *Ding* (thing), which is the root in the German for "condition" (Be*ding*ung).—Eds.

68. Volkelt: relaxing of the thing category; melodies, etc., rhythms.—Cassirer. Probably a reference to Hans Volkelt, *Über die Vorstellungen der Tiere: Ein Beitrag zur Entwicklungspsychologie* (Leipzig and Berlin: Wilhelm Engelmann, 1914), pp. 79ff. and 125–126ff., where he discusses "rhythms" and "melodies" in the perceptions of animals. See above, Part I, Chapter Two.—Eds.

state if we attempt to describe it according to our own viewpoint's category of the thing. Uexküll has presented the program for this; beginning with animal behavior, he reconstructs the animal's surrounding world and inner world. It is conditioned through the nature of the living subject, it always contains a complete group of actions, not just reactions. Each living creature displays a specific organization, a structure—and its "surrounding world" and "inner world" take shape according to these structures: connaitre—co-naître.

Only with mankind does this life complex become a knowledge complex; instead of the circles of life just *standing* in one another, now there is knowledge of one another among the circles of life. Mankind attains an eye for the other circles of life; this can be attained, however, only by mankind's learning more and more to ignore or look away from itself. This learning to "look away" consists in not introducing the available human category of the thing into the worlds of other living creatures,[69] a world that is not fixed in terms of things.

How does the situation look with regard to the "higher" animals? The first level of "representation": it appears to precede language, to be what first makes language possible—"mediated" behavior—"tools." With that the "preliminary" level of the concept of the thing [is] achieved. We will have to attribute some kind of "object-related" view to the higher animals. An "opposing world," an "objective" reality, as the "objectified" starts to appear.

[A. The "Object Character" of Language]

But on the whole the working out of this "objectified" reality is bound to language. Its beginnings lie in the animal realm, but the step that [is] taken here, the step to "representation," attains a basis and stability only when it is able to bring forth the organ of language. The perception of things, objectification in terms of objecs, is perfected only in language. It draws forth the core of the thing, the substance of the thing. This core is really something more negative than positive, as Plessner has rightly seen.[70] It amounts to a

69. Volkelt-(spider); sea urchin; rhythmic-periodic.—Cassirer. See Volkelt, *Über die Vorstellungen der Tiere*, "Die Nichtdinghaftigkeit des tierischen Umgebungsbildes," pp. 61–66. See above, Part I, Chapter Two.—Eds.

70. On the "core of the thing," see Plessner, *Die Stufen des Organischen und der Mensch* (Berlin: Walter de Gruyter, 1928), pt. 2, chap. 3, sec. 2: "Der Doppelaspekt in der Erscheinungsweise des gewöhnlichen Wahrnehmungsdinges," pp. 81–85.—Eds.

new kind of "separation," a separation also from the individual perceptual basis.

The animal can in a certain sense let something in its awareness stand as a representation for something else, but it does not thereby yet have the X of the thing, the pure thing-schema. This schema first comes about through language, and it does so by thought finding a whole new way of taking hold. Thought must remain in contact with the sensory, but it holds fast to sensory signs. The sign acquires functional value (meaning) for it, and by means of this functional value of meaning, mankind advances beyond the immediacy of sensory awareness. Now the "object" is also there for mankind even if it is not represented by one of its sensory aspects ("characteristics"). It has "being" because it has a "name." This [is] the correct core of "nominalism": *nomen* dat esse *rei*.[71] The name is the origin of the category of the thing. Only as a speaking creature does man have a world opposite him.[72]

UEXKÜLL'S *GEGENWELT*—"SCHEMA"

This theory is correct, but it suffers from one shortcoming: it conceives this schema all too narrowly as an "image," as a spatial schema.[73] The schema must be expanded, from the sphere of pictorial *rappresentazione*[74] to the

---

71. "The name gives being to the thing." See Kant, "Von einem neuerdings erhobenen vornehmen Ton in der Philosophie," *Werke*, vol. 6, p. 493, where he mentions the scholastic formula *forma dat esse rei*.—Eds.

72. Humboldt: Man lives with things in the manner that language brings them to him.— Cassirer. See Humboldt, "Ueber die Verschiedenheit des menschlichen Sprachbaues un ihren Einfluss auf die geistige Entwicklung des Menschengeschlechts," *Werke*, 4 vols. (Darmstadt: Wissenschaftliche Buchge sellschaft, 1963), vol. 3, p. 434: "Man lives with things mainly—even completely—depending on the way language presents them to him, since his perception and action depend upon the way he conceives of things."—Eds.

73. On "Schema" in Uexküll, see *Umwelt und Innenwelt der Tiere*, 2d ed. (Berlin: Julius Springer, 1921), p. 168: "In the *Gegenwelt* the objects in the environment are represented through Schemata, which, according to the organizational plan of the animal, can be very general and can encompass very many kinds of objects." On the "schema," see *Theoretical Biology*, trans. Doris L. Mackinnon (New York: Harcourt, Brace, 1926), pp. 92–97.—Eds.

74. The Italian spelling for pictorial representation in art is a common term in Aby Warburg's writings on art and culture. See the passages listed under "Rappresentazione," in the index to Aby M. Warburg, *Gesammelte Schriften*, Bibliothek Warburg, Unter Mitarbeit von Fritz Rougemont hrsg. von Gertrud Bing, 2 vols. (Leipzig and Berlin: B. G. Teubner, 1932), vol. 2, p. 714. Aby Warburg (1866–1929) founded the Kulturwissenschaftlichen Biblio-

larger sphere of representation in general. And it is the word that here truly carries the "representative function." Man is relieved by words of the need to make "pictures" of things. In this way mankind arrives at a relatively imageless "view" of the world. Animals do not possess such a view as a nonperceptual "representation." The "thing" as a mere X, as an ideal point of unity, is not accessible to immediate sensory awareness. It functions as such as an ideal point of unity, and this function goes back to the action of language. Uexküll has shown very well how every "surrounding world" and "shared world" depends upon such actions, not upon mere "reactions."[75]

Here we are in the midst of nonpragmatic, ideal "action," the activity of pure representation. The viewpoint of usefulness is much too narrow. The ideal function begins much earlier; even the act of simple expression can never be reduced to mere goal-directed action as Darwin sought to do.[76] The form of shared life, as represented by expressive means, is earlier than that of acting upon things. So here too: "making present" is an ideal final goal.

Pathological cases offer the negative instance of this. Where the linguistic web has become undone, the web of things also becomes undone. We have cases of agnosia where the fixed forms of objects and their meanings become obliterated. Along with the names disappears the expression of the object and it can no longer be recognized as what it "is." The "thing" loses its "stability." It assumes an unsteady state—a knife: "for cutting," a fork: "for eating."[77]

The perceived "use" takes the place of the significative meaning. This is closer to the realm of animals: prey, partner for pairing, "something" to eat or drink. In apraxia the thing is no longer recognized outside of its immediate usefulness. It is not *the* knife, *the* fork, but only for cutting, for eating, in the practical sense; it can only be recognized *in concreto* and made use of *in concreto*.

---

thek Warburg in Hamburg. Cassirer developed much of his philosophy of symbolic forms in Hamburg at Warburg's library.—Eds.

75. This reference is probably to the detailed discussion of reflex and other actions in Uexküll, *Theoretical Biology*, pp. 271–280.—Eds.

76. *Marginal note:* The sphere of Life (Action-sphere), to which the animal is limited, for Man becomes 'a sphere of vision' (beginning of all 'Speculation').—Cassirer.

77. Such pathological cases are discussed in *PSF*, vol. 3; see pt. 2, chap. 6, "Toward a Pathology of the Symbolic Consciousness," pp. 205–277.—Eds.

B. The "Object Character" of Language in Contrast to That of Myth

Myth as a total phenomenon already encompasses the three dimensions of expression, representation, and signification. On the last of these: there are also "abstract" myths—the Roman "special gods" of an abstract kind, gods of the "situation," and so on.[78] But the emphasis here is in the sphere of expression. The world of myth is not composed as a whole of things with the structure of objects; it is a world of demons, hence, it is not bound to spatial-temporal limitation, to the here and now of the thing.

In the thing sphere (and hence in the logical sphere of language in general) being is essentially characterized as demonstrable being: as something here and now. It is accordingly in a "now" only by being in a "here." It has its specific place in a fixed schema of space and time, and out of this perceptual identity, which is bound to language, develops logical identity (the "principle of identity" as an expression of the constancy of the name: that designated by a specific name "is" something unchanging in its character).

This does not hold at all for myth—here demonstration does not dominate, but expression and manifestation do. The "same" thing can, in fact must, manifest itself at different places in space and time—and must appear in completely different shapes, without ever ceasing to be the same.[79] But this has nothing to do with "collective thought." Rather, this is an example of the nature of the mythic object, which is "manifestative," not "demonstrative."

Here is the root of mythic thought—myth as a form does not of course remain at this level. The momentary demons become the figures of gods. But this transition into the sphere of representation (from that of expression) is possible only through the decisive cooperation of language: the

---

78. Material in Usener.—Cassirer. See Hermann Usener, *Götternamen: Versuch einer Lehre von der religiösen Begriffsbildung* (Bonn: Friedrich Cohen, 1896). On the Roman special gods, pp. 76.—Eds.

79. Cf. Chapter Totemism, *Language and Myth* and material in Lévy-Bruhl.—Cassirer. See *PSF*, vol. 2, pt. 3, chap. 2, sec. 1, pp. 175–199: "The Community of All Life and Mythical Class Formation: Totemism." There is no chapter in *Language and Myth*, trans. Susanne K. Langer (New York: Dover, 1953), specifically titled "Totemism," although discussions in this work are relevant to Cassirer's point. For Lévy-Bruhl, see *PSF*, vol. 2, p. 183 n., which refers to ethnological material on felt identity in Lévy-Bruhl, *How Natives Think*, trans. Lilian A. Clare (New York: Washington Square Press, 1966), pp. 216ff.—Eds.

name first creates the "personal god."[80] On the other hand, the course of language is to move on to representation and objectification. Here too language shows how these spheres are originally entwined and grow together. It does not immediately overcome the "demonic" object by means of the "schematic" and representative object; rather, the word is itself demonic. Only gradually does a separation come about.

[C. The "Object Character" of Science]

The last stage, the stage of theoretical knowledge, creates a new form of objectification. It is in a certain sense directed as much against language as it is directed against myth. It advances beyond language's category of the thing and hence beyond its way of schematizing. The world of myth and of animals is not yet thing-like; the world of science is no longer thing-like. Here too, of course, a slow, continuous development [takes place], for science cannot begin without [drawing upon] the formulations of language. In fact, insofar as science is "descriptive" it remains essentially representative in character. It develops further language's activities of classification, ordering, and division. But even as mere classification it creates completely new "viewpoints."[81] It deals not with what exists per se, but with the order of being, and this order requires, even in the morphological sense, more than mere configurations. It requires principles (for example, genetic phenomenology). The way in which "characteristic features" are determined follows therefore from completely different points of view.

[First step:] In any case the task remains to establish characteristic features of some kind. In the perceptual, representational sphere, "groups" are formed and brought together in "concepts"—the concept "dog" as a monogram of imagination.[82]

Second step: the "models" of physics, quasi-perceptual, schematizations.

---

80. Usener cf. Language & Myth.—Cassirer. See Usener, *Götternamen*, p. 334. In *Language and Myth*, p. 72, Cassirer writes: "The Name and nature of the god are the same thing. Thus the polyonymy of the personal deities is an essential trait in their very being." Cassirer then quotes Usener's *Götternamen*: "For religious feeling, the power of a god is expressed in the abundance of his epithets; polyonymy is a prerequisite for a god of the higher, personal order."—Eds.

81. Whale, Fish.—Cassirer.

82. See the comment in Kant, *Kritik der reinen Vernunft, Werke*, vol. 3, pp. 143f. (A 142 / B 181). *Critique of Pure Reason*, p. 183: that "the *schema* of sensible concepts, such as of figures in space, is a product and, as it were, a monogram, of pure *a priori* imagination."—Eds.

Third step: level of pure significance, principles instead of models. That [is] the course of scientific explanation.

[1. Three Forms of Space]

Explication by means of the problem of space:[83]

α) Expressive space (Myth)
β) Representational space (demonstrative article)
γ) Significative space (Nothing from the intuitive essence of space enters into the four-dimensional order.)

[These levels are:] below the level of things—the thing—beyond the level of things.

[The] course of religion [is] quite analogous! [It leads] beyond the "image" and the "Name."
[The world has a] pure content of meaning, which is no longer a mere representative content.

[2. Three Forms of the I]

The same [holds] for [the phases of the] "I."

I as *physical* individuality (as my own "body").[84] [There is] no "knowledge" of one's own body in the world of the lower animals. Bodily movements do not even belong to an environment of one's own.

I as concrete, pragmatic I. Activity [serves] as the roots of concepts in language. Concepts in language arise from action, just like the mythic figures. [This leads to the] singling out of the "individual" I from the sphere of the "collective." Myth and language [serve] here as the vehicle.[85]

I as "geist." [This is the] transpersonal "sphere of meaning."[86]

---

83. A discussion of different ways of understanding space is found in Cassirer's essay "Mythic, Aesthetic, and Theoretical Space," trans. Donald Phillip Verene and Lerke Holzwarth Foster, *Man and World* 2 (1969): 93–111.—Eds.

84. Cf. Uexküll.—Cassirer.

85. See vol. I and II.—Cassirer. On the role of "action" in language and in myth, see esp. *PSF*, vol. 1, pp. 285–287; vol. 2, pp. 199–218.—Eds.

86. Cf. the page: Spranger and Plessner, underlined passages.—Cassirer.

[3. Three] Types of Metaphysics

α) Sphere of expression (Klages)[87]
It puts life above geist and sees in everything intellectual only a tearing apart and alienation from life: Romantic yearning after the paradise of life. But paradise is closed. Plessner's concluding chapter: Mankind is only what it makes of itself.[88]

β) Bergson—Mauthner (language). Take over from the introduction chapter.[89]

γ) What is knowable "reality"?
Haeberlin—Schlick to be contrasted![90]

Our metaphysics: life's becoming truly aware.[91] Life's going back to its "ground" means of course its destruction,[92] but it is preserved in the sphere

---

87. *Marginal note:* Mat. Ples. concluding chapter.—Cassirer. It is not clear if this is a reference to material on Plessner in Cassirer's drafts for his concluding chapter or to material in the concluding chapter of Plessner's *Die Stufen des Organischen und der Mensch*, a work that Cassirer cites in his concluding chapter.—Eds.

88. Reference to Plessner's view that man must as an "excentrically organized" creature "first make" himself what he is. See Plessner, *Die Stufen des Organischen und der Mensch*, p. 309.—Eds.

89. Folder 184a, in which this manuscript is contained, also includes a text with the heading "For the introduction," but neither Bergson nor Mauthner is mentioned in it.—Eds.

90. Carl Haeberlin or Paul Haeberlin? Carl Haeberlin (1878–1947), M.D., author of *Die Forschungsergebnisse von Ludwig Klages* (Kampen auf Sylt: Niels Kampmann, 1934); Paul Haeberlin (1878–1960), Swiss philosopher and pedagogue, personally acquainted with Cassirer. See Peter Kamm, *Paul Häberlin. Leben und Werk* (Zürich: Schweizer Spiegel Verlag, 1981), vol. 2, p. 110. Moritz Schlick (1882–1936), founder of the Vienna Circle of Logical Positivism. Schlick's essay "Erleben, Erkennen, Metaphysik" is mentioned below, but a comparison might also be intended with Schlick's essay "Vom Sinn des Lebens" in *Symposium: Philosophische Zeitschrift für Forschung und Aussprache* 1 (1927): 331–354.—Eds.

91. "Gewahrwerden." See the discussion of Goethe's notion of "Gewahrwerden," above in Part II, Chapter Two.—Eds.

92. This involves an untranslatable play on the words "zu Grunde gehen," which literally means "going to the ground," but usually has the sense of "being destroyed." Cassirer's manuscript reads, "Zurückgehen des Lebens in seinen 'Grund'—dadurch muss das Leben freilich 'zu Grunde gehen,'" i.e., "Life's going back to its ground or basis must thereby destroy what it was." With self-awareness, the phenomenon of life is no longer naively what it is, but has become elevated to self-consciousness. On this notion of "zu Grunde gehen," see Klages, *Vom kosmogonischen Eros* (Munich: Georg Müller, 1922), p. 48: "*Ekstase* is not the soul discarding the body, but rather the discarding of self and hence of intellect.—But in such a case, every *Ekstasis* of a creature possessed of intellect will go through two phases: the phase in which the I *passes away* [*untergeht*] and the phase in which life is *resurrected*."—Eds.

of geist. The substance of life has become a subject,[93] the pure sphere of meaning, above both the thing and the personal.[94]

93. See Hegel, *Phänomenologie des Geistes, Sämtliche Werke*, vol. 2, p. 22. *The Phenomenology of Spirit*, par. 17, pp. 9–10: "In my view, which can be justified only by the exposition of the system itself, everything turns on grasping and expressing the True, not only as *Substance*, but equally as *Subject*."—Eds.

94. In this whole sentence Cassirer is paraphrasing Ludwig Klages, who holds the diametrically opposite view of the relationship between "mind" and "life." See Klages, *Vom kosmogonischen Eros*, p. 48.—Eds.

Appendix

The Concept of the Symbol:
Metaphysics of the Symbolic
c. 1921–1927

[*1. Metaphysics of Being and of Life*]

THE metaphysics that we combat is twofold, and its claims seem to derive from opposing presuppositions. The worldview of "Symbolic Idealism" is opposed both to the metaphysics of dogmatic Realism and to the metaphysics of so-called Positivism. It combats something which, despite all their apparent differences, is a common basic feature in both of them: that they see the source of intellectual life and its functions in some kind of "reproduction" and "mirroring" of some "reality" given independently of them. In the older metaphysics this reality is the absolute being of things; in Positivism it is the, no less absolute, givenness of "simple" sensations. In contrast to these views, the fundamental starting point of our way of looking at things is that no separation can be made between some positively given being and the intelligent [*geistig*] functions, which are presumed to apply subsequently to this material. We have access to no "Being" of any kind—be it metaphysical or psychological in nature—prior to and independently of intelligent action, but only in and through this action. Even the very idea of severing the two from each other, of contrasting in our imagination a purely passive "givenness" with intellectual [*geistig*] "activity" is deceptive. There is no form of "Being" for us outside of these different kinds of action (in language, myth, religion, art, science) because there is no other form of determinacy. The error in these abstract philosophical doctrines always arises because they tacitly assume in the discussion that the results of a particular energy of mind are given and they remain unconscious of its preconditions. When, for example, "Positivism" regards sensations as simple "givens," this overlooks that what we call a "simple sensation" always contains at least its fixation through language and hence

223

linguistic concept formation (in brief: the "energy" of language as such). It is only because positivistic logicians overlook this, so to speak, prelogical, intellectual work of language, or fail sufficiently to appreciate its full value, that they arrive at the erroneous notion of a given prior to all activity of mind. On our view, the general and particular, sensory and intellectual, passive and actual, "impression" and "expression" cannot be separated at all; we only possess these two aspects "at once" and together. Therefore there is no "being" of any kind except by virtue of some particular energy ("nature," for example, only by virtue of artistic, religious, or scientific energy) and without our taking this relation into account, the concept of "being" would be completely empty for us. Being acquires an intelligent organization for us only through the sequence of symbolic "forms"; but these are symbolic activities. We have no concept for the way the "world" looks if we abstract from all activity of mind—if we, so to speak, assume the zero point of intelligence [*Geist*]. We can only explicate the particular concept of being applicable to each particular level of intellectual activity and determine by analysis what is characteristic of it. This is what we have tried to provide in the foregoing analyses of the energies of language, art, religion, and logic.

This gives us in fact a fundamentally new way of seeing. The older metaphysics—as well as psychological Positivism, which begins with the univocal "being" of the "world" or of "sensations"—entangles itself again and again in unsolvable contradictions and antinomies in the interpretation of this supposedly unitary being. The different worldviews (for example, that of "knowing" and those of belief, of "religion" and of empirical science and of metaphysics, and so on) contradict one another, were incommensurable. Yet each of them claimed to give and represent the One, true Being!

These contradictions cannot be resolved as long as one clings to the notion of Being as a univocal, certain starting point. We find over and over again that the readings we attain of this supposedly unitary Being are in truth wholly different.

Here a turn must occur: "subjective, instead of objective." What we need is not the "unity" of the thing, the absolute object, but the unity of geist, of the intellectual energy as such in all the various "symbolic forms." That is what the philosophy of symbolic forms has tried to give and provide (whereby of course we may not confine ourselves to the energy of "knowledge" [*Erkenntnis*] as Kant did).

Realistic metaphysics agrees with empiricist Positivism in that they both think in terms of substance: they begin with the unitary "simplicity" of the thing, of the existing "world" as present at hand. But gradually there turns out to be no way for us to grasp this supposed "simple unity." It constantly falls apart into a variety of conflicting "viewpoints."

It is different with symbolic idealism, *which begins not with the simple unity of the thing (substance), but with the unity of function.* This unity of *action* and the plurality of possible symbolic viewpoints are not opposed to one another as hostile opposites, but stand in a necessary correlation. The unity of geist is to be found only in the plurality of symbolic forms, not as a substantial unity but as a functional plurality. Geist becomes one through its conscious awareness of its identity (as action in general) in the plurality of various activities. In each of these a particular world arises (the worlds of science, religion, art), but the unity of these "worlds" is rooted in a common origin, in a principle of action, as the philosophy of symbolic forms shows. That is the true unity, the critical-ideal unity (of action), the sole unity to which we can attain, in contrast to the dogmatic-substantial—in truth, unattainable—unity of "Being" (of the Absolute, the *Thing* in itself).

We begin not with the primordial fact of so-called Being, but with that of "Life."[1] To this fact, however, this dispersion in a multitude of different directions is quite essential—and that precisely is the "primary phenomenon" of Life itself, that it asserts its deep unshakable unity in this divergency. The philosophy of symbolic forms seeks to represent the nature and full development of this primary phenomenon, but it naturally cannot go back to its "Why," and it does not raise this question, but recognizes here the necessary and inescapable "limit of conceptualization."

[2.] On the Idealism of the Symbolic Function

If we are to carry out this idealistic viewpoint, we must of course here too arrive at a final point of identity. What does this assumed identity between the object, the "Absolute," and the symbolic function consist of?

The "Absolute," "Being" insofar as it is conceivable for us at all, is taken up for us in the primary phenomenon of life. The highest that we can conceive of is life—the rotating movement of the *monas* around itself.[2] This

---

1. Cassirer gives a brief discussion of this interpretation of "Life" in his essay "Language and Art II" (1942), *Symbol, Myth, and Culture* (New Haven: Yale Univ. Press, 1979), pp. 193–195.—Eds.

2. Paraphrase of Goethe, *Maximen und Reflexionen*, Schriften der Goethe-Gesellschaft, 21, ed. Max Hecker (Weimar: Goethe-Gesellschaft, 1907), no. 391. See above Part II, Chapter One, and the following discussion.—Eds.

motion consists in the creation of ever new forms—*Gestalts*—and in their destruction. Here we stand indeed before a primary phenomenon, which can be given only verbal expression but not given any further "explanation." This primary phenomenon of the production and transformation of forms corresponds to the basic phenomenon of the symbolic function. The "adequation" here refers not to an object but to the process of motion and change itself. Each function embraces this process within its own characteristic motion, within its own characteristic shaping and changing of shapes. The only way for us to make this whole "primordial process" present to us is by reference to the totality of this specific function.

The movement of "geist" gives expression in its language to this primordial movement, but it then breaks itself down into individual, specific, special movements, and so on.

[3. Philosophical Knowledge]

It is characteristic of philosophical knowledge as the "self-knowledge of reason" that it does not create a principally new symbol form, it does not found in this sense a new creative modality—but it grasps the earlier modalities as that which they are: as characteristic symbolic forms. As long as philosophy still vies with these forms, as long as it still builds worlds next to and above them, it has not yet truly grasped itself.

Philosophy is both criticism and the fulfillment of the symbolic forms. [It is] criticism because it turns away from the transcendental "object," because it grasps these forms as the active intellectual construction of reality, not as directed toward some external "Absolute," and because it tries to overcome the symbolistic character of the "sign," even to "eliminate" the sign and attempt to attain to "adequate" knowledge, without signs.

This tendency is introduced by the particular symbolic forms themselves. In the course of their development they all turn against their own "system of signs"—so religion turns against myth, cognitive inquiry against language, the scientific concept of causality against the sensory-anthropomorphic-mythic conception of causality, and so forth.

But philosophy does not want to replace the older forms with another, higher form. It does not want to replace one symbol with another; rather, its task consists in comprehending the basic symbolic character of knowledge itself.

We cannot cast off these forms, although the urge to do so is innate in us,[3] but we can and must grasp and recognize their relative necessity. That is the only possible ideal liberation from the compulsion of symbolism. Such a compulsion is involved in every application of a positive form, in every positive "language."[4] We cannot overcome it by casting off the symbolic forms as though they were some husk and then behold the "Absolute" face to face. Instead, we must strive to comprehend every symbol in its place and recognize how it is limited and conditioned by every other symbol.

The "Absolute" is always simply the completely relative, which has been carried through to the end in a systematic overview, and the absoluteness of geist in particular can be nothing else and cannot try to be.

[4. The Basic Opposition of Modern Philosophy]

Here perhaps [we can] take up the basic opposition of modern philosophy—the distinction expressed in such catchwords as rational–irrational; life and thought; intuition–concept; existence–value, and so on, and so forth.[5]

Our treatment moves quite outside this opposition—it cannot even [be] grasped by means of it. For "symbolism," as we understand it, is in fact actually the true mediation of the seeming opposition. It is the true μεταξύ-, which explains the μέθεξις-, the participation of "appearance" in the "idea," of "life" in "thought," of the eternal flux in the created form. The modern theories of "life" are altogether insufficient because they single out only the negative, the merely natural, the biological element. (Even in Bergson we have nothing but this biological element.)

3. ("The light dove . . . !")—Cassirer. A reference to Kant's comment about the drive of reason toward limitless expansion. See Kant, *Kritik der reinen Vernunft*, in *Werke*, vol. 3, p. 39 (A 5 / B 8f.). *Critique of Pure Reason*, p. 47: "Misled by such proof of the power of reason, the demand for the extension of knowledge recognises no limits. The light dove, cleaving the air in her free flight, and feeling its resistance, might imagine that its flight would be still easier in empty space."—Eds.

4. Cf. on the relationship of art and conceptual knowledge the good comments in Konrad Fiedler, cf. sheet 86.—Cassirer. No such sheet 86 could be found.—Eds.

5. Overview of the forms of modern Lebensphilosophie in Rickert, Philos. des Lebens; cf. Frischeisen-Köhler's review of Rickert's book in the *Kant-Studien.*—Cassirer. Heinrich Rickert, *Die Philosophie des Lebens: Darstellung und Kritik der philosophischen Modeströmungen unserer Zeit* (Tübingen: J. C. B. Mohr [Paul Siebeck], 1920); Max Frischeisen-Köhler's review, "Philosophie und Leben: Bemerkungen zu Heinrich Rickerts Buch: 'Die Philosophie des Lebens,' *Kant-Studien* 26 (1921): 112–138.—Eds.

But that way we never come to the real problem of "life" as something more than mere "existence" bound to nature, something that just takes place, namely as an intelligent [*geistig*] process. In life alone we do not have such intelligence, such "being for itself." We find this only in the form that life gives to itself—and this form does not disclose itself to us either in mere vegetative-biological existence or in biological development, but only in free activity, that is, in the creation of symbolic forms (language, myth, art . . .). Hence it is in these that "life" first attains to "form" (to *eidos*)—in which it reconciles itself with "form."

The concept of "concrete intelligence" [*des konkreten Geistes*] therefore experiences its realization only in these symbolic forms—the dialectic is balanced out, but continues then naturally within each of the particular symbolic forms (the overcoming of the "image" through the image, and so on).

The meaning of "life" in this sense was more deeply recognized by Fichte, Schelling, and Hegel than by the "moderns." They overcame the antitheses of life–thought (Fichte), life–reason (Schelling) through the new idealistic concept of geist, which negates mere "life" (as dasein), in order then to "posit" fully developed concrete life—to arrive at being for itself, and so have "Subject" come from mere Substance.[6]

Geist attains to the form of life by breaking away from its mere immediacy—this is most obvious in the "symbolic forms," in language, art, knowing. These are themselves of course something "mediated," not the so-called "in itself" of things. But only by virtue of this mediacy, in the creation and destruction of these forms (dialectical process herein . . . see earlier: dissolution of the image worlds),[7] can geist come to possess and know itself—and there is no other, "higher" form of reality than this self-knowledge of geist. Here it knows itself as One and Many, as immediate and mediated, as unity, as a synthesis of life and form. This unity (synthesis) of life and form is the true concept of geist, its "essence."

---

6. Historical: the naturalistic concept of Life, of the immediate, of belief for Jacobi. Criticism of Jacobi through Fichte, Schelling, Hegel. Fichte: Life is not actually not-philosophizing, and so on. / Schelling, Hegel (bad infinity, bad immediacy in Jacobi).—Cassirer. See Fichte, "Rückerinnnerungen, Antworten, Fragen," in *Sämmtliche Werke*, ed. J. H. Fichte, 8 vols. (Berlin: Verlag von Veit & Comp., 1845), vol. 5, p. 343: "*Life* is actually *not-philosophizing*; *philosophizing* is actually not-living, and I recognize no more adequate definitions of these two concepts than this."—Eds.

7. This could be a reference to the discussion of Klages. See above, Part III, "For the Concluding Chapter," note 94.—Eds.

[5. The Symbolic and the Intuitive]

To be developed: the basic difference between the symbolic and the intuitive.

The notion of pure intuition appears to be in direct conflict with the course of the mind's development toward symbolic processes. Leibniz already (logically) distinguished explicitly between intuitive and merely "symbolic" knowledge.[8] The former kind of knowledge grasps the object in its pure essential nature—the other is satisfied with a "sign" of the object. Such immediate "intuitive" knowledge appears here [to be] incomparably more valuable; such an intuitive understanding would be a divine understanding, an absolute understanding. In contrast to this, our "discursive" understanding (which needs "images")[9] is an inadequate, merely symbolic (significative) understanding.

Yet, regardless of how high this ideal of a purely intuitive understanding or *intellectus archetypus* stands in Leibniz's or Spinoza's metaphysics, Leibniz's work as a logician moves entirely in the sphere of the significative, of the *characteristica generalis*,[10] which for him is the model of all knowledge. For us as human beings, "knowledge" is given in no other way but in this form, only through the power and function of "signs."

But there is necessarily a dialectical conflict between these two trends—toward the "intuitive" and toward the "symbolic"—no matter how cor-

---

8. See Leibniz, "Meditationes de Cognitione, Veritate et Ideis," *Die philosophischen Schriften von Leibniz*, ed. C. I. Gerhardt, 7 vols. (Berlin: Weidmann, 1875–1890), vol. 4, p. 423. See Leibniz, *Philosophical Papers and Letters*, ed. and trans. Leroy E. Loemker, 2 vols. (Chicago: Univ. of Chicago Press, 1965), vol. 1, p. 450: "I think of a chiliogon, or a polygon of a thousand equal sides, I do not always consider the nature of a side and of equality and of a thousand (or the cube of ten), but I use these words, whose meaning appears obscurely and imperfectly to the mind, in place of the ideas which I have of them, because I remember that I know the meaning of the words but that their interpretation is not necessary for the present judgment. Such knowledge I usually call *blind* or *symbolic*; we use it in algebra and in arithmetic, and indeed almost everywhere. When a concept is very complex, we certainly cannot think simultaneously of all the concepts which compose it. But when this is possible, or at least insofar as it is possible, I call the knowledge *intuitive*. There is no other knowledge than intuitive of a distinct primitive concept, while for the most part we have only symbolic knowledge of composites."—Eds.

9. "Bilder" bedürftiger. A reference to Kant's comparison of our discursive understanding ("intellectus ectypus"), "which needs images," with the notion of an intuitive mind ("intellectus archetypus"), which does not. See Kant, *Kritik der Urtheilskraft, Werke*, vol. 5, p. 487. *The Critique of Judgment*, §77, pp. 292f.—Eds.

10. See sec. XI [Characteristica generalis], in Leibniz, *Philosophische Schriften*, vol. 7, pp. 184–189. See *Philosophical Papers and Letters*, vol. 1, pp. 339–346.—Eds.

relatively conditioned we may conceive them to be. The turn toward intuition stands in opposition to the symbolic direction of thought, and it seeks to gain predominance by an *Aufhebung* of the contents of the symbolic forms. Typical examples: the criticism of language through the call for a "pure" representation (without concepts and language)[11] of basic experiences, of perceptions . . .

Berkeley—F. Mauthner.[12]

If we could only pull aside the "curtain of words" and so on . . .[13]

Religion—Mysticism—pure knowledge of God without the intermediation of any "image," God as "complete Nothingness" as attained only through an *Aufhebung* of the determinacy of images (of all the symbolic functions of the concept and the image).

This opposition is expressed differently in the antithesis of "culture" and "life." For all "culture," the entire development of "geist," leads away in fact from mere "life"—into a realm of symbolic, hence merely significative and not immediate, "living" forms. This is the case with science, language, and even art. But the demand for pure "intuitionism" (Bergson) cannot be fulfilled: paradise is bolted fast, and we must make the trip around the world (Kleist, "Marionettentheater" . . .).[14]

---

11. Cassirer discusses Berkeley's call for a representation of experience without concepts in his *Das Erkenntnisproblem in der Philosophie und Wissenschaft der neueren Zeit* (Berlin: Bruno Cassirer, 1920), vol. 2, esp. pp. 286f. and 297–309.—Eds.

12. Mauthner is briefly mentioned in *PSF*, vol. 1, p. 188 n., but Cassirer applies his views in criticism of Nicolai Hartmann in "Erkenntnistheorie nebst den Grenzfragen der Logik und Denkpsychologie," *Jahrbücher der Philosophie* 3 (1927), p. 88.—Eds.

13. See Berkeley, *A Treatise concerning the Principles of Human Knowledge*, in *Works of George Berkeley*, 4 vols. (Oxford: Clarendon Press, 1901), vol. 1, sec. 24, p. 255: "In vain do we extend our view into the heavens and pry into the entrails of the earth, in vain do we consult the writings of learned men and trace the dark footsteps of antiquity. We need only draw the curtain of words, to behold the fairest tree of knowledge, whose fruit is excellent, and within the reach of our hand."—Eds.

14. Cassirer refers here to Heinrich von Kleist's essay "Ueber das Marionettentheater" (1810): "Paradise is bolted fast, and the cherub far behind us; we must travel around the world and see whether perchance an entrance can be found somewhere from the rear." See *H. von Kleists Werke*, ed. Erich Schmidt with Georg Minde-Pouet and Reinhold Steig, 4 vols. (Leipzig and Vienna: Bibliographisches Institut, n.d. [1905]), pp. 133–141, quotation on p. 137. See Cassirer's discussion of this Kleist essay in "Geist und Leben in der Philosophie der Gegenwart," *Neue Rundschau* 41 (1930): 244–245, translated as "'Spirit' and 'Life' in Contemporary Philosophy," in *The Philosophy of Ernst Cassirer*, ed. Paul A. Schilpp (La Salle, Ill.: Open Court, 1973), pp. 857–880, esp. pp. 857–858. The translation is on p. 858.—Eds.

All culture takes place in and proves itself in the creative process, in the activity of the symbolic forms, and through these forms life awakens to self-conscious life, and becomes mind.

The negation, the annihilation of the symbolic forms, in order to return to life as something immediate would be therefore simultaneously to kill the mind [*Geist*] itself—for the mind exists, unlike life itself, only in the totality of these symbolic forms. And yet this tendency to return to the immediacy of life (in opposition to the striving toward symbolic form as the striving toward mind) is itself of course a ubiquitous phenomenon in all cultural development—comparable to a negative key signature. But if this curtailment of the activity of the symbolic forms were consistently carried through, it would lead to a complete quietism toward culture itself. (This quietistic ideal [is] a basic feature of all mysticism. In the seventeenth century [it is] most energetically opposed by Leibniz—who supports the positive significance of the symbolic forms! Leibniz's concept of culture[15] is essentially informed by this!)

On Romantic conceptions of this same idea.

[6. Metaphysics and Logic]

The manner in which this metaphysics—to our understanding—simultaneously comprehends and gives a foundation to all the previous levels of symbolism (language, myth, art, science) and, on the other hand, also relativizes them is most evident in its attitude toward logic.

The entire development of "pure logic" leads to the formulation of logical "contents" independent of the psychological sphere, to the pure being of logical "objects" independent of the processes in which they appear to the consciousness of particular individuals.

Experience—and *Validity*

The development of the concept of validity (Material perhaps in Liebert?)[16]

---

15. Cassirer explains Leibniz's cultural ideal in contrast to quietistic religious ideals, in his *Freiheit und Form* (Berlin: Bruno Cassirer, 1916), pp. 84f.—Eds.

16. Arthur Liebert, *Das Problem der Geltung, Kant-Studien* Ergänzungsheft 32 (Berlin: Reuther & Reichard, 1906).—Eds.

Historical Development

Leibniz: Doctrina juris . . .[17]

first step . . .

[On the] dispute about Psychologism and Antipsychologism in the eighteenth century (Tetens, Lossius), cf. *Erkenntnisproblem.*[18]
The interpretation of the Platonic *Idea* as "validity":[19] Lotze, Cohen, Natorp (as content of a relation), Husserl's "third realm."[20]

All this is doubtless unassailable within the sphere of logic itself, but the

---

17. This probably refers to the following passage from "Juris et aequi elementa," pp. 19–34, in *Mittheilungen aus Leibnizens ungedruckten Schriften*, ed. Georg Mollat (Leipzig: H. Haessel, 1893), pp. 21f.: "Doctrina juris ex earum numero est, quae non ab experimentis, sed definitionibus, nec a sensuum, sed rationis demonstrationibus pendent et sunt, ut ita dicam, juris, non facti" (The science of jurisprudence belongs to that number of cognitions, which derive not from experience, but from definitions, and depend upon proofs not based upon the senses, but grounded in reason and in which the object of concern is therefore validity and not questions of fact).—Eds.

18. Tetens and Lossius are discussed in *Das Erkenntnisproblem*, vol. 2, pp. 574–582.—Eds.

19. The interpretation of the Platonic idea as *Geltung* was set out in Hermann Lotze, *Logik*, 2d ed. (Leipzig: S. Hirzel, 1880), bk. 3, chap. 2, p. 509. Eng. trans. Bernard Bosanquet, 2d ed., 2 vols. (Oxford: Clarendon Press, 1888), vol. 2, pp. 205f.: "What we do possess *as* truths is in virtue of the identity of every such content of perception with itself, and of the constancy of identical relations which obtain between different contents. Thus we readily understand the significance of Plato's endeavor to bind together the predicates which are found in the things of the eternal world in continual change, into a determinate and articulated whole, and how he saw in this world of Ideas the true beginnings of certain knowledge." This interpretation was taken up in Hermann Cohen, *Platons Ideenlehre und die Mathematik*, Separat-Abdruck aus dem Rectoratprogramm der Univ. Marburg vom Jahr 1878 (Marburg: Elwert, 1879), pp. 12–17, esp. p. 14: "The idea of existence, as an Idea, is only ἀλήθεια, not οὐσία according to the negative significance of this word; it designates existence as such, in abstraction from all qualitative determinacy, in the validity of ὄντως ὄν, as the object of ἐπιστήμη." On the interpretation of validity as the holding of a relation, see Paul Natorp, *Platos Ideenlehre* (Leipzig: Dürr, 1903), p. 196. There Natorp writes about the highest species of being: "This is, according to the clearest explications, namely those in the *Phaedo*, rather the 'Being' of the *function of judgment*. This means in general, however: the *holding [Bestand] of relations*; be they the original logical [relations], in which the basic mathematical relations are comprehended, or be they relations to ends, or temporal relations of events and laws in the usual sense of natural laws. If we understand law in its broadest significance to mean every expression of the general holding of a relation, then the idea has the general meaning of a law."—Eds.

20. Not a technical term in Husserl; Cassirer is probably referring to the ideal in contrast to the physical and psychical. See Cassirer's use of this term above, p. 187, where it serves as a designation for a "'realm of pure forms,' that is given to us in a pure vision."—Eds.

point to recognize is that the "content" referred to here is nothing other than the highest logical symbol. Logic cannot go further than the unconditioned validity of a truth because validity and relation are the only categories that it has at its disposal. In the end, these categories (these "symbols") themselves appear to it again and again in an objective form.

Just as myth transformed everything into life in accordance with its function, so logic transforms everything in accordance with the nature of its basic function into "contents" [*Bestand*] and "validity" [*Geltung*]. Hence, for the former all "nature" becomes personal force; for the latter it becomes a matter of law (example of the transition in Boyle).[21] But these two standpoints are not absolute; neither of them gives us "the" essence per se; rather, they give us a specific viewpoint, under which we observe it. This is the solution to the antinomy.

Just[22] as for the former [myth] all "existence" [*seiende*] is necessarily changed into gods and demons—so all existence is necessarily changed for logic into truth.

No longer the πράγματα, but rather the ἐν τοῖς λόγοις σκοπεῖν τῶν ὄντων.[23] This is the tremendous step that takes place with Plato and through which he is distinguished from the "physicists," who are also mythologues.

And the same holds for Descartes: la vérité étant une même chose avec l'être.[24]

This is especially fascinating in the Eleatics, because in them both forms are immediately interwoven. Existence is brought to thought, the concept. But the "concept" itself still has a half mythical meaning, as the goddess of truth.[25]

---

21. See the discussion of this point regarding Boyle in Cassirer, *Das Erkenntnisproblem*, vol. 2, pp. 430–434.—Eds.

22. This text was added to the bottom of the page and continues in the margin of the next. It is given here in what seems to be its logical place.—Eds.

23. See Plato *Phaedo* 99E4–6: ἔδοξε δή μοι χρῆναι εἰς τοὺς λόγους καταφυγόντα ἐν ἐκείνοις σκοπεῖν τῶν ὄντων τὴν ἀλήθειαν. *Collected Dialogues*, p. 81: "So I decided that I must have recourse to theories, and use them in trying to discover the truth about things."—Eds.

24. Cassirer quotes this in his dissertation, "Descartes' Kritik der mathematischen und naturwissenschaftlichen Erkenntnis" (1899), published as a supplement to his *Leibniz' System* (Marburg: Elwert, 1902), p. 83 n. It is from a French translation of Descartes' *Méditations métaphysiques* (1824), méditation 5, p. 312: "la vérité étant une même chose avec l'être." See Descartes, *Meditationes*, *Oeuvres de Descartes*, vol. 7, p. 65: "patet enim illud omne quod verum est esse aliquid." *The Philosophical Writings of Descartes*, vol. 2, p. 54: "for it is obvious that whatever is true is something."—Eds.

25. Reference to Parmenides frag. B 1 (Diels, vol. 1, p. 150; Freeman, pp. 41f.).—Eds.

[This is the] Midas gift of myth and of logic! This is only truly grasped by the metaphysics of symbolic thought!

In the final, highest insight we must naturally rise to the concept of validity [*Geltung*], but we cannot for this reason do without the concept of life! On the contrary, it is final—a life itself in which we "participate" in changing symbols! Even the concept of "content" [*Bestand*] is—only a semblance![26]

This is how we see a solution to the conflict between logicism and psychologism.

26. In German: "ist—nur ein Gleichnis!" Allusion to Goethe, *Faust* II, lines 12104f.: "Alles Vergängliche / Ist nur ein Gleichnis." Goethe, *Faust*, *Goethe's Collected Works*, vol. 2, ed. and trans. Stuart Akin (Boston: Suhrkamp/Insel, 1984), p. 305: "All that is transitory / is only a symbol."—Eds.

Index of Personal Names

Personal names occurring in Cassirer's texts, his footnotes, and the editors' introduction

Achilles, 92
Adler, Max, 140*n*52
Aenesidemus, 116
Anaxagoras, 6
Aristophanes, 133
Aristotle: and doctrine of *nous,* xix; Bergson's criticism of, 48; on *praxis* and *poiesis,* 130, 183*n*153; and metaphysics, 154; conception of Socrates, 184; and Pythagorean conception of number, 197; and *eidos,* 198
Augustine, Saint, xix

Bachofen, Johann Jakob, 25, 88–90
Bacon, Francis, 26
Baeumler, Alfred, 88*n*106
Bergson, Henri, 36*n*3, 170; metaphysics of life, xi, 8, 29, 47–50, 157, 227; conception of intelligence, 53, 59–60; and problem of expression, 124; and *durée vécue,* 138, 169; contrasted with Descartes and Husserl, 172–75; and Heidegger, 201–2, 209–10; and types of metaphysics, 219; and "intuitionism," 230
Berkeley, George, 230
Bethe, Albrecht, 95
Böhme, Jakob, 156*n*97
Boll, Franz, 184*n*154
Boyle, Robert, 233
Bréhier, Emile, 206
Brun, Rudolf, 94*n*120
Bruno, Giordano, 156
Bühler, Karl, 52*n*36, 130*n*12, 146–47, 151–52, 163*n*112, 165, 172*n*127, 183*n*153
Byron, Lord, 23

Caesar, 163
Campanella, Tommaso, 156

Carnap, Rudolf, xix, 123, 125
Cassirer, Ernst: biographical details, ix, xiii–xiv
Cassirer, Toni: organization of Cassirer's papers, xiv; on *The Philosophy of Symbolic Forms* (vol. 4), xx–xxi, xxiii, xxiv
Cohen, Hermann, 149, 232
Cohn, Jonas, 125, 146*n*66
Comte, Auguste, 36–37
Croce, Benedetto, 81
Cusanus, 32, 198

Darwin, Charles, 38–39, 215
Descartes, René, xix; skepticism of, 116, 135; and "reflection," 136; and existence of matter, 137–38; and the *cogito,* 144–45, 169–76, 178, 181; and idealism, 188–89; and truth, 233
Dewey, John, 179
Diderot, Denis, 131*n*19
Dilthey, Wilhelm, xi, xix, 8, 120, 140*n*51, 143–44, 161–65
Duhem, Pierre, 200*n*23

Eckhart, Meister, 30
Empedocles, 195
Epicurus, 30, 196
Eschenbach, Wolfram von, 135

Fabre, Jean Henri, 76
Fichte, Johann Gottlieb, xix, 178*n*139, 228; and consciousness, 28–29; philosophy of religion, 101–2; conception of the "I," 128*n*5, 129*n*8, 140, 181–82; metaphysics of ethics, 158
Fiedler, Konrad, 81–85, 227*n*4
Fischer, Kuno, 182*n*150

Freud, Sigmund, 157*n*100
Freyer, Hans, 186*n*166
Fries, Jakob Friedrich, 118
Frischeisen-Köhler, Max, xxii, 227*n*5

Goethe, Johann Wolfgang von, 162, 207; conception of primary phenomena, xviii, 127–30, 131–33, 136–38, 141, 149, 152–53; and language, 17–18, 75; and the aesthetic, 79, 81; conception of nature, 105, 200; his *Prometheus* fragment, 110; and self-knowledge, 185, 186*n*164
Goldstein, Kurt, xii
Gundolf, Friedrich, 163–64

Haeberlin, Carl, 219
Haeberlin, Paul, 219
Hamann, Johann Georg, 90
Hartmann, Nikolai, 196
Hegel, Georg Wilhelm Friedrich: nature of his system, xvii–xviii, 154; and Romanticism, xix, 159–61, 165–66; concept of history, 86, 104; knowledge of objects, 144; concept of the true as the whole, 193; contrasted with Heidegger, 204; contrasted with Kierkegaard, 205; and meaning of "life," 228
Heidegger, Martin, xi, xix, xxii, xxiv, xxvi, 141, 178*n*139, 180, 181*n*148, 200–211
Helmholtz, Hermann von, 199
Hendel, Charles W., ix, xiv, xxi
Heraclitus, 61, 107, 154, 156, 162, 188
Hercules, 98
Herder, Johann Gottfried, 70, 88, 205
Heyse, Hans, 194*n*6
Hitler, Adolf, xx, xxiii
Hobbes, Thomas, 145
Hölderlin, Friedrich, 162
Homer, 92
Hönigswald, Richard, 116*n*3, 117, 143
Humboldt, Wilhelm von, 16, 214*n*72
Hume, David, 118–19, 145, 168, 194
Husserl, Edmund: conception of phenomenology, xvii, 148–49, 151; and basis phenomena, 137; and descriptive psychology, 143; phenomenology of the "I," 169, 171–73, 178; and "monadic" theory of knowledge, 175–76, 180–81; conception of "third realm," 232

Jacobi, Friedrich Heinrich, 119–20, 124, 228*n*6
James, William, 147, 178–79

Kant, Immanuel, 135, 136; divisions of his philosophy, 3; and theoretical knowledge, 21, 149, 151, 164–65; and problem of philosophical anthropology, 34–36; and aesthetics, 45, 81; conception of critical philosophy, 53, 55–57, 64*n*56, 188–89, 194, 224; and being, 141*n*54; conception of metaphysics, 153; doctrine of "apperception," 178, 181; his "Averroism," 205
Kierkegaard, Sören, xi, 201, 203, 205, 206
Klages, Ludwig, xix, xxvi, 23–27, 29–32, 59, 106, 124, 219
Kleist, Heinrich von, xix, 230
Köhler, Wolfgang, 69
Köning, Josef, 194*n*6, 209
Krois, John Michael, xv, xxv
Külpe, Oswald, 146

Lange, Carl Georg, 147
Langer, Susanne K., xxiii
Leander, Folke, xx, 179*n*143
Leese, Kurt, 156*n*97
Leibniz, Gottfried Wilhelm, 154, 189, 194*n*5, 232; basis of his philosophy, 124; doctrine of perception, 139; concept of the monad, 197; and *characteristica generalis*, 229; concept of culture, 231
Leonardo da Vinci, 79*n*86, 81
Lessing, Gotthold Ephraim, 162
Lévy-Bruhl, Lucien, 68, 76*n*82, 216*n*79
Liebermann, Max, 79
Liebert, Artur, 231
Lipps, Theodor, 148–49, 152
Litt, Theodor, 110*n*142, 116*n*3, 131*n*18
Lossius, Johann Christian, 232
Lotze, Rudolf Hermann, 232
Lumholtz, Karl Sofus, 76*n*82
Luther, Martin, 203

INDEX OF PERSONAL NAMES

Mach, Ernst, 145*n*64, 193*n*3
Maier, Heinrich, 184*n*158
Manheim, Ralph, xxiii
Mannhardt, Wilhelm, 70
Marx, Karl, 178*n*139, 180
Mauthner, Fritz, 219, 230
Meister Eckhart, 30
Messer, August, 147*n*70
Münsterberg, Hugo, 146, 147

Natorp, Paul, 54*n*39, 56–58, 126*n*33, 138*n*47, 143, 149–52, 232
Nelson, Leonard, 118
Newton, Isaac, 105, 200
Nicholas of Cusa, 32, 198
Nietzsche, Friedrich, xi, 8, 27–28, 178*n*139, 179–80
Noiré, Ludwig, 142
Novalis, 162

Ortega y Gasset, José, 139*n*50

Parmenides, 154, 156
Pascal, Blaise, 208
Petzäll, Åke, xiv*n*20
Plato, xix, 135*n*35, 184; doctrine of becoming, 15, 20; idea of the Good, 103; doctrine of Ideas, 109, 156, 179, 187–89, 197–99, 232; as historical figure, 131; image of the cave, 174; and truth, 207
Plessner, Helmuth, 37*n*6, 44–45, 62*n*52, 213, 218*n*86, 219
Plotinus, xix
Prometheus, 110–11, 130*n*15, 159
Protagoras, 180*n*147, 187

Rádl, Emanuel, 95
Reid, Thomas, 117, 124
Richter, Raoul, 116*n*3
Rickert, Heinrich, xxii, 8*n*8, 207, 227*n*5
Russell, Bertrand, 86*n*101, 147*n*72, 178*n*139

Scheler, Max, xi–xii, xix–xx, 37, 39, 62*n*52, 124, 163*n*114
Schelling, Friedrich Wilhelm Joseph von, xix, 89–90, 156–57, 228
Schiller, Friedrich, 46, 204, 208
Schilpp, Paul Arthur, xxiii
Schlegel, Friedrich von, 29
Schlick, Moritz, xix*n*28, 219
Schopenhauer, Arthur, xi, 27, 123, 140*n*51, 179
Schrödinger, Erwin, 126
Simmel, Georg, xi, xxvi, 8–15, 19, 130*n*13, 154*n*90, 186*nn*166, 167, 205
Socrates, 133–35, 184–87, 189
Spencer, Herbert, 37
Spengler, Oswald, 105–8, 199
Spinoza, Benedictus de, 154, 196, 197, 207, 229
Spranger, Eduard, 99*n*128, 161*n*108, 218*n*86

Tasso, Torquato, 129
Tetens, Johann Nicolaus, 148, 232

Uexküll, Jakob von, xxiv, 42–45, 52, 62–65, 213, 214–15, 218*n*84
Usener, Hermann, 216*n*78, 217*n*80

Verene, Donald Phillip, xv, xxv
Vico, Giambattista, 103
Vignoli, Tito, 68–69
Volkelt, Hans, 65–66, 76*n*84, 95*n*121, 212*n*68, 213*n*69

Wach, Joachim, 199*n*22
Warburg, Aby, xiii, xxiv
Werner, Heinz, 68*n*64, 69*n*68
Weyl, Hermann, 22*n*28
Wolfram von Eschenbach, 135
Wundt, Wilhelm, 40

Xenophon, 184

Made in the USA
Middletown, DE
23 July 2020